The Age of Catastrophe

ALSO BY JOHN DAVID EBERT

The New Media Invasion: Digital Technologies and the World They Unmake (McFarland, 2011)

The Age of Catastrophe
Disaster and Humanity in Modern Times

JOHN DAVID EBERT

McFarland & Company, Inc., Publishers
Jefferson, North Carolina, and London

LIBRARY OF CONGRESS CATALOGUING-IN-PUBLICATION DATA

Ebert, John David, 1968–
 The age of catastrophe : disaster and humanity in modern times / John David Ebert.
      p.   cm.
  Includes bibliographical references and index.

  ISBN 978-0-7864-7142-3
  softcover : acid free paper ∞

  1. Disasters — History — 20th century. 2. Disasters — History — 21st century. 3. Disasters — Social aspects — History — 20th century. 4. Disasters — Social aspects — History — 21st century. 5. Civilization, Modern — 20th century. 6. Civilization, Modern — 21st century. I. Title.
  D24.E24 2012
  363.3409'04 — dc23   2012031717

BRITISH LIBRARY CATALOGUING DATA ARE AVAILABLE

© 2012 John David Ebert. All rights reserved

No part of this book may be reproduced or transmitted in any form or by any means, electronic or mechanical, including photocopying or recording, or by any information storage and retrieval system, without permission in writing from the publisher.

Front cover photographs © 2012 Shutterstock

Manufactured in the United States of America

McFarland & Company, Inc., Publishers
  Box 611, Jefferson, North Carolina 28640
  www.mcfarlandpub.com

Acknowledgments

Special thanks to William Irwin Thompson, Drew Burk, Stu Grimson, Jacques de Beaufort and Lawrence Phillip Pearce for reading versions of the manuscript at various stages of completion.

"How could we manage to analyze today's technical progress if we don't analyze its accidents?"

— Paul Virilio

Table of Contents

Acknowledgments — v
Introduction: The End of Natural Disasters — 1
A Brief Note on Civilization's Loss of Command Over Its Environment — 11

Part I: Disasters of Paleomodernity — 17

One. The Sinking of the *Titanic* and the Fate of the Mobile City — 20

Two. On the *Hindenburg* Disaster and the Technologization of the Soul's Descent to Earth — 28

Part II: Disasters of Neomodernity — 37

Three. The Plane Crash at Tenerife: What It Unconceals — 40

Four. The Disaster at Bhopal and the Collision of the Biosphere with the Chemosphere — 50

Five. Being-*Outside*-the-World: Thoughts on the Space Shuttle Disasters — 61

Six. Back from History: Some Implications Regarding the Accident at Chernobyl — 72

Seven. The Amsterdam Cargo Plane Crash and the Derailment at Eschede: Parallel Accidents — 85

Eight. The Aum Shinrikyo Nerve Gas Attacks As an Attempt to Recode Japanese Society — 97

Nine. The Columbine Shootings and the Absence of Meaning — 109

Table of Contents

Part III: Planetary Scale Disasters — 125

Ten. On the September 11 Terrorist Attacks — 129

Eleven. Hurricane Katrina and the Flooding of New Orleans — 139

Twelve. Sichuan, 2008: The First Man-Made Earthquake — 150

Thirteen. A Satellite Collision in the Exosphere: Some Ontological Consequences — 161

Fourteen. Tiny Blue Globe: Reflections on the BP Oil Spill — 168

Fifteen. On the 2011 Tohoku Earthquake, Tsunami and Fukushima Meltdown — 177

Postscript: Global Accident — 185

Appendix: A Disaster Timeline — 191

Chapter Notes — 197

Bibliography — 207

Index — 213

Introduction: The End of Natural Disasters

Age of Revisions

There seems to be no escaping it.

With record tornadoes and floods in the Midwest; a massive drought from California to Florida; a gigantic earthquake, tsunami and nuclear accident in Japan; anomalous floods in Vermont and New Jersey unleashed by Hurricane Irene; more flooding in Australia; an earthquake in New Zealand; devastating fires in Texas; and another earthquake in Turkey, the year 2011 has gone down as *the* most expensive for "natural" disasters ever.

Catastrophe, it seems, is becoming something of a way of life for us. Indeed, it has become the new norm for civilization.

But, of course, the very word "catastrophe" means a "reversal of what is expected." It is a Greek word, a compound of "*kata*," meaning "down," and "*strophe*," meaning "turn" or "reversal," as in "a reversal of fortune." Catastrophes, then, are supposed to be *exceptions* to the normal run of things. They are *disruptions* of the banal world of seriality and repetition, of days carbon copied from one another, in which the hell of the same unfolds with single-minded and relentless monotony. Catastrophes are singularities which irrupt into such sequences with bizarre and atrocious anomalies of human suffering.

But on a planet in which catastrophes are becoming a daily occurrence, the classical understanding of the word no longer seems to fit. It has to be revised—along with everything else—and modified to fit the changed circumstances of an upside down world in which catastrophes are now the norm and banality is increasingly becoming the exception.

Catastrophe has become our new environment, a total surround, inside which we exist, but without noticing the strangeness of it, precisely because of its very ubiquity.

Nowadays, it seems that every time I turn on CNN or read the *New*

Introduction

York Times, one fresh catastrophe or another is in process of unfolding somewhere on this planet (and not of the political kind, either, which is another matter) but rather the kind of catastrophe that threatens to unhinge the very order of civilization itself. As I write this, Hurricane Irene has just made her way up the Eastern seaboard, nearly submerging Vermont and washing entire towns into the sea. In the Pacific Ocean, meanwhile, typhoons are ravaging the Philippines, where they threaten China and Japan, while just days ago, another anomaly, a 6.0 earthquake, struck the East Coast, putting a crack into the Washington Monument.

All this appears not to be just business as usual, either, as the political right would like us to think, for climate experts and geological scientists are now saying that earthquakes are on the rise in both frequency and intensity, while Category 4 and 5 hurricanes have *doubled* in number since the 1990s, since which decade the hottest years ever recorded are now on file.[1]

Of course, these are all "natural" catastrophes, but one of the arguments you will find me making in this book is that there is no longer any such thing as a "natural" catastrophe, since all such catastrophes now occur on a planetary stage that has been tampered with by human beings, those ex-simians turned atmospheric architects whose greenhouse gas emissions have so altered the biosphere that it is now virtually impossible to point to a strip of earth anywhere on the planet that has not been somehow "managed" by the human hand. The 2008 Sichuan earthquake, for instance, has gone down as the world's first man-made earthquake. Now, it seems, we are even capable of engineering our own quakes.[2]

All disasters nowadays, to one degree or another, would seem to be man-made, and so the old conceptual dichotomy of "civilization vs. nature" has become one of those outdated polarities of the kind that Derrida used to love to deconstruct, and which therefore no longer fit with the postmodern, or, rather, "ultramodern" situation. Our engineering projects have become so entangled with the earth's bio and lithospheric processes that anything which happens in the human order sends ripples out through the natural order and vice versa. The human hand, nowadays, seems to be perennially hidden behind the disasters and catastrophes which routinely befall us.

This is, indeed, a truly novel situation. In the days of the ancients, whenever earthquakes, storms and floods transpired, the ancients could always pray to their gods to show them some form of mercy, since they knew that Other forces were involved in the causes of these phenomena. Like the Levinasian Other which troubles and disrupts the self closure of the "I circuit," forcing an ethical singularity in which "I" must now take the problems and concerns of the "Other" into account within my own personal ethical feedback loop, so too, the civilizational closure of the ancient world was constantly being forced to take the "Other," the cosmic Other, in this case, into account, as their cities were disrupted by the wrath of the gods in the form of floods, earthquakes and tsunamis. If a catastrophe befell a Sumerian city—for instance, if its population was deported and the city destroyed—then it was assumed that the city's patron deity had withdrawn her favor from the city due to one or another offence on the part of its rulers. Likewise, if catastrophe befell a particular ruler or dynasty of ancient Chinese civilization—if, for example, the Shang Dynasty was overthrown by the rulers of the Chou—it was assumed that another, supernatural Order was involved, a heavenly order that had withdrawn the so-called Mandate of Heaven from that line of rulers and transferred it to the new dynasty.

But the existence of this Other order can no longer be factored in when considering the human civilizational equations, since humanity has taken upon *itself* the management of the planetary ecosystems that were once delegated to the order of the gods. It is not the Eye of Horus that now watches us from above, but the electronic eye of the satellites cluttering up the earth's Thermosphere. It is not the gods who move rivers around anymore with earthquakes and floods, but the U.S. Army Corps of Engineers, as for instance, in the case of their constraining of the Mississippi River into a single mighty channel, which then contributes to the erosion of the coastal wetlands as an unintended by-product, thus clearing a path for gigantic hurricanes coming in off of waters warmed by rising global temperatures.

We can't pray to Huracán, the Mayan god of hurricanes, to show us mercy anymore. That option is no longer available to us, for the gods, as Heidegger once pointed out, have withdrawn from us into concealment. Neither can we pray to the gods of earthquake—Poseidon or Geb—to show us mercy when we are building the world's largest dams and reservoirs along fault lines that create seismic tremors due to the massive displacement of water. Our technologies have become cosmospheric in scale. And we have replaced the old order of the Other, the divine Other, with a humanly manufactured and engineered cosmosphere inside which we are now sur-

Introduction

rounded and encased. It is we *humans* who are now causing what used to be referred to as "natural catastrophes" and before that were revelations of the wrath of the divine Other. But now we have replaced the order of the gods with a human, man-made order, and it is we humans who are, in one way or another, inevitably to be found at work in the wings of the stage shifting things around. Our catastrophes are no longer caused by gods at war with one another — such as the war between Athena and Poseidon which caused the sinking of Atlantis — but rather *engineers* and *city planners* whose projects are at war with one another's. It is *their* failure to agree that results in huge catastrophes which bring down disasters of cosmic scale and scope onto our cities.

So with the technological conquest of the earth by Western — now actually planetary civilization — we *know* where the "causes" are coming from, and they can no longer be blamed on the gods. *We* are at fault for the state the earth now happens to find itself in, for we have taken over the roles once formerly occupied by the gods of old. Human beings now find themselves responsible for planetary management — and mismanagement — and so there is no one else left to pray to in order to show us mercy in the situation that has come about. If we want mercy, we had better start rethinking the layout of the current civilizational order, since we were the ones, and not the gods, who set it up in its present configuration.

Hence, with a new planetscape of impossibly intertwined entanglings of earthly biorhythms and colossal human engineering projects, our *language* with its stratum of old-fashioned terms like "accident" and "catastrophe" is going to have to change in order to catch up with current events. The word "accident," for instance, used to imply something man-made, but not anymore. Hurricane Katrina was both natural catastrophe *and* man-made accident. It is a Derridean undecidable, for since the hurricane itself was the result of global warming (or at least, exacerbated by it), it can no longer be said to have been merely "natural."[3] It is impossible to draw the line anymore between "natural" and "man-made" with anything like the conviction with which such designations were drawn during, say, the Steam Age.

So, all the old vocabulary has to be thrown out: "catastrophes" are no longer anomalies, as the word implies, but have become civilization's new default mode; "accidents" no longer refer merely to man-made disasters like car crashes, train derailments and plane crashes but to what in reality are Derridean undecidables; and "disasters," which imply something cosmic (the word "astral" points to the heavens), now mostly have their origin in things as banal as human engineering of the earth's ecosystems gone awry. Thus, *none* of the old vocabulary fits the new situation anymore, and that is part of the reason why it is so difficult for us to understand what is going on all around us. Our thinking is constrained along the lines of these old words, but one cannot, of course, understand new situations without new concepts to go along with them.

Mass Production of Catastrophes

The past couple of decades, meanwhile, have seen more catastrophes — of both the man-made kind like industrial accidents — *and* "natural" catastrophes — that is, those involving a cosmic scale of warring elements — than any previous decade of human history. You might argue with this point, but then you will have the insurance companies to contend with, which, as theoretician Paul Virilio points out, have recently claimed that man-made catastrophes have overtaken natural catastrophes in frequency by about 70 percent since the 1990s.[4] However, keeping in mind the of the concepts I have pointed out above as a caveat (our concepts, just like our cities, are being eroded by these new events) natural catastrophes, too, in the traditional sense, have been on the rise. Not only was the year 2011 *the* most expensive year for natural disasters ever recorded, but it seems that *every* year which comes along sets some new disaster record that tops those of the previous year (2010, for instance, has tied with 2005 as the warmest on record, with 2009 following close behind).[5]

Some geologists are now pointing out that earthquakes have been occurring with more frequency in the past fifteen years than ever before, and their magnitude on the Richter scale also seems to be growing.[6] The 9.1 earthquake in the Indian Ocean in 2004, for instance — the one which caused the destructive tsunami that killed 300,000 people — was followed by the magnitude 8.0 Sichuan earthquake in 2008. Then came the 7.0 earthquake in Haiti in January of 2010; a 7.0 temblor in the Ryuku Islands of Japan in February of 2010; an 8.8 earthquake in the same month on the 27th in Chile (which caused another, smaller, and hence, less famous, tsunami); a 9.0 earthquake in Japan in March of 2011; the 7.6 earthquake in the Kermadec islands of New Zealand that July; and the rare and bizarre 6.0 quake on the East Coast of North America. That September, a 7.1 quake rumbled through the Aleutian islands off the shores of Alaska and this was followed, in turn, by a series of earthquakes that hit Guatemala in the same month, while a 7.2 earthquake in November struck Turkey, killing hundreds of people. And finally — perhaps most sinister of all — a 4.0 earthquake that rumbled through Youngstown, Ohio, on December 31 and which appears to have been man-made.

Of course, there have always been earthquakes and now with the aid of our real time media we hear about them the moment they occur all over the planet. But we have also had the luxury of electric media ever since the invention of the telegraph in the middle of the nineteenth century and our media haven't gotten any faster since then, just more ubiquitous. Geologists are indeed saying that the earthquakes are coming with more and more frequency. The norm allows for the occurrence of one magnitude 8.0 quake per year, but they have been occurring at about twice that rate during the past decade or so.

Stepping back, then, from the earth and viewing it as a scale model on a display table in front of us, it becomes possible to see how the practice of fracking — i.e., injecting water and chemicals into deep wells in order to force natural gas out of the earth — near Youngstown, Ohio, which has been linked with a series of unusual earthquakes that have been occurring there since March of 2011, shortly after drilling started in 2010,[7] or the burning red rivers of nickel tailings in Sudbury, Ontario, or the open pit coal mines of Sparwood, British Columbia, or even the concentric layers of copper mines in Bingham Valley, Utah, all begin to add up to a lithosphere that can hardly be considered to be in tip-top shape. And when we add on the world wide construction of colossal dams — many of them, as at Three Gorges Dam in China, built along fault lines — oil drilling, pipelining and the siphoning off of groundwater from our ever more and more arid aquifers, then the suspicion begins to sink in that human engineering projects may be somehow destabilizing the earth's crust, as though it were becoming more and more irritable at the pesky human parasites feeding off of its dermis.

Some climate scientists have even connected the recent increase in seismic activity to global warming. The melting of glaciers, this theory goes, relieves pressure off of tectonic plates in Greenland and Antarctica, which then begin to shift around and kick up more undersea tectonics and volcanic activity. The resulting sea-level rise, furthermore, makes for heavier oceans, which then apply *more* weight to plates globally, causing not only an increase in seismic activity but also a greater frequency of tsunamis which do, indeed, seem to be on the rise.[8] This may sound like fringe science to some, but as anyone with a little acquaintance with the history of science knows, new ideas — including Wegener's theory of plate tectonics itself— are often treated as part of the lunatic fringe until further observation confirms them. In this particular case, I'm placing my bets with the fringe group.

So the age of natural disasters, together with Acts of God, can now be put to rest. We are moving on into a new epoch, an age of man-made global and planetary disasters which are surrounding and hemming us in like an army besieging an ancient walled fortress. Civilization is now encompassed by disaster, which has become its new environment, an environment which emerges into shocking visibility in the work of our poets and artists — like the car crash paintings of Andy Warhol or Anselm Kiefer's installations of cities in ruins.[9]

Indeed, every generation or so, H.G. Wells' 1898 novel *War of the Worlds* has to be remade, since the scenario of the invasion of society by an antagonistic Other is really a dramatization in metaphoric picture language of the fact that we are always having to adjust our sense ratios to accommodate the impacts of new technologies, which disrupt them with catastrophic consequences. Thus, Orson Welles' 1938 radio version of the novel was a dramatization of the invasion of democratic society by fascism, whereas Byron Haskin's 1953 movie version was an envisioning of the invasive new electromagnetic environment configured by television. Steven Spielberg's recent updating of the film in 2005, however, takes place under the shadow of 9/11 as well as a whole series of environmental disasters which transpired in the first five years of the 21st century. The point of Spielberg's version of the story, then, seems to be that we are now surrounded by catastrophes everywhere we look, for catastrophe has invaded our civilization like an alien attack. A general paranoia, consequently, now saturates our field of awareness regarding not only other cultural agendas that are in conflict with our own but also regarding the current ecological situation, with all its storms, hurricanes, tsunamis, etc. which pose such a hostile threat to planetary industrial civilization taken as a whole. Our technological civilization, in other words, is presently at war with the entire world.

Introduction

A Frayed and Torn Cosmic World Picture

Suffice it to say, though, that this is not a "how to" book. I personally do not have the answers for what we need to do in the face of these catastrophes. I leave that to the world's climate scientists, civic engineers and city planners. I am no pragmatist.

This book, instead, is written as an attempt to increase *awareness* of the situation that we're in. Decisive action can only result when a clear mental image exists in the mind of just what the parameters of the situation look like.

What the reader of the current book *will* find, however, is a description of the evolution of catastrophes since the sinking of the *Titanic* in 1912. When one lines them up and compares them with each other in a manner similar to the comparative morphologist of the nineteenth century who lines up his animal skeletons beside one another looking to identify homologies between them, as I have done here, certain patterns begin to come into view.

When the German composer Karlheinz Stockhausen said that 9/11 was the greatest work of art ever created, what he said was true in a certain sense, since catastrophes function in a way that is *analogous* to works of art. That is to say that, like great works of art, they provide glimpses into hidden aspects of Being, making evident certain ontological structures that would otherwise be invisible to our normal mode of perception. The space shuttle disasters, for instance, reveal that the idea held by the ancients of a two world ontology, in which the laws of the heavens beyond the earth were substantially *different* from those below it, was actually correct. The shootings at Columbine bring into relief the entire cosmology of the suburbs and show us, very clearly, what is *missing* from its world picture. Hurricane Katrina uncovers what happens to human rights when the polisphere encasing the human being inside of a city collapses and those rights disintegrate, thus changing the ontological status of the human being from a citizen to something more like that of Agamben's *Homo Sacer*.

All catastrophes reveal hidden aspects of Being. Each one of them can be examined, as they are in this book, in just the way that a forensic investigator reconstructs the lifeworld of a crime victim in order to find out how the singularity of his death occurred as a sudden disruption within the continuity of that lifeworld. Each catastrophe, likewise, occurs within the very specific parameters of a certain lifeworld embedded in a cosmosphere that can be carefully reconstructed piece by piece. And, since every cosmosphere is imperfect, creating, at best, only a partial Image of the world as a whole, the investigator of the accident or catastrophe finds that each disaster reveals a hidden flaw built into each cosmosphere, showing the point of its incompletion or else the fatal assumption made as a design error that is capable of rupturing the whole system.

The main point of this book, then, is that *catastrophes are three dimensional realizations of a society's hidden cosmological flaws*. Redundancies, errors, misalignments and fatal incompletions in a society's World Image translate into the physical world in the form of its particular brand of disasters. In our case, a steady rise in the abundance of such disasters indicates that our World Image is becoming less and less adequate for mapping reality, for the catastrophes point to where seams become visible in this cosmic image, seams that reveal zones of misalignment with the Real. The cosmological maps of Western ultramodern civilization, then, are more riven with scars, tears and frayed edges than perhaps any other such maps in history. Otherwise, the disasters proliferating all around us wouldn't be on the rise.

The following book, then, far from being a mere collection of pessimistic broodings, is a sort of exhibition of catastrophes, each exhibit complete with its own photos and charts and diagrams (as it were) full of revelations about the way we humans situate ourselves, either comfortably or not, within the cosmos as a whole. The ontological implications, once fathomed, need to be mulled over, and possibly, as I have suggested above, for the express purpose of discarding the worn out cosmology in question, or else revising the current world picture to fit the new modifications suggested by the catastrophe.

Nietzsche, at the end of the nineteenth century, said that we were living in an Age of Comparisons in which each civilization could compare itself, for the first time, to every other in history. But today his statement needs to be revised, for now we are living in an Age of Revisions, in which almost nothing is certain anymore. And in an age of such uncertainties, the cosmospheric maps are in a state of flux, constantly being drawn up, discarded and redrawn to suit the circumstances newly modified by the course which Events have taken. A similar age came in at the end of the Medieval world, when all the maps of the ancients from Galen and Ptolemy onward had to be redrawn to fit the new data that was coming in daily as the result of voyages to new continents and the discoveries of new worlds

Introduction

in the heavens. Something similar is going on right now, for we find ourselves in an age of what Zygmunt Bauman has termed "liquid modernity," an age in which no structures seem capable of solidifying for very long. Consequently, a great opportunity is now available to us to redraw all the maps, and to do so in accordance with the data that is given us by a forensic examination of the catastrophes, disasters and accidents of Industrial civilization, now reaching both the temporal and spatial limits of its life cycle.

At the end of history—which attained its completion with World War II—we now find ourselves living in an age in which catastrophes have replaced Events in the sense in which the philosopher Alain Badiou has defined Events, that is, as occurrences of historical singularities with great consequences for the subsequent unfolding of culture and society. But the catastrophe is not an Historical Event: it is too random, aleatory and wayward for that. It is a kind of *non*-event — the temporal equivalent of Marc Auge's non-places — that does not fit *into*, but rather exists *outside of*, any meaningful sequences of cultural history. The catastrophe, unlike the Event, does not create History, it only ruptures and splinters it into random bifurcations of sequences that break away from each other, hurling off into realms of semiotic vacancy.

But ignoring catastrophes, like ignoring history, only leads to repeating them. Those architects who will be in charge of the new world ahead of us, especially before the new maps of the cosmosphere resolidify, should take this present opportunity to heed the data which a careful examination of these catastrophes reveals. The ontological and cosmological revelations which I have found in them should be taken into account and carefully considered before *any* new maps are drawn up.

There will never be a catastrophe free society, but it *is* possible to have a society in which catastrophes are kept to a necessary minimum, thus reverting the signification of the word itself back to its original Greek connotations of "an *unexpected* reversal," rather than an expected daily occurrence.

A Brief Note on Civilization's Loss of Command Over Its Environment

One of the constitutive aspects of Martin Heidegger's analysis of the worldhood of the world — of its nature as *a* world — is that the objects around us making up our daily lives create a kind of closed referential totality such that we scarcely notice them. That is, the objects that surround and comprise the everydayness of our world have a tendency to withdraw from us and *blend in* to the world which they compose. They only stand out when they *break down*, become unusable or otherwise damaged. At that point, the object becomes *conspicuous* — Heidegger's example of the broken hammer has become proverbial — and stands forth into our awareness *as a problem*. The object no longer blends in but has now shifted into a theoretical mode in which it has become a problem for the human intellect to solve.[1]

But as the following chapters should, if I have done my job right, make abundantly clear, we are now surrounded, everywhere we look, by broken technological artifacts that have stood forth from the background of global consumer society and made themselves conspicuous through the increasingly ubiquitous phenomena of accidents and catastrophes. *Technology as a whole,* that is to say, has now come into question as the result of this pile-up of broken down machines that have come crashing forth from out of the background of our awareness and into the field of our concern. Technology, as was once the case during, say, the nineteenth century, no longer forms an unnoticed and therefore subliminal world-round inside which we are contained, but now stands forth into the clearing of our mentality as something that has become a problem to be solved, and therefore, impossible to ignore. The entire technological landscape has now shifted into the mode of Heidegger's broken hammer, and so it must now be theorized about as a problem.

A Brief Note on Civilization's Loss of Command

Apparently, the decade of the 1930s was the point at which this took place, for it wasn't until then that books written about technology in the abstract began to appear, beginning with Oswald Spengler's *Man and Technics* in 1931[2] and Lewis Mumford's *Technics and Civilization* in 1934.[3] Heidegger's famous essay "The Question Concerning Technology" was first delivered in its earliest form as one of his Bremen Lectures of 1949, while Marshall McLuhan's *The Mechanical Bride* soon followed in 1951.[4] Jacques Ellul's *Technological Society*, furthermore, appeared in its original French version in 1954,[5] while the later books of McLuhan, such as *Understanding Media,* soon followed.[6]

Once any subject — and in this case, we are concerned with technology — has shifted into the mode of discussion, worry and theory, you can be sure that that subject is being noticed precisely because it has become a problem.

It was Arnold Toynbee, furthermore, who, in his monumental *A Study of History*, pointed out back in the 1930s that one of the conspicuous signs of a disintegrating society is a slow, gradual loss of command of its ability to control its environment.[7] A decreasing technical and artistic ability, he insisted, was one of the symptoms — though not the cause — of the breakdown of a civilization.

The great civilizations have each had their own particular stylistic bias; that is, like human individuals, they all did one thing better than the others. For the Egyptians, this was their elaborate articulation of the rituals and technologies associated with the Afterlife; for the Greeks, it was a keen aesthetic sensibility; for the Hindus, a superior religious development; for the Mesopotamians, an advanced hydraulic civilization based upon an extremely complex irrigation system; and for the West, it has been a machinic specialization evident from as early as the stirrups and iron horseshoes of the fifth century.

Consistent with this logic, then, a breakdown in one or the other of these areas of expertise in their respective civilizations should be an unfailing marker that the society in question had reached the limits of its mortality, and was beginning to enter the initial stages of its senescence. And indeed, when one surveys the evidence, this does appear to be the case.

In ancient Egypt, for instance, a gradual loss of competence in the technical abilities attending the mortuary practices of its ancient cults becomes evident around the period of the 22nd Dynasty, in which the elaborate imagery associated with tomb decoration begins to disappear.

A Brief Note on Civilization's Loss of Command

Coffins become shoddier and shoddier from this point on and by the 25th Dynasty, the famous canopic jars were artistically inferior as well. By this point, the Egyptians were even beginning to forget their own traditions, for the two jars associated with the falcon, Qebehsenuef, and the jackal, Duamutef, were confused and inverted such that the jackal became associated with Qebehsenuef and the falcon with Duamutef.[8]

It was the great Near Eastern scholar Thorkild Jacobsen, furthermore, who noticed that the shift in Mesopotamia from the homeland of the Sumerians in the south near the Persian Gulf, to the north with the coming of the Babylonians, and then even further north with the Assyrians, paralleled a gradual depletion and exhaustion of arable soils along the banks of the Tigris and Euphrates Rivers. Jacobsen suspected that this shift was not accidental but mapped out the slow, inevitable salinization of the soils due to the failing Mesopotamian irrigation system. The shifting of each Mesopotamian kingdom further and further north was symptomatic of its southern neighbors' gradual loss of command over their land, as their canals silted up, and their soils became ruined by salt.[9]

In ancient India, a gradual loss of command over the religious sphere begins to become evident from about the twelfth century on, where a certain sugary sweetness appears first in Jayadeva's *Gita Govinda* and then with the gradual rise and spread of the sentimentality of the *bhakti* cults with their Krishna avatars and circling gopis.[10] The sophistication of yoga and philosophy slowly gave way to the kitsch of folk art and popular piety.

And in Classical civilization, as is well known, the decline in Greek sculpture and statuary that began to set in from the Hellenistic period was tantamount to the rise of melodrama, realism and bombast — first evident in the "Wagnerian" art of Pergamene — which became slowly rigidified and calcined until, with the severe and imposing Roman portrait busts, this great art came to its end.

But these, of course, are only some of the most conspicuous examples of the phenomenon. We need only think of a few others — the loss of the Hinayana Buddhist control over the great irrigation tanks on the island of Ceylon; the loss of the ability of the Polynesians of Easter Island to create their stone statues, which had become legend already by the time of Captain Cook's arrival in the eighteenth century; or the ghostly, dust-blown ruins of desert oasis cities like Petra and Palmyra — in order to remind ourselves that the phenomenon is not at all a rare one, for *every* civilization is mortal and *all* eventually lose their ability to shape and command Form in the effort to reverse Entropy into higher, more complex dissipative structures.

And this is no less so in the case of our modern Western civilization, as the following catalogue of disasters reveals. Indeed, the increasing banality of disaster, its overwhelming everydayness, points to the fact that the West is slowly losing its grip over its environment, namely, its ability to command Nature by manipulating its forces with machines and technological apparatuses. It was precisely this ability — first evident in the windmills, waterwheels and mechanical clocks of the twelfth and thirteenth centuries — that marked the emergence of Western civilization as a unique society entering upon the stage of world history with a style of unprecedented technological mastery over Nature. An ever increasing abundance of catastrophes, however — whether defined as "technological" or "natural" — means that more and more turbulence is building up in the system of the West's great global megamachine, and as any student of chaos theory knows, turbulence can only increase so much before the system snaps into a phase change governed by an altogether different systemic attractor.

Everywhere we look nowadays, upon the distant horizons — like those tiny burning villages and shattered boats and windmills in the dim backgrounds of the paintings of Bosch and Brueghel — planes are falling, cars are crashing and buildings are crumbling, their foundations washed away into the sea by the ever-swelling tides and tsunamis brought forth by rising sea levels and global earthquakes. It would appear that we are entering into the early stages of a mortal illness that is spreading throughout the West and is revealing itself through the pile up of disasters as the West's gradual loss of command over its own particular environment, namely, the orb of the earth itself.

But, after all, the great cavalcade of machines cannot continue to unfold forever. Sooner or later, the sheer abundance and profusion of them is bound to generate so much entropy in the environment that it will cause far more problems for us than the machines will actually solve.

Once, long ago, at the dawning of Western civilization, its creaking windmills and chiming clocks shone with a kind of divine aura to the Gothic monks who brought them into being as revelations of a whole new age, a Third Age, that is, of the Holy Spirit — as articulated by Joachim of Flora — during which the Spirit would descend to earth and reveal a New macro-order of world history to those initiated into the secrets of the Machine and its inner workings.

A Brief Note on Civilization's Loss of Command

But now, the Machine has become more of a source of fear and apprehension than a revelation of the interior workings of the mind of God. It has shifted its ontological status from a mechanization of the Holy Spirit, to a threatening mechanical demon sent up from Hell — like those homicidal robots in the *Terminator* movies — to harry and hound the human being to the edges of his Final Days.

We never know, anymore, when the elevator we are riding in is going to stop; or the balcony we are leaning on to look over the atrium of some hotel is going to give way; or whether the roof of the stage at a rock concert is going to come down on our heads. Technology, these days, can no longer be trusted.

We simply never know when it is going to turn against us, for it is becoming increasingly more and more expected that it will fail, give out, and bite back when we least expect it to.

Thus, the arc of Western culture, long past its noon, and long since having diverged with the ever rising arc of technology which surpassed it long ago, is coming, lightly, to rest upon the earth, while somewhere, not too far ahead of it, the arc of technology, too, is now coming down from the heavens like a falling satellite whose orbit is decaying as it comes crashing toward the earth.

Who knows where the pieces will land?

Part I: Disasters of Paleomodernity

Paleomodernity is a name which I have given to that phase of modernity which begins around the time of the Industrial Revolution and lasts down to about the outbreak of World War II, at which point this epoch gives way to what I have called Neomodernity. It is a wholly unoriginal designation that parallels the distinctions made by the European sociologists Ulrich Beck and Zygmunt Bauman, who call the two epochs "first and second modernity" in Beck's case, and "heavy and light modernity" in Bauman's. Bauman has characterized heavy modernity in his various books as an age of massive engineering projects, center — periphery models in industry and the economy, the building and extension of nation states into empires and general cultural stability all around. Light modernity, by contrast, or, as he usually calls it, Liquid Modernity, is an age in which the nation state is in process of disintegration and massive engineering projects have given way to the microworld of the small and the ever smaller in the realm of electronics, quantum mechanics and genetic engineering. Liquid Modernity, moreover, as the designation implies, is a time in which change is happening so fast that nothing can ever crystallize into shape and take any kind of lasting form for very long. Individuals, in such an age, can no longer expect to work one job all their lives but must be constantly prepared to adapt and adjust to new and different jobs which, every day, render old skills obsolete. Truths and knowledge, in such an age, are changing so rapidly that it is scarcely an exaggeration to say, as Bauman does, that what is considered "true" today may not be so any longer when one wakes up tomorrow morning. It is an age, in other words, of cultural meltdown and disintegration.[1]

But it was the German sociologist Ulrich Beck who spotted a difference between these two ages in the kinds of accidents and disasters which

Part I: Disasters of Paleomodernity

take on form inside them, a distinction which I find useful enough to borrow as this book's guiding metanarrative schema. The accidents of the first modernity, as he puts it, have very specific boundaries which confine them spatially, temporally and socially, boundaries which are largely missing from the occurrence of such disasters in the second modernity.[2]

Disasters of Old Modernity such as, for instance, the sinking of the *Titanic* and the destruction of the *Hindenburg*—disasters which I have chosen as archetypally demonstrative for this age — are events which occur in very localized and specific parts of the world, and they are events whose consequences remain largely confined to those regions. They have, in other words, a definite beginning, middle and end, like a novel, and they are also very, very concrete in that the effects and circumstances surrounding their occurrence is largely perceptible to the immediate senses.

With the later disasters of Neomodernity, on the other hand, as Beck points out, such as in the cases of Chernobyl or Bhopal, this is no longer the case, since such accidents occur on a much larger scale with much more difficult to understand causes, and their consequences, moreover, remain open ended. These are accidents which affected vast geographical regions with invisible antagonists — chemicals in the case of Bhopal, radiation in the case of Chernobyl — whose effects continue to unfold into the present day. There are, for instance, still unborn children who will bear birth defects from radiation poisoning as the result of the Chernobyl disaster, and in that sense, the temporal boundaries of that disaster remain unconfined, or at least, unknown (and probably unknowable). In Bhopal to the present day, moreover, the lives of the disaster victims remain an uncertain affair of continuing health complications such as respiratory difficulties, heart arrhythmias, sleep disorders and other ongoing forms of life-disrupting wreckage. Indeed, the Bhopal chemical plant, still standing, continues to poison the groundwater in the region.

It is also difficult in such disasters to know who to blame, for they are largely the result of state and corporate organizational incompetence. Anyone who tries to sue a corporation knows how difficult it is to do so successfully, since responsibility in such organizations is skillfully diffused throughout the network of the company and sometimes even rests in the hands of obscure and shadowy state officials.

In the case of the crisp and classically bounded lines of the *Titanic* and *Hindenburg* accidents, by contrast, it is known precisely who was responsible — J. Bruce Ismay, White Star Line, etc. — and direct measures

Part I: Disasters of Paleomodernity

could therefore be taken to improve safety standards in the respective industries within which these accidents occurred. In the case of the *Hindenburg*, the entire passenger airship service was discontinued, while in the case of the *Titanic*, trans–Atlantic sea travel continued on with new safety regulations implemented, such as adequate number of lifeboats, new wireless code regulations, etc.

The effects of these old-fashioned industrial accidents, moreover, are usually known with a fair amount of precision: we know exactly how many people died in both cases and we also know that in the future, there will not be *more* people killed as the result of consequences from these particular accidents. They have very specific temporal and spatial boundaries, in other words.

These accidents, then, are small and local by contrast with those of Neomodernity, and also with those which we are experiencing today on a planetary scale, such as global warming and terrorist threats, both of which surround and implicate everyone on the planet as potential victims.[3]

So, as this book unfolds, we will see the accidents grow ever larger, more diffuse, non-linear and complex, until with those of the final chapters, we will watch as the entire planet is engulfed by a new species of accident that is no longer local, but global in extent. Indeed, global accidents would appear to accompany globalization as its inextricable shadow and side effect.

We will begin, however, with two old-fashioned industrial accidents from the days of Paleomodernity, when a certain naivete still characterized the technological project as a whole. The sinking of the *Titanic* and the explosion of the *Hindenburg* were small and local, taking place in the North Atlantic Ocean 400 miles off the coast of Newfoundland in the one case, and in Lakehurst, New Jersey, in the other, but yet, their occurrence decisively opens up a new age for Western industrial civilization, an age in which a slow and gradual loss of the ability to retain command over ever larger and larger technological systems begins to dawn.

It is an age — the Age of Catastrophes — that comes suddenly into view in 1912 with the sinking of the *Titanic*, and an age whose ending — as the direct result of the altering of the planetary atmosphere with greenhouse gases — is also now coming slowly into view, somewhere within the space of about a century from now, when the entire surface of the planet will be restructured in unimaginable ways.

One

The Sinking of the *Titanic* and the Fate of the Mobile City

Iceberg

The RMS *Titanic* struck an iceberg at 11:40 on the night of April 14, 1912, and sank just a little over two hours later, at 2:20 on the morning of the 15th. The ship had just embarked upon her maiden voyage and was headed for New York City carrying 2,223 people, having departed from Southampton on April 10. The ship was under the command of one Captain Edward J. Smith, a veteran seaman of some 40 years, and had been constructed by the Belfast shipbuilding firm of Harland and Wolff as part of White Star Line's three ship project — together with the *Olympic* and the *Gigantic*— of rivaling Cunard's twin steamers, the *Lusitania* and the *Mauretania*. It was the largest man-made moving object ever built at that time in the world.

Traveling at a speed of 21.5 knots, and in an area roughly 400 miles off the coast of Newfoundland, the ship struck a 10,000-year-old piece of melted Greenland ice which had been pushed slightly further south than usual by the so-called Labrador Current, a cold current following the contours of Labrador, Newfoundland and Nova Scotia while pressing up against the warming Gulf Stream to its immediate south. The collision caused a 90-meter-long series of ruptures to open up on *Titanic*'s starboard (or right hand) side as the result of faulty rivets which had been mixed with slag and were therefore of inferior quality and gave way under stress.[1] The ship had been designed to stay afloat if all four of its forward compartments were flooded, but not the fifth. The ruptures, however, ensured that water seeped into all *five* compartments and, as a result, the ship was "mathematically doomed" to sink at that point.

Famously, there were only twenty lifeboats onboard — 16 wooden lifeboats and 4 collapsibles — enough to save a theoretical 1,178 people, although in reality only 711 were saved, due to the loss of two of the collapsible boats and the failure to fill the others to capacity. The other 1,513 passengers, accordingly, drowned (or else froze to death) in the cold waters of the icy North Atlantic.

The survivors were rescued by the *Carpathia*, which arrived on the scene at approximately 4:10 that morning.

Mobile City

The sinking of the *Titanic* is *the* archetypal accident of the age of what I have called "Paleomodernity" or "Old Modernity," an age which is succeeded by "Neomodernity" or "New Modernity" at around the time of World War II. Paleomodernity begins somewhere around the year 1800 with the rise of the Industrial Revolution when the burning of coal as the first fossil fuel of the Carboniferous Age began to heat up an army of steam engines whose metabolism colored the grayish skies of England a sooty dirt brown. Old Modernity is thus Fossil Fuel Era I, and it is characterized by an initial assault on the earth's atmosphere in the form of thermodynamic engine by-products of carbon dioxide gasses which slowly begin to build a new heat dome over the earth. As theoretician Peter Sloterdijk points out, the demolition of the old cosmology of angelic spheres surrounding and encasing the earth with the rise of the Copernican cosmology was here traded off for the creation of a new kind of technologically produced greenhouse sphere composed out of carbon gasses and methane within which civilization was now to be enshrouded henceforth.[2]

But also characteristic of Old Modernity was the creation of the nation state as a political enclosure sealing off European ethnic groups into bounded and contained vessels of state within which they could take on their identities as part of "imagined communities"—à la Benedict Anderson—held together by literacy and a shared language.[3] The nation state was *the* great political structure of this age and, together with its colonial extensions, began to carve out huge swaths of the earth as nationalistic empires unto themselves. This race for Empire inevitably laid down the basis for the coming of the First World War which would provide the crucible within which the nation states of Old Modernity would begin to melt down and disintegrate.

Also central to the structure of Old Modernity was the project of replacing the natural order of things with a Human Order. This was the motivation for the colossal engineering projects which characterize this age from the Crystal Palace in London (1851) and the Eiffel Tower in Paris (1889) to the giant dams, bridges and skyscrapers of the American 1930s. The Human Order is the attempt to create a kind of invisible dome within which the laws of nature hover in eternal suspension so that the process of human cultural formation can take place within the anthropogenic space created by the dome. In order to do this, however, the state has to come into being so that it can guarantee the safety of its citizens as they proceed with the task of building civilization, while the natural order of chaos and lawlessness, of predators and prey, of the strong against the weak, is suspended by a kind of process of reverse entropy. These various culture spheres (i.e., the French Culture Sphere, the German Culture Sphere, etc.), normally invisible, were, however, in the middle of the nineteenth century, beginning to become visible in their engineering equivalents in the form of the iron and glass architecture first used by the French architect Fontaine who, in 1829 used wrought iron to construct the glass roof of the Galerie d'Orléans, a part of the Palais Royal in Paris.[4] This was soon followed by Rouhault's design of the Greenhouses of the Botanical Gardens in Paris in 1833 (the Conservatory of the Jardin des Plantes), which became the inspiration for all subsequent iron-framed buildings, including the famous Crystal Palace, the Parisian Arcades and the various train stations and libraries that became a signature of this age. Culture exists within an *invisible* dome, a kind of terrarium, that is built to keep chaos out, and these engineering marvels were beginning to make *visible* this metaphysical principle of the civilizational membrane that functions as a kind of cellular wall of operational self-enclosure. (The glass and iron dome above the *Titanic*'s main staircase is a direct descendant of this architectural tradition.)

The wall is the principle archetype, traditionally speaking, by way of which culture has demarcated itself in opposition to nature, and so yet another structural characteristic of Old Modernity was precisely a sharp tension existing between the spheres of Culture and Nature, one in which it was thought to be the business of culture to subdue and conquer nature with a man-made order that would replace it altogether on a mass scale. The Medieval walled city — Carcassone is archetypal here — is the exemplar of the self-contained city state, but in the nineteenth century, the actual physical walls surrounding European cities had long since disappeared (brought down by gunpowder in the fifteenth century) to give way to the

One. The Titanic

various invisible walls erected by cultures themselves in the form of things like language barriers and artistic style forms.

It was in the nineteenth century, however, that for the first time in history cities began to become portable. That is to say, with the so-called Transport Revolution pointed out by Paul Virilio, in which, with the advent of the railroad and the steam engine and the coming of ships, hot air balloons and dirigibles, civilization began to be something that could be moved about in component pieces from one place to another.[5] Railroads were used to pack up cities and transport their goods elsewhere, which gave way — mid century — to the birth of department stores like Kendal's in Britain and Au Bon Marche in Paris. Indeed, these early department stores — Wanamaker's in Philadelphia being a classic example — were sometimes developed out of converted train depots.

The French philosopher Paul Virilio has termed the sphere of vehicles and bodies in motion the "dromosphere" (after *dromos*, the Greek word for speed). It is a very old sphere, one that goes back to the epoch of the first men mounted upon horseback during the rise of the Indo-Europeans of the fifth millennium B.C. (Evidence for the earliest instance of a horse cult was unearthed at the site of Dereivka in the Lower Dnieper basin dating from around 5000 B.C., where a horse's skull, together with the longbones of its left foot, were found buried in the ground as offerings. Antler cheek pieces for riding horses were also found at this site located not far from the Caspian Sea.[6]) Indeed, the dromosphere is composed of anything that carries human bodies about through space, including both metabolic vehicles like horses and camels, and technological vehicles such as cars, ships, planes, etc.

With the rise, during the nineteenth century, of ever larger and larger vehicles for moving bits of civilization about through space, the dromosphere — long since integrated into the polisphere (the latter being a term I have given to the realm of cities and pedestrians) which, throughout history, has often been the target and enemy of the mounted armies of the dromosphere — began to become dominant over the polisphere. That is to say, the animal *principle of motion* began to overtake the archaic plant-like *principle of rooted stasis* that came into being, once upon a time, with the agricultural revolution of the Neolithic and the invention of the first protocities in walled towns and villages rooted to specific geographies that often later became the targets of mounted warriors on horseback. Nineteenth-century transport technology, to put it otherwise, is mechanized zoology.

Part I: Disasters of Paleomodernity

Indeed, we may say that the overarching principle of nineteenth-century civilization, taken as a whole, was that of Motion, for we see it everywhere we look. Stasis, that artifactual characteristic of high civilizations everywhere — in Buddhism it is even sublimated into a religion — begins, for the first time in history, to crumble and actually becomes the *exception* while motion becomes the new *rule*: trains, balloons, dirigibles, bicycles, steam driven automobiles and boats. *Motion* pictures. Muybridge. The Gatlin gun. The Kinetoscope, the Bioscope, the Zoescope, etc., etc. People scrambling about through the ancient framework of the polisphere by means of ever greater and more modernized technical forms of new mobility. Indeed, motion of the physical body through the cavernous spaces carved out by these world cities into the earth becomes, at this time, *the* signature of Modernity. The titles of Verne's novels —*Around the World in 80 Days; A Trip to the Moon; Five Weeks in a Balloon; 20,000 Leagues Under the Sea; Journey to the Center of the Earth*—shift and squirm with this restless energy of putting the body in a machine and setting it into motion around, beneath, across or away from the surface of the earth.

Consequently, by the time we arrive at the construction of the *Titanic*, and her sister ships, the *Olympic* and the *Gigantic*, the principle of speed has so overwhelmed and taken control of the polisphere, that with the largest man-made moving object in the world at that time, what we are really confronted with is the world's first moveable city. The *Titanic* is nothing if not a miniaturized city capable of moving about through space. It is the sort of technological mutation which results when the stratum of the polisphere is so completely overlaid by that of the dromosphere that the polisphere, from henceforth, is forced to express itself through new, mobile entities such as a "floating city," to use another of Verne's book titles. The principle of "rain, steam, speed," to quote from Turner's painting, has so overwhelmed the city that it has caused a piece of the city to actually detach itself and become mobile.

But this, of course, now means that, for the first time, whole populations of people, thousands at a time, are put in motion at dangerously high speeds which are more proper to the dromosphere than they are to the polisphere. As a result, these populations are now subjected to the creation of the world's first technologically induced mass catastrophes. To put an entire city of three thousand people in motion across the North Atlantic is simultaneously to invent the first mass industrial catastrophe — together with the creation of the first industrial refugees from such a dis-

One. The Titanic

aster — for it is, of course, one of the structural properties of the dromosphere that its vehicles often collide with one another. In ancient history, cities could not rise up like a creation out of a Miyazaki movie and go walking about the landscape, where they crash into each other; in those days, they had to translate their motive power into sieging armies that were then unleashed upon other cities, which erected technologies of obstruction against them. In this ancient scenario, the city with its technologies of obstruction came up against the sieging armies of the dromosphere with their technologies of ballistics, but by the nineteenth century, the city's ancient, and very persistent, resistance to the dromosphere had collapsed and given up its defensive fortresses and obstacles of obstruction to allow the dromosphere to take it hostage.

The result: when bicycles are in motion, they are at risk of crashing into pedestrians; with cars in motion, they are not only at risk of crashing into pedestrians, but also into other cars. With *entire cities* now in motion across the earth, however, the risk factors grow to epic proportions, for it is now *geological formations* — which cities, once upon a time, had used to build and construct themselves around, beneath, above and beyond — that become the primary object which these mobile cities are at risk of crashing into. Hence, the 2008 Sichuan earthquake in China, with its construction of the massive Three Gorges Dam — the world's largest dam, ever — was tantamount to the crashing of the Chinese polisphere into the geological lithosphere, causing the world's first man-made earthquake. With the *Titanic*, however, the *geomorphic* (i.e., having been shaped by tectonic forces without being a lithic object proper) formation crashed into was a 10,000-year-old piece of melted Greenland ice that had strayed too far south into the shipping lanes.

The collision, then, of this mobile city with a piece of Greenland ice seems — strangely enough — to be an allegorical foreshadowing of our current climatological situation, for the collision of industrial civilization with the earth's geo- and biospheres is now resulting in a particular anxiety on the part of our climate scientists regarding the fate of the Greenland ice sheet. That ice sheet is melting at an alarmingly fast rate and our climate scientists now point out that if carbon dioxide concentrations in the atmosphere reach 500 parts per million — which they are scheduled to do by about 2050 (currently they are at about 392 ppm)[7] — then this will soon drag the earth's global mean temperature up to about a 3 degree increase, an amount sufficient to tip the Greeland ice sheet into an irreversible catastrophic process of melting. This will raise sea levels by about 7 meters, enough to flood most of our coastal cities and make living in them too difficult to manage.[8]

It seems, then, that all our mobile cities have crashed into the earth as though it were a separate object from the paved roads which they inhabit, resulting in a cosmic accident capable of generating sufficient heat to melt the polar ice caps and raise the global sea levels.

In a dreamlike, allegorical kind of way, it is almost as though the whole drama of global warming had been actually *caused* by the *Titanic*'s crashing into that one piece of Greenland ice, which, on a magical level, at least, set loose a whole series of chain reactions that have resulted in the hot era that we are now in process of entering. (The global mean temperature has already risen by nearly one degree since the 1950s.) But this is, of course, poetic thinking and I don't mean it literally, only figuratively.

However, the accident of the *Titanic* does seem to be the overture to the whole opera that is now entering its third and final act, the Era of Fossil Fuel III (Neomodernity, beginning just after the Second World War, was Fossil Fuel Era II) in which vanishing oil reserves combine with disappearing water sources as the world's great rivers dry up due to diminished rainfall and the spread of massive desertification across Europe and North America. Soon, it seems, our mobile cities are destined to become static once again, mired — like the rusting hulks of the beached ships littering the dried up floor of the Aral Sea — as huge, lumbering ruins of steel and concrete in windblown deserts subject to Great Dust Bowl conditions of soil erosion and vanishing vegetation.[9] The other cities, the coastal ones, meanwhile, like the *Titanic* itself, will be submerged by the world's oceans, where they will lie glittering beneath the waves, remembering their days of hurried magnificence and glory as an epoch long since buried in the past.

Indeed, it seems that the age of floating cities heralded by the advent of the *Titanic* will soon be over. Eventually, the dromosphere will uncouple, as it was in the beginning, from the polisphere, only this time it will take the form of camel and horse riding nomads dragging the crumbling carapaces of creaking automobiles behind them just as horses once used to pull carriages. These nomads, and their particular dromosphere, will exist, once again as in the ancient past, in a world of smooth spaces whose surfaces will be entirely denuded of cities. The American Midwest, as one such area, will be transformed into a vast Sahara-like desert — as it once was —

uninhabitable save to these groups of horse-riding nomads who will drift across its empty spaces as nomads have always done, camping in the ruins of deserted farm houses and abandoned cities.

But that is a vision — according to climatologists like James Lovelock and Mark Lynas — for the southern latitudes. In the far northern latitudes, things will be different, for there, on the coasts of the North Sea, something else will likely transpire, as a society with vastly reduced human populations may once again see civilization of a new and unprecedented kind flourish with the disappearance of the Arctic ice.[10] Indeed, the shores of the Arctic Sea may become host to a new kind of Mediterranean civilization with its comparatively warm climate encasing a new polar society sprawling across hitherto unused tracts of land in Greenland, Siberia and northern Canada. The North Atlantic civilization, by then long since faded into myths and legends remembering a vanished age of Mechanical Giants, may well give way to a Northern Arctic civilization.

Who knows?

Two

On the *Hindenburg* Disaster and the Technologization of the Soul's Descent to Earth

Explosion

On Thursday, May 6, 1937, at 7:25 P.M. local time, the German passenger airship LZ129 *Hindenburg* exploded into flames as it was attempting to land at Lakehurst Naval Air Station in Lakehurst, New Jersey. Within 34 seconds, the entire ship, the largest air vehicle ever put into the sky, was consumed by flames. Of the 97 passengers onboard, 35 were killed (plus 1 member of the ground crew).

The *Hindenburg*, though, had already been up and running for over a year, with 62 successful flights behind it, 10 of those flights having already traversed the same route from Frankfurt, Germany, to Lakehurst. In fact, the German company DELAG (*Deutsche Luftschiffahrts-Aktiengesellschaft* or "German Airship Travel Corporation") founded in 1909, had, in its 27 years of passenger airship service, a *perfect* flying record with no passenger accidents whatsoever. In this respect, it was unique amongst all the other airship companies of France, Britain and the United States, all of which had suffered serious airship catastrophes by 1937 and had, consequently, mostly gone out of service.

Thus, the mystery of what caused the *Hindenburg*— the world's finest and most sophisticated airship product at that time — to suddenly burst into flame with little apparent provocation has been debated by experts since 1937, and various theories, such as sabotage by a terrorist who might have planted a bomb in the girders of its Duralumin frame, have been suggested over the years. But the problem now seems to have been credibly solved by one Greg Feith, a former American senior air safety investigator with the National Transportation Safety Board.[1]

According to Feith, the airship had generated a static build up of electricity on its outer skin due to the storm that had just passed through the naval station. The ship's pilot, one Max Pruss, as he approached the mooring mast on the ground, made a sharp left turn when the wind changed direction, and since the craft was not designed for making sharp turns, this caused one of the ship's rear bracing wires, located inside the ship near gas cell number 4, to snap and puncture the cell, thus creating a hydrogen leak. But as the ship's wet mooring ropes made contact with the ground, this conducted the electrical charge to flow from the metal frame of the ship down to the ground, thus creating a differential. The craft's skin, however, was still highly charged with static electricity due to the atmospheric conditions, and this caused a spark to jump from the outer skin to the metal frame, thus igniting the leaking hydrogen, which then roared through the ship and consumed it within a mere 34 seconds.

I'm no engineer, but the theory seems perfectly plausible to me, and I see no reason to reject it out of hand. For the time being, then, we will let it stand as the likeliest explanation for the disaster.

Building a New Cosmosphere

By contrast with the wreck of the *Titanic*, in which the great dromospheric vessel was destroyed by water and ice and slipped down through a crack in the earth into the Underworld below, with the *Hindenburg* we have an accident which, cosmologically speaking, has an exactly opposed semiotic, for the airship is a dromospheric conveyance of the Upper World — the realm of the Spirit in traditional cosmology — which comes down out of the air and is destroyed by fire, like the descending tongues of flame of the Holy Spirit at Pentecost. Fire and air were the elements in ancient cosmology associated with the Upper World, while earth and water were those belonging properly to the earthly world below. Between these two accidents, the human world of the mesocosm exists as a thin crust of habitation in between two *very* ancient and archaic realms, realms for which, as these accidents make clear, we are in the process of building technological equivalents.

Most ancient cosmologies from the time of Paleolithic shamanism on down were structured along the lines of this three layered vision of the human world caught in between the spiritual forces of the heavens above and the earthly, or chthonic forces, of the realm below. (This is reflected,

Part I: Disasters of Paleomodernity

for instance, in the archetypal opposition of the bird and the snake: note that the Titans in Greek myth were normally associated with serpents.) Our accidents and catastrophes, then, seem to be revealing to us the degree to which we are not only *not* rid of the ancient cosmologies of traditional mythological man, but are actually translating the images of that two dimensional visionary world, for the first time in history, into mechanized three dimensional equivalents. It is almost as though the ancients were providing us with a blueprint for the entire endeavor of the construction of industrial technological civilization.

With aerial technologies, for instance, we have been engaged all throughout the twentieth century in building mechanized equivalents of the various spirit vehicles found scattered throughout the ancient myths and tales of traditional societies everywhere from the fiery chariots of Ezekiel or Phaeton to Daedalus's wings; or the Hindu cosmic sun bird Garuda (the national airlines of Indonesia are called Garuda Airlines) to the Eagle of Zeus who picks up Ganymede and makes off with him; *all* are prototypes and forerunners of our airplanes, space shuttles and satellites.

This mechanization of the realm of the Spirit began at the end of the eighteenth century, when, in 1783, Pilâtre de Rozier and the marquis d'Arlandes made the first, short flight into the heavens with a hot air balloon in Versailles. They were followed less than a fortnight later by Professor Jacques Charles and Marie Noel Robert in a hydrogen balloon launched from the Tuileries.[2] It was in France, then, that we began to rise up off the ground and venture into the Troposphere for the first time in human history. But the problem with hot air balloons is that they can't be directed very easily and so, in the middle of the nineteenth century, the steam engine was crossed with the gas balloon to create the first dirigibles — also accomplished in France — which enabled these airships to go at specific speeds in particular directions. The internal combustion engine was brought onboard the dirigible by the end of the century, but it was the Germans who, with Count Ferdinand von Zeppelin, created the first great rigid airships by giving to the dirigible an internal skeleton in the form of aluminum girders.

From 1900 on, when von Zeppelin's LZ1 made its first flight into the air from Lake Constance, dirigibles became bigger, longer and better as he gradually perfected them. Indeed, in his mind, they were conceived as warships for dropping bombs on the French, and during World War I,

Two. The Hindenburg Disaster

that is exactly what they were used for, since it was in that war that the Germans invented the practice of the aerial bombardment of cities with their attacks on London, Liege and Antwerp using zeppelins loaded with bombs. (The first such attack took place on August 25, 1914, when the Germans launched zeppelins against the city of Antwerp, killing or wounding some 26 people. In May of 1915, London became a target for the first time.) But most of these airships were eventually shot down by British biplanes with incendiary bullets, and so the zeppelins then had to be designed to go higher than the British planes could reach (up to 20,000 feet, whereas the British planes could only fly up to 13,000), eventually climbing up to the stratosphere.[3] But when the British then countered by designing planes mounted with new Rolls Royce combustion engines that could carry them up to 22,000 feet, from whence they could then proceed to bomb the German airships, the zeppelins had seen the end of their day as warships, and so after the war, Count von Zeppelin's company, DELAG, was forced into secularizing its airships strictly for usage as fee paying passenger travel for the very rich.

Thus, with all these events, for the first time in human history, technology is extended *vertically* into the cosmosphere surrounding the earth. We have already seen how the dromosphere, Virilio's realm of vehicles in motion, has, throughout history, been extended *horizontally* across the surface of the earth, where it often comes into conflict with the polisphere, or the realm of cities. In this case, though, the dromosphere is extended vertically for the first time into a new smooth space constituted by the troposphere, the sphere of the weather. Since, as the philosopher Gilles Deleuze has pointed out, nomads have historically favored the realm of the smooth spaces of vast, flat horizontal plains such as deserts and steppes (nomads, in their centauric form of assemblage as man *plus* animal, are the typical constitutive elements of the dromosphere), it becomes possible to see how the atmosphere constitutes an ideal plane for colonization by the technosphere, since it is the ultimate realm of smooth space, freed of all obstructions (above the weather, at least).[4]

With the colonization, then, of the troposphere by hot air balloons, dirigibles and airships, we see the beginnings of the first attempts to recreate the ancient cosmology of whirling planetary spheres, governed by angelic intelligences, surrounding the earth. With these new mechanized spirit vehicles, accordingly, the first layer of the human project of creating a technologized cosmosphere is laid out: the atmotechnological layer of vehicles making use of the dome of the sky as a new plain for modern techno-nomads to roam at will. Later on in mid-century, with the creation of commercial airlines and supersonic jets, a higher, secondary layer of technosphere will be created as the stratosphere above the troposphere is colonized with a layer of faster moving vehicles than those of the airships and hot air balloons which had earlier colonized the troposphere. The atmotechnological layer is then succeeded, as it were, by the sonotechnological layer, where jets capable of travelling faster than the speed of sound will find their proper habitat.

Thus, the evolution of dromospheric vehicles on the ground below as a gradual increase in speed of moving the human body about through space, which had hitherto unfolded within the striated spaces of the cities (and were, correspondingly, constrained, as a result) is now mirrored in the technicization of the cosmosphere surrounding the earth as a series of concentric shells composed out of speeding technological components of dromo-technologies, with the machines conquering each new sphere moving ever faster and faster the further away these spheres are located from the earth. Finally, with the launching of satellites and space stations after the 1950s, the thermosphere beyond the stratosphere was colonized with bits of machinery orbiting the earth at speeds of *thousands of miles an hour*. Indeed, there seems no limit to the speeds to which the human body can be subjected, as each layer of constructed technosphere puts the body into motion faster than the one beneath it. Thus, a thermotechnological layer is added to the sonotechnological and atmotechnological layers below.

In the ancient cosmology of the concentric spheres surrounding the earth, the higher you went, the lighter and more luminous — the closer to God — became the beings inhabiting those realms. Dante, on his ascent through these outer spheres, encounters saints and eventually angels of ever more and more refined spiritual substance. In our technological recreation of this cosmosphere, on the other hand, the higher one goes, the faster the body moves as it drifts away from the earth, now defined as the realm of slow moving entities damned to mere biological locomotion.

In technological civilization, in other words, speed becomes a new kind of soteriological force that is capable of inducing ecstatic trance states that are equivalent to the spiritual ecstacies of the ancient world. When training astronauts are subjected to intense G-forces in the centrifuge that whirls them around at high levels of acceleration, they sometimes have near death experiences. Thus, Bernini's sculpture of Saint Theresa in orgas-

Two. The Hindenburg *Disaster*

mic ecstacy as she is penetrated by the arrows of the Spirit gives way to the image of the enthralled astronaut looking out the tiny port window beside him as the lunar landscape speeds past him and he recites his Genesis cosmology to an audience located thousands of miles away down on the earth below, rapt in front of their television sets at the prospect of this cosmic fusion of speed and spirit in Modernity.

The problem comes, however, when the human body is moved by means of these conveyances *downward* toward the earth, for the body, and the dromospheric conveyance carrying it, must shift gears and move ever more and more slowly as it approaches the earth once again. (Just as upon awakening, the astral body must shift gears out of the dreaming state as it retrofits itself back into a physical body that it must now adjust to.) In ancient cosmology, by contrast, the soul dropping downward through the spheres on its way toward birth in a physical body on the earth actually fell *faster*, since with each sphere that it passed, it acquired some element that made it heavier and heavier as it approached the earth. The earth, remember, was in those days at the center of the universe precisely because it was made out of earth, the heaviest of all four classical elements. All bodies, correspondingly, fell toward the earth as a central basin of attraction precisely because it was located at the center of the cosmos.

Consider the disaster of the space shuttle *Columbia* in 2003 — which is a kind of replay of the *Hindenburg* disaster at a higher technospherical level — which shows what happens, or the danger of what *can* happen, anyway, when shifting from one of these outermost spheres to a lower one. Upon encountering the earth's atmosphere, the shuttle, just like the *Hindenburg* as it approached the earth, exploded into flames and was consumed in a matter of seconds. It had, as it were, crashed into the invisible dome separating the biologically habitable realm of the World Below from the biologically hostile outer surrounding space of the World Above.

Catastrophes, then, often mark the invisible membranes of boundaries between worlds. Just as the space shuttle *Columbia* marked the boundary of the point of entry into the earth's atmosphere, so the *Hindenburg*'s approach to the earth marked the boundary where the troposphere meets the striated spaces of the polisphere below. In atmospheric terms, the friction generated by the meeting of the troposphere with the earth's outermost geological crust generates weather in the form of static electricity, lightning, tornadoes and such. And it was at precisely this level of friction between the Upper World and the mesocosm of the human world below that the

Part I: Disasters of Paleomodernity

Hindenburg exploded as it encountered this lower sphere, moving too quickly in relation to it to maneuver successfully without undergoing structural stresses that caused its interior bracing wire to snap.

Navigating from one sphere to the next is a function of deceleration. Where two worlds meet — in both ancient mythology as well as in our modern technological reconstructions of them — there always exists a liminal zone of danger in which the unprepared human biological vessel may be torn to pieces by the friction generated at the meeting point of the spheres. In ancient history, it is precisely at the boundaries of our cities, for example — where, atop the battlements, mounted archers rained arrows down and soldiers poured Greek fire upon the armies besieging the walls below — that were the most dangerous zones of these ancient polises. Even in death itself, the body is shattered and must be left behind as the soul crosses the invisible boundary from one sphere of existence to another.

So, too often it happens that in our technicization of the cosmologies of the ancients, we fail to take into account that their cosmologies might actually have reflected not just symbolic but also *real* aspects of the physical world that are not necessarily obvious to the senses but which were clearly intuited in these ancient myths nonetheless. The dangers of crossing boundaries from one cosmosphere to the next seems to have been one of their main intuitions.

Today, we build our machines and then thrust them heedlessly at, around, above, below and into the earth, with little expectation that they will ever meet any form of resistance by unseen forces.

But one of the revelatory functions of catastrophes, such as the disasters of the *Hindenburg* or the space shuttle *Columbia*, is that they often make such invisible boundaries visible. Indeed, *every* disaster reveals some hitherto hidden facet of the human technological interface with the earth and its cosmic rhythms — usually in the nature of a misalignment — a facet that would not otherwise have come into visibility in any other way. It is important, then, that we learn from them about the hidden, unseen nature of the forces and various fields of resistance which their occurrence unconceals for us.

For almost invariably, where there is an accident, there exists an invisible threshold of one sort or another which has not successfully been taken into account. Nowadays, though, it is true, we hear on a routine basis about one catastrophe or another which has occurred somewhere on the planet, and seems to be occurring all over the planet with ever greater and

Two. The Hindenburg Disaster

greater frequency and level of devastation. Indeed, catastrophes, unlike in times past — as I have pointed out in this book's introduction — are currently becoming the planet's norm, rather than its exception. And this can only mean that planetary industrial society is now running up against boundaries, limits and invisible walls just about everywhere it turns. We are not, apparently, paying attention to what we are doing or where we are going. We are behaving somewhat like the proverbial child with the new toy on Christmas Day who runs off with it, oblivious to everything else around him, while he trips and falls.

How long technological civilization can continue to develop and colonize the planet and its surrounding cosmosphere, with the increasingly frequent occurrence of such catastrophes mounting all around us, is a matter that, as of yet, remains to be seen.

Part II: Disasters of Neomodernity

Neomodernity is the period which begins just after World War II — and which includes such economic structures as GATT, the IMF, the World Bank and the UN — and extends down to about the last decade or so of the twentieth century. The accidents which occur after the year 2000 or so tend to take on a planetary scale and significance — just about the time during which the creation of economic globalization (along with *its* structures, such as Global Free Trade Agreements, NAFTA, the World Trade Organization, the Internet, etc., etc.) begins to go into full swing — and so they are addressed in this book's third section as a separate group.

The disasters of Neomodernity, though large and open ended, as Ulrich Beck has shown, are not yet, for the most part, planetary in scope.[1] However, they are — from Bhopal and Chernobyl clear on down to Columbine — of very great significance *cosmologically* and *ontologically* speaking. That is to say, they bring into question the very nature of the human mode of being in the world as a technological entity.

They are *world-spheric* disasters which pose a threat to all traditional modes of human existence. Bhopal and Chernobyl, taken by themselves, are accidents which threaten human life in an ontological manner. They assault the very possibility of the mode of human being-in-the-world *inside* cultural containers — what Peter Sloterdijk calls Anthropogenic World Islands ("You insert apes and out come humans")[2] — which act as extensions of his immune system to isolate and protect him from the *not*-culture world that surrounds and ever threatens him with non-existence. The space shuttle disasters bring into question the possibility of his existence as an outer-earthly being (that is, in space stations and space craft located above the troposphere, not, as in the case of Katrina survivors, outside the polisphere), suggesting very strongly that such an existence is simply not viable. The sociological disaster of Columbine, moreover, brings into question the validity of the human being's existence as a suburban being-in-the-world located *outside* of History and its meaning producing processes of culture and semiotic formation, tending to imply that such a worldless existence — worldless, that is, in the sense in which gas stations and shopping malls have replaced museums and cathedrals — will only produce atrocious acts of violent-laden quests for new systems of meaning. Such is also illustrated by the AUM Shinrikyo subway attacks in Tokyo in 1995 although, unlike Columbine, those attacks were not generated out of a suburban semiotic vacancy, but rather out of a semiotic collision between two mutually incompatible modes of human being-in-the-world: existing, that is, either as a sign-circulating global consumer or as an ecstatic, symbol-constructing animal. (Just as photosynthetic cyanobacteria produced the oxygenated atmosphere as a by-product of their metabolism, so too, the human animal produces a symbol world as a by-product of his *Existenz*).

Each of these disasters implies that the very way of our being human, of existing in the world in a properly *human* way, that is to say, as an animal that produces meaning, is in jeopardy. The catastrophes discussed in this section are, one and all, assaults on human semiotic systems of meaning, assaults which threaten his mode of existence as an essentially culturally creative being. It took the human animal over 30,000 years to construct his symbol world — and an additional five or six million years to construct his upright hominid body — but now it is possible that he may *dis*-construct that symbol world in a matter of decades and in the process return to a way of life in which he vanishes from the earth by blending back in with the landscape in the reduced form of roving human wolfpacks and warring tribes, like those spear-wielding beings in the paintings of Odd Nerdrum. (And notice that one of the things missing in Nerdrum's post-apocalyptic tribal landscape is maps and map-makers, though he features just about every other primordial human activity. By that time of the world, he suggests, people will wish precisely *not* to know what the earth looks like or where things upon its surface are).

Taken all together, these catastrophes tend to suggest that the human way of being in the world *as* human — in contradistinction say, to that of the animals — is on the verge of collapse, with an attendant danger of the human being reverting back to a mode of cultural exile. That is to say, he is in danger of being a creature whose technological projects threaten to exile him from the sphere of symbolic cognition altogether. The essence of being human is to produce culture — i.e., systems of signification — which fathom the very nature and significance of what it is to *be* at all.

Persistent technological breakdown, however, as catalogued by the catastrophes in this book, points to the danger of dismantling and removing the very conditions, ontologically speaking, which make it possible for the human being to create signification at all. If he is surrounded by catastrophe on all sides, then the very environmental conditions which allow him to build cities and create works of art may disappear. And in that case, the human being will find himself in danger of becoming an *exospheric* being — i.e., exiled from his own culture spheres — on the surface of his own planet.

Should that happen, we can expect a long and brutal slide down into barbarism and anarchy. By that point, the Finns, as Joyce predicted, will once again *be* awakened. Indeed, it was the good old-fashioned professor Kenneth Clark who pointed out in his BBC series *Civilization* that the Vikings, though they had culture, since they *did* produce works of art, nevertheless, did not have *civilization*, properly speaking, since they were nomadic (at least, early on) and therefore hostile to the very idea of living in cities — the principle and anchor of civilization — wherever they went. In our present circumstances, it is the other way about: we have civilization — for now — but it is the symbol producing realm of *culture* which is vanishing over the horizon behind us. Skyscrapers, shopping malls, sports stadiums, apartment buildings: these things may be component parts of *civilization*, but they are not *culture*, which means *thinking* about these things and then building systems of meaning to trap their significances in the lines of a poem, in the strokes of a brush or behind the shutter of a camera. Electronic technology has liquidated much of high culture, and the pop culture that now remains as the tides of civilized, metaphysical society recede, is a poor excuse for culture of *any* kind. But soon, even that may disappear beneath an onslaught of mounting technological and ecological catastrophes.

Three

The Plane Crash at Tenerife
What It Unconceals

Vectors in the Four-Dimensional World

The most catastrophic plane crash in aviation history took place on March 27, 1977, on Tenerife Island, one of the Canary Islands located just to the northwest of Morocco. At 5:06 in the afternoon, two 747 jumbo jets collided on the runway of a small airport on the island, killing 538 people. A proliferation of errors, ominous events and misjudgments led up to the crash; errors and events which, when carefully analyzed, illuminate certain otherwise hidden ontological structures of the technological society.

The accident's multiple strands of intertwining causes began with a terrorist attack. The Fuerzas Armadas Guanches ("Guanches Armed Forces"), the militaristic wing of the Movement for Self Determination and Independence of the Canary Archipelago — a separatist movement fighting for independence from Spain — detonated a bomb in a flower shop at the airport on Gran Canaria. The group had already launched their movement on November 1, 1976, when they set off a bomb at the Galerías Preciados department store in Las Palmas de Gran Canaria.

The civil aviation authorities immediately ordered the airport closed and diverted all of its incoming flights to Los Rodeos Airport on the island of Tenerife, a small commercial airport with only a single runway and one taxi strip connected to it by a series of four exit passages. The two planes that crashed were both 747 jumbo jets that had been diverted to the small airport: these were KLM Flight 4805 out of Amsterdam, and Pan Am Flight 1736, originating from Los Angeles, and just arriving at the islands from JFK International in New York, where it had stopped to change out its crew. The Dutch plane had 234 passengers and 14 crewmembers, while the Pan Am aircraft was carrying 380 passengers, with a crew of 16. The

Three. The Plane Crash at Tenerife

KLM was piloted by Captain Jacob Van Zanten, a respected and highly competent pilot who had trained his first officer, Klaas Meurs, himself. The Pan Am flight was under the command of one Captain Victor Grubbs.

Los Rodeos was, to say the least, ill equipped to handle the sudden influx of traffic. It was just after noon on a Sunday and there were only two air traffic controllers working in the control tower. Five large planes had been diverted to Los Rodeos, and its taxiway was therefore thoroughly cluttered with craft. The only method allowing planes to take off was to taxi along the single runway to its end, turn around and then launch in the opposite direction from which it had taxied, a practice known as "runway back taxiing."

The Dutch plane had landed first and allowed its passengers to debark into the airport terminal while the captain had the plane refueled. This proved to be a major mistake, for the added extra weight of the fuel, some 55 tons, rendered the plane too heavy to take off in time to avoid crashing into the Pan Am aircraft which, meanwhile, had arrived at the airport and was now part of the general traffic jam.

While the KLM plane was refueling, a heavy fog began to roll in, reducing visibility to some 300 meters. The legal threshold for takeoff was 700 meters of visibility, but in spite of this stipulation, the KLM, after fuelling, restarted its engines and taxied out onto the runway. The Pan Am flight behind it was instructed to follow. The two aircraft, rolling along at about 10 mph, trundled out onto the single runway as the fogbank began to erase it with a white blanket. Neither of the planes was able to see the other.

The Pan Am was then instructed by the control tower operators to move off the runway by taking the third exit on their left, which would have been passageway C-3. However, since there were no markings to identify the exits, the crew became confused about which exit to take: had the operator meant the third exit from the first one, which, in that case, would be C-4, the last available exit before the end of the runway, or had he meant for them to exit via C-3? The problem with C-3 was that it forked back at a difficult angle that would have required them to make a very awkward turn in the opposite direction, whereas C-4 sloped away at a gentle 45 degree angle and seemed the logical one to take. The plane rolled past C-3 and hovered at C-4 in a state of indecision.

By this point, the KLM on the runway ahead of them had reached the end of the strip and was now turning around to point in *their* direction, although neither plane was aware that the other was only half a mile away. The air traffic control tower was not equipped with ground radar, and the two operators could not actually see the planes through the fog. Their attention was also divided by a soccer game they happened to be listening to on the radio.

Captain Van Zanten, on the KLM, meanwhile, was worried that, because of flight duty restrictions on the length of time he could fly, if the craft didn't take off soon, he would have to shut the flight down and remain stranded at the airport overnight with all his passengers. He was anxious to *go*: he had already fuelled up his plane with enough gas to get back to Amsterdam and he didn't want to be stranded on the island overnight.

After lining up, then, Van Zanten began to advance the plane's throttle for "spin-up," a test to verify that the engines are operating properly for takeoff, but his co-pilot Meurs, surprised, burst out, "Wait a minute! We don't have ATC clearance." "I know that," replied the captain, with some embarrassment. "Go ahead, ask." The pilot radioed in for clearance, and the tower gave them permission to fly the route once airborne, but this was not yet permission to take off. However, the captain, apparently interpreting this as permission to take off, said, forcefully, "We're going." The co-pilot, reluctant to embarrass his captain a second time, remained silent as the plane shot forward.[1]

The ATC then asked the Pan Am plane if they were off the runway yet, but the pilots replied that they were still, in fact, there. The controller then told KLM, "Stand by for takeoff, I will call you," but he hadn't heard the captain's intention to go ahead, for the captain had said this to his crew and not into the radio. A simultaneous call from the Pan Am crew caused interference on the radio frequency, so that the KLM crew did not hear Pan Am say that they were still taxiing down the runway.

Just after the KLM began its takeoff roll, the tower told the Pan Am crew to report when the runway was clear. The KLM flight engineer, Willem Schreuder, overhearing this with some anxiety then said to captain Van Zanten, "Is he not clear, that Pan American?" But Van Zanten merely replied, as if in a trance, "Oh, yes," and continued throttling up to speed.

At this point, the Pan Am was just beginning to turn off the runway when Captain Grubbs, now seeing the KLM approaching, shouted, "Goddamn, that son of a bitch is coming straight at us!" and hit the throttle full force to try and steer the plane out of its way.

Van Zanten, sighting the Pan Am, tried to avoid the collision by taking off early, tilting the plane back sharply until its rear tail struck sparks from the pavement. But, as we have seen, he had already fatally overloaded the plane with 55 extra tons of fuel, and as it began to lumber into the air, it hit the top of the Pan Am at a right angle, shearing off the entire roof of its fuselage. The number one engine of the KLM, which was doing 160 mph at that point, broke off in the collision, and the pilots quickly lost control of the plane, which smashed into the pavement at a point about 500 feet beyond the Pan Am. The heavy fuel load burst into a flaming incandescence which rapidly engulfed the plane, killing everyone onboard. There were no survivors from the KLM.

There *were* some survivors on the Pan Am plane, though, who were presently making their way out of their seats and down to the ground from the plane's left wing. But as one survivor has described it, the burning plane was rapidly collapsing inward, and the screams of still living passengers were soon silenced as the flames sucked away all their oxygen and suffocated the ones who were too slow, or too encumbered, to make it out of their seats in time.

Sixty-one out of a total of 380 passengers survived the burning wreck of the Pan Am.

Anti-world

Stepping back from the glare of the wreckage in order to gain some perspective on this catastrophe, we now turn to the world of books and discourse in order to remind ourselves of Heidegger's point that, when a tool breaks, such as a hammer, it becomes suddenly conspicuous, standing out from the contextual background of its web of referentiality. "When a thing in the world around us becomes unusable," Heidegger states,

> it becomes *conspicuous*. The natural course of concern is brought to a halt by this unusability. The continuity of reference and thus the referential totality undergoes a distinctive disturbance which forces us to pause. When a tool is damaged and useless, its defect actually causes it to be present, conspicuous, so that it now forces itself into the foreground of the environing world in an emphatic sense.[2]

Tools, that is to say, are normally *used*, not thought about; consequently, while being used, they fuse harmoniously with the specific task that is being performed as part of a particular lifeworld. The tool disappears into the web of referentiality surrounding it: nails for the hammer to hit, other tools to repair it, this desk, that toolbox, etc. Each thing presupposes each other thing, while the sum total of them all adds up to the making of a particular world. When the tool breaks down, such as when the head falls off of my hammer, it stands out abruptly from this web of referentiality, becoming a problem. It is now not something to be *used*, but rather something that has to be *thought* about.

In science (and in traditional academic philosophy from Descartes to Husserl), it is in this latter mode — a mode which Heidegger calls *Vorhandenheit*—that objects are analyzed by isolating them out of their contextual web of worldly interrelationships and plugging them into the geometrical lattice of a Cartesian grid, where they are then theorized about. This is what Newton did, for instance, to the planets when he plugged them into an abstract mathematical phase space and derived from them the laws of motion and universal gravitation. But in the process, such objects are, as it were, "deworlded," or divorced from the real world in which they normally function invisibly in their smooth-flowing mode of *Zuhandenheit*.

In fact, the entirety of the technological world that science has been constructing since about the year 1800 is a world made up precisely of such deworlded objects which have no relationship whatsoever to their cultural, and environmental, surroundings. Indeed, it is as though many of these objects — buildings, bridges, highways — have dropped down out of the sky from nowhere and sifted like a layer of technological sediment over the older world of culturally authentic artifacts that long since preceded them. Industrial technology, in other words, has been engaged in building a "non-world" or "anti-world," a world, that is, composed of what Marc Auge has termed "non-places."[3] These are places such as airports, train stations, shopping malls, parking lots, gas stations and the like, which are indifferent to the cultural circumstances of their surroundings and which therefore have no aura to them, as Walter Benjamin would say, because they are not embedded in history. There is nothing culturally significant about them, for they did not emerge as the result of historical unfoldings of artistic processes, but were simply realized for their functionality and placed wither they fall. They are akin to the theoretical objects of science, existing in a featureless and invisible phase space which they have realized in four dimensions as the result of feats of modern engineering. Aesthetically speaking, however, such non-places are worthless.

The plane crash at Tenerife, then, functions for us like Heidegger's broken hammer: the crash brings the airport as *an entire system* abruptly into view. It now stands out as a problem: it becomes conspicuous as a world unto itself, a bounded world of vectors, forces, lines and quantities that has been constructed following the principles of science and engineering. It is, in short, a non-world, for it is an artificial island of technology that bears no organic relation to the cultural — or even geographical — circumstances of the Canary Islands. This airport could exist anywhere on the planet and it would still look and function in exactly the same way.

Such microworlds, though they are culturally indifferent, nonetheless have quite specific effects on human relations, for inside them people are transformed into pure entities: they are simply there, one quantity among many, to be moved about through a grid of mechanical relations like functions in a quadratic equation. They are, in fact, no longer people but rather take on the character of the non-world itself, that, namely, of pure moving quantities shorn of significance and depth of any kind, like skeletons walking through X-ray machines. Indeed, X-ray machines at airports really do reveal the abstract way in which people inside such systems disappear as subjectivities and reappear as theoretical entities, or units of mass moved about by quantitatively measurable forces. They, too, are filtered through the mode of *Vorhandenheit* as purely theoretical objects. If, as Foucault says, social institutions can create human subjectivities by disciplining them, they can also — in today's world, anyway — shear such individuality clean away from their bones.[4]

The depth and struggle that is borne out of living a life of signification, that is to say, of generating meaning for oneself by creating values and remaining faithful to one's own truth events — in Alain Badiou's sense[5] — all of this is a matter of complete indifference inside such a world system as an airport, as indifferent as is culture itself taken as a whole. Indeed, this is perhaps why, in recent years, airports have tried to incorporate art into their terminals, as a way of subliminally recognizing the victim that has been sacrificed in order to make the mechanical system work. The slaughtered victim — like the stacked buffalo and antler horns decorating the streets of the towns of the Old West — whose death makes the functioning of the system possible, is taken up inside the new world to become a merely decorative art object.

Thus, the pressure of such a mechano-world, in order to function, leaves so little room for human flexibility that decision-making is often constrained to unfold along the lines of the system. And when such a system comes under stress, it exhibits perturbations that can often manifest themselves through warped and distorted forms of human judgment that then reflect the turbulent nature of the system under stress.

As we have seen, multiple causes piled up to form the catastrophic bifurcation of the crash at Tenerife: the fog, the divided attention of the air traffic controllers, Van Zanten's decision to refuel, etc. But authorities investigating the crash singled out Captain Van Zanten's disregard of ATC clearance for takeoff as *the* overriding cause of the accident. If he had waited for clearance, the argument goes, the accident simply wouldn't have happened. But he was impatient to get the plane off the ground so that he wouldn't have to spend the night on the island with his passengers. And indeed, Van Zanten's single-minded determination to get back to Amsterdam before the close of his working day stands out as a glaring fact in any discussion of the causes of the accident.

Van Zanten's situation, moreover, is one that can be identified as a phenomenon of technological fatigue which I will call here "closed-circuit machinic symbiosis." The captain, that is, at the time of takeoff, had become an extension of the tightly mechanized world within which he was embedded and constrained. His thinking had shifted *out* of the human world and its concerns, and was operating in the mode of Heidegger's *Vorhandenheit*, in which thinking becomes an extension of the machine itself.

To a man with a hammer in his hand, everything looks like a nail. This famous quote from Mark Twain sums up the problem neatly: technology, at the time we are using it, very often uses *us*, that is to say, imposes upon us its functionality and causes our decisions to override all other considerations. At the time we are using it, the tool, as it were, has hijacked our consciousness, closing it off from conscious relational awareness with other human beings, while we engage in a single closed-circuit task with the tool we are using. The man who is sawing lumber on an electric saw is so engaged in his task that we dare not disturb him, lest he cut off his fingers. The same goes for someone driving a car: the machine demands the full attention of a hyper-aware and alert consciousness in order to operate it, for if consciousness is distracted by other claims, such as cell phones or people arguing with us, fatalities can result.

In Captain Van Zanten's case, we have a similar principle at work: his consciousness had closed into a feedback loop with the aircraft that he was piloting to the extent that he wasn't taking in data from other human beings. He had become an extension of the machine and was determined,

Three. The Plane Crash at Tenerife

no matter what, to get the plane off the ground. All other data that were inconsistent with this single-minded purpose were disregarded. The critical faculties of his higher brain functions had disappeared somewhere into the circuitry of the craft as his consciousness fused with the plane to the point of becoming a servo-mechanism of it. Thus, at the very moment of attempting to physically leave the ground, Van Zanten's consciousness had actually fallen and become captured by the machine.

Jarring his consciousness loose from this machine symbiosis would have required an external fulcrum of the sort of authority that co-pilots didn't have back in the 1970s. Nowadays, pilots cannot take off without a cockpit consensus. But in 1977, there existed no means of extricating Captain Van Zanten from his capture by the machine. He had *fallen*, like the Gnostic Anthropos who falls into matter and becomes caught by it, and was unable — as we all are nowadays, in fact — to extricate himself from its possessive grasp. The story of the crash at Tenerife, then, becomes illustrative of *today's* Gnostic myth, that, namely, of the human soul's fall, sinking and capture by the machine.

The very opposite phenomenon of such possession by the machine is that of possession of one's consciousness by traditional spiritual entities: the Muse who, for instance, seizes the poet in a moment of rapt attention when the pure lines of a breathless verse surfaces into view in his mind; or the *daimon* of inspiration which is channeled by a philosopher in the midst of composing his work; or the rapt seizure of a Sufi mystic in the ecstatic trance of his whirling dervish; or the dance of a Kung Bushman who sends his soul out into the visionary realm to commune with astral animals and bring back knowledge of how to make paintings. These are all examples of people functioning in cultural contexts that are *not* dominated by the constant demands which machines make upon our consciousness at every waking moment. In a culture *not* dominated by machines, the space of human consciousness is freed up to channel *other* entities, entities that bring cultural forms into being, entities whose visions serve as catalysts with which to build worlds of authenticity, meaning and value.

World and Machine

Thus, the plane crash at Tenerife reveals the structure of the airport *as such*, as an anti-world (one opposed, that is, to traditional culture worlds) exerting its machinic demands upon human consciousness in order to navigate successfully about through its labyrinth. The transformation of human consciousness into an extension of machinic consciousness can be carried to such a point that, if the human being remains unaware, he can find himself in a situation in which the system demands that decisions be made *in favor of the system*, rather than from the viewpoint of properly human considerations. This is one reason why, for instance, courtesy and politeness are so famously scarce inside airports: the all-encompassing dictates of the system shear them clean off the bones of human relations in which *everyone* inside the system exists only for the sake of running the system efficiently. In an inhuman environment, human beings are no longer human, but rather tools of systemic efficiency.

The airport itself, of course, is but a localized instance of a more general technological world system that has been laid down like a new and artificial stratum across the surface of the earth. Local cultures and authentic traditions are today everywhere being squashed and flattened out by the imposition of this technological anti-world that is so hostile to cultural values. Heidegger, I'm afraid, had it right: this anti-world built by science is so dangerous because it is utterly value-neutral, and, therefore, nihilistic.[6] And the more it is built up across the surface of the globe, the more of its indifferent nihilism it brings along with it. Human culture, local traditions, and *real* values are simply pushed aside in favor of ever more and more shopping malls, gas stations and convenience stores. Museums, book stores and locally-owned businesses, meanwhile, are vanishing in order to make room for these structures, structures which are scandalously *void* of any values beyond those of mass consumerism.[7]

The terrorists who attacked the Gran Canaria airport, on the other hand, were precisely engaged in culture — historical concerns, the historical project, specifically, of attaining independence from Spain. Hence their attack on the airport was a historical event while the plane crash, on the other hand, embedded as it was inside of a global anti-world, was *a*-historic, and therefore culturally meaningless. It is a non-event, like Marc Auge's non-places. The terrorists specifically bombed an airport, and before that a department store, because both structures are types of non-places indifferent to historical and cultural values. The targets of terrorist attacks, as Marc Auge points out, are so often non-places like airports, shopping malls and office buildings precisely because such places signify the *absence* of meaning, the stripping of all values from the world that technopolis represents, and which are therefore totally opposed to the kinds of historical — cultural struggles within which they find themselves engaged.[8] Indeed, the technological stratum that is currently being erected over the surface of the earth is the greatest threat to cultural authenticity that the planet has ever seen. Islamic fundamentalists actually do not have it wrong at all: local culture and traditional religion — for religion builds culture — *are* worth fighting for, even at the point of a gun. Nowadays, it seems, no one will take you seriously without one.

The battle between World and Machine is a battle of values, and which side the individual of today finds himself on will determine his fate and destiny within the world system as a whole. As culture disappears and is replaced by the art of the motor, i.e., video graphics the size of buildings, as in Shanghai, pixelated images and various other forms of "art" at the speed of light, the world *as* world shrinks from a horizon of meaning and tradition to become merely a local colony of consumerism. The ancient, vanishing world of Mona Lisas, Picassos and Rodins becomes a collection of historical fossils that are then gathered up and put on display in museums which become advertisements for the nostalgic days when human beings were once, long ago, before mechanization took command, capable of this sort of thing.

Nowadays all we seem to be able to do well is figure out better methods for making smoother highways across which our historically evanescent automobiles travel, increasing the distance between physical human beings, who become ever more and more remote from each other, while cultural authenticity, correspondingly, fades from existence.

And in the end, what will be left?

Four

The Disaster at Bhopal and the Collision of the Biosphere with the Chemosphere

Airborne Toxic Event

The worst industrial accident of all time occurred in India, on December 3, 1984, at just about fifteen minutes past midnight. The Union Carbide India Ltd. pesticide plant leaked a toxic chemical known as methyl isocyanate (MIC for short) into the air, which northwesterly winds blew over the city of Bhopal, where it created a sort of gas dome that sealed itself off — since the chemical is heavier than air and therefore sinks — and assaulted the breathable living space of the poor of the city.[1] The official death toll stands at roughly 3,800 people, but local estimates hover somewhere closer to 10,000. In subsequent years, this number rose to over 20,000 as the slow, temporal creepage of the chemical disturbed and disrupted the nervous systems of the survivors, resulting in a high incidence of birth defects, respiratory diseases and gynecological problems.[2]

Whereas dromospheric crashes (like the one we have just seen at Tenerife) happen with sudden, terrifying force and are usually over in a matter of minutes or even seconds, with industrial accidents of this sort, the temporal evolution unfolds more slowly, over the course of hours — even days, months, years — as though events were suspended in a gravityless orbit hovering somewhere above the earth. In the case of Bhopal, events began their ponderous motion at about 8:15 on the evening of the 2nd when a worker at the plant, performing routine maintenance, connected a water hose to part of the plant's labyrinthine skeleton of pipes. It was essential to keep the system clean by flushing out the dirt, but by 8:45, dirt was already clogging the system and causing the water to back up into one of the main pipes that snaked throughout the plant.

The factory manufactured a pesticide known as Sevin, which was used on Indian crops to kill bugs. Sevin contains some dangerous chemicals, such as phosgene — the very same substance used in the gases hurled at soldiers in the trenches of World War I — and MIC, which Union Carbide was using as an intermediate to synthesize production of the pesticide. MIC is a type of chemical which cannot be allowed to mix with water, otherwise it produces an exothermic reaction that causes deadly vapors to escape and poison anyone in the vicinity.[3]

At the plant, the MIC was stored in three large tanks that were buried underground beneath a concrete bunker like the reliquary mound of a king. These tanks were each 40 feet long, 8 feet in diameter and could hold approximately 42 tons of MIC. At about 10 P.M., water entered one of these tanks in large amounts (no one seems to be certain quite how this happened) and began to create a runaway chemical reaction that soon raised temperatures inside the tank to over 200 degrees Celsius. The MIC in the tanks is normally kept under pressure with inert gas in order to prevent anything from getting inside the tank, but now that the pressure was disappearing, the gauge inside the plant read "zero." However, since the gauge had been broken for weeks, this was assumed to be a faulty reading.

In fact, safety procedures had been designed to prevent water from ever backing up so far into the plant, since as each pipe is cleaned, a thin metal strip known as a slipblind can be inserted between couplings, and the bolts of the seal then tightened to create an impenetrable obstacle. However, this procedure was no longer being practiced at the plant, although if it had been, the accident might never have occurred.[4] Many safety systems at the plant, furthermore, had been deliberately turned off in order to save Union Carbide money: the refrigeration unit, for instance, that would have kept the MIC from boiling had been shut off since May of that year, while a device known as a Vent Gas Scrubber, which was designed to neutralize toxic gas before it spread into the air, had been switched off for maintenance. The MIC tank alarms, furthermore, had ceased working four years ago.

The plant was, in short, in a poor state of disrepair. And this was not just due to slovenliness, either, but to specific instructions on the part of Union Carbide, which had told workers *not* to replace leaking pipes, and even fined many of them for refusing to deviate from safety protocols that would save the company money. Union Carbide has itself admitted that most of its safety systems were not functioning on the night of the catastrophe.[5]

Part II: Disasters of Neomodernity

At just after midnight, then, a worker who ran out to the concrete sarcophagus could hear a rumbling noise as the concrete began to fracture. The tank itself did not burst: instead, a pressure relief valve blew, and released 50,000 pounds of the toxic gas out into the night air of Bhopal, where it was carried by winds over the slums of the city, slums which were located too close to the plant. A ten meter high wall of gas closed down over the area.

A large number of sleeping men, women and children were soon woken up by itching, burning, watering eyes and incessant coughing, for MIC gas seeks out mucous membranes and any wet spots on the body and destroys the lower respiratory tracts of the lungs. Vomiting, diarrhea, frothing at the mouth, and then death, soon follow. The gas cloud was a chemical textile woven out of phosgene, MIC, carbon dioxide, carbon monoxide, hydrogen cyanide, hydrogen chloride, oxides of nitrogen and monomethyl amine.

Soon, a mob of screaming people were evacuating the city, some running, others jumping on the sides of buses, grabbing rickshaws, anything at all that would carry them away more swiftly from the toxic cloud's slow, creeping death.

Somewhere between 100,000 and 200,000 people have sustained permanent injuries which have cost them such problems over the years as faulty vision, menstrual disruptions, cardiac failure, breathing difficulties, immunological and neurological disorders.[6] Birth defects in this region are high, and women and men who have attained marriageable age are generally shunned as marriage partners since they are perceived, with all their health problems, as burdens.

The victims of the disaster demanded compensation from Union Carbide, but the Indian government settled with them in 1989 for a mere 470 million dollars which, parceled out over 500,000 people amounted to about 500 or so dollars per person. The victims, to this day, are actively seeking reparations from Union Carbide, which is now, however — as of 2001— owned by Dow Chemical.

The factory building itself, furthermore — a rusting labyrinth of steel and corrosion that is being slowly reclaimed by the surrounding vegetation — has been preserved at the site by the Indian government for purposes of investigation. However, toxic chemicals are still leaking from the plant into the groundwater, continuing to cause health problems for the nearby population.

Four. The Disaster at Bhopal

How Lifeworlds Are Ruptured

The Bhopal disaster, when viewed topologically as though via satellite from above, was indeed an accident, but it was an accident that *structurally* replicates the type of assault on an enemy's living conditions which theoretician Peter Sloterdijk terms "atmoterrorist." In his book *Terror from the Air*, Sloterdijk points out that the prototype event for this kind of an attack dates from April 22, 1915, when the Germans used chlorine gas on French-Canadian troops at Ypres.[7] The use of phosgene gas, which was even more effective, soon followed. These attacks, according to Sloterdijk, represented something new in the history of warfare, for they were the first occasions in which, not the bodies of soldiers proper, but the actual *atmospheric envelope* that enabled them to exist was assaulted. All subsequent terrorist attacks of the 20th century evolved from this type of attack, in which an enemy's living conditions, the very milieu in which he lives and breathes, is turned against him. These chlorine, phosgene and mustard gas attacks, in other words, actually made visible — "explicate" is the term Sloterdijk uses — a previously known, but consciously subliminal fact, namely that societies presuppose invisible structural conditions that enable them to exist in the first place. Once the conditions of these envelopes, or spheres, are ruptured, livability and breathability within those spaces is no longer possible. The best way to assault large aggregates of people, then, is to destroy the spherological envelope inside which they are encased and which sustains their existence: hence, the firebombing of German cities in World War II, the Sarin nerve gas attacks on the Tokyo subway in 1995, the gassing of the Jews with Zyklon B, etc.

So, the Union Carbide "accident" at Bhopal, though it was, technically speaking, an "accident," nevertheless perfectly replicates the structure of these kinds of attacks, and the fact of this resemblance, furthermore, is not "accidental" at all. What the Bhopal disaster reveals is the essential antipathy of the multinational corporation to all human communities whatsoever, indeed, to all *biospheric* systems whatsoever. The biosphere and the multinational corporation are based upon mutually opposed systems of technics.

A community, whether human or biological, is a set of living conditions that implicates all of its members in a communal strategy of survival and mutual concerns such that the very existence of the community is at stake if these conditions are not met. If I look at a microbial "community"

Part II: Disasters of Neomodernity

in a petri dish, what I see is a collection of bacteria mutually engaged in constructing a system that makes the existence of the entire community possible. If I look down at the earth from a satellite orbiting above it, what I see are thousands of interlocking ecosystems, including human ones, engaged in activities that are mutually beneficial for the members of those ecosystems. If any of the conditions which make those systems possible fails, then the entire system collapses. Paul Hawken, in *The Ecology of Commerce*, cites the example of a reindeer community that was imported to Saint Matthew Island in the 1940s: beginning with a population of 29 reindeer, it was thought that there was enough trees, plants and shrubs to sustain a total of about 1,600 to 2,300 animals, but by 1963, this number had exploded to 6,000. Soon, the overpopulated reindeer herds were decimated by disease and starvation such that by 1966 there were only 42 reindeer left alive on the island.[8] Thus: destroy one of the conditions that make the system possible, and the entire system collapses.

Multinational corporations, on the other hand, are based upon a technical system that specifically reverses this set of figure-ground relations: they are machines designed to make only a tiny percentage of the population wealthy by extracting one or two resources from a functioning biosystem and exploiting it such that the remaining ability of the system to survive is left in question. The only thing that matters, from the point of view of the corporation, is profit. Context, contexts of all sorts, whether human, cultural, animal, etc., are seen as irrelevant "externalities."

Thus, multinational corporations like Union Carbide, Monsanto, Bechtel, etc., exploit resources and leave human and ecological systems behind to collapse in the wake of their processes of extraction and exploitation.

In the case of Bhopal, what becomes evident is the collapse of a human community as the result of an attack on the very bio-conditions which make that community possible: the MIC gas cloud ruptures the human lifeworld of Bhopal, actually causing it to collapse and deflate like a popped balloon. At that point, the city's inhabitants may as well have been cut loose into outer space, for the breathability of their air was about the same.

Now, if we multiply this disaster as a merely localized phenomenon of a planetwide collision between corporate megasystems and the biosphere, and then speed up the film, we can begin to see the lifeworld bubbles of one community after another collapsing and popping with the rapidity of cylinders in an internal combustion engine.

The ultimate end result of this process can have precisely *one* outcome: the disappearance of the biosphere and the victory of the lithosphere.

One day, Earth may look just like Mars.

How World-Spheres Collide

But that is only one vector of approach to Bhopal; others are possible. Union Carbide, as a multinational, was merely the midwife of another, special category of accident, one in which the technological world of the chemosphere collides with the human biosphere as the result of a dromological speed up via capitalism.

Our technical systems can be conceived as a series of spheres, just the way the ancients used to imagine the cosmos as a set of planetary crystalline spheres set one inside the other. Thus, the dromosphere is composed of all moving vehicles; the polisphere of the city as a defended fortress against the dromosphere; the mediasphere of all communications technologies from Sumerian clay tablets to tablet computers; and the chemosphere, or the realm of the manipulations of matter by means of chemically applied technologies.

The biosphere — which is presupposed by all of these technospheres — is in turn dependent upon the chemosphere for its existence. If you deleted the biosphere, as Ken Wilber points out somewhere, then the entire human technosphere would collapse, useless. The same goes for the chemosphere, for if it were suddenly deleted from existence, life could no longer exist. The biosphere is based upon and presupposes the chemosphere, since all living things are made up of chemicals in varying combinations.

But it is important to note that in the organization of biological matter, the chemosphere has not been allowed to dominate; the entire existence of the biosphere depends upon the fact that the chemosphere has been subordinated to it, wrapped up and, as Gilles Deleuze would put it, "folded" into it.[9] Physical matter is so intricately folded and refolded, that eventually interior subjectivity emerges as the result of this topological folding. Or perhaps Deleuze is wrong and a spirit world, a sort of *anima mundi*, is involved. Either way, the chemosphere has to be brought under the dominance of living matter in order for the latter to function smoothly. If the chemosphere erupts into the biosphere and begins to hijack it, disaster results: cancer, illness, disease, etc.

Part II: Disasters of Neomodernity

Now, there are two aspects to this chemosphere: there is the chemosphere that evolved naturally, which is based upon the earth's ability to manipulate its own materials, produce chemical reactions and evolve living things. But then there is the human technological chemosphere, which evolved in such a way that human beings gradually took over and learned to mimic the self-making or "autopoietic" properties of the earth's own chemosphere, beginning with the mastery of metallurgy and pottery during the so-called Pottery Neolithic that falls somewhere around 7000 B.C. At this time, new kinds of pyrotechnologies began to be invented in northern Iraq, Syria and Iran, such as two-chambered kilns which enabled the raising of temperatures so that very fine, thin pottery bowls could be made, like the famous Samarran or Halafian pottery; and also, dating from about this time, the beginnings of metallurgy, first evident in the form of the various copper trinkets of jewelry found adorning the dead in graves. The practice of disposing of the dead by cremation began to come in at this time, too.

The technological chemosphere, however, underwent further complexification when it evolved out of the matrix of Alexandrian culture in the first century or so B.C. where, in the Egyptian port city of Alexandria, Greek philosophy was crossed with Egyptian technology to produce alchemy. Eventually, this new science of manipulating chemical matter was picked up by Nestorian Christians who disseminated it on their travels along the Old Silk Road, and the Arabs, apparently, received it from them. The Arabs, in turn, brought their alchemical texts and their alembics along with them into eleventh- and twelfth-century Almoravid Spain from whence Latin and Jewish scholars translated these Arabic texts and introduced the practice of alchemy into Europe, where it continued down into the 17th century.

Alchemy, however, was not just a science, but a kind of spiritual discipline for manipulating matter in order to release the Spirit that was thought to be trapped inside of it. The alchemist, in his laboratory, put various kinds of matter — urine, dung, metals, sulphur, mercury — through distillations and purifications in order to achieve the epiphany of a purified substance known as the philosopher's stone or *lapis exilis* which was thought to enable the transformation of base metals into gold.

The ontology of alchemy was derived from the philosophy of Aristotle, in which it was thought that all matter was based upon combinations of the four elements in various measures.[10] The theory was that if you could adjust the various ratios between such principles as the hot, the cold, the wet and the dry, then you could change one form of matter into another. If elemental water was based upon the combinations of the cold and the wet, then, theoretically speaking, if you changed the wet into the dry, you would have a solid: ice. And so on.

But when the atomist paradigm was discovered and brought into the scientific consciousness of the 17th century amongst natural scientists such as Robert Boyle, Isaac Newton or Descartes, the ontological rug, as it were, was pulled out from under alchemy, since the atomistic paradigm is completely antipathetic to Aristotle's elemental paradigm. The favoring of the atomistic ontology left alchemy out to dry, as it were, for the world was now composed of tiny building blocks, atoms which, when jostled, brought all the various substances of the world into being as the result of their vortical motions.[11] At this point, chemistry was born, and the periodic table of the elements slowly began to compose itself as, one by one, various elemental substances — hydrogen, nitrogen, oxygen, etc.— were isolated, named and categorized. The four classical elements of antiquity soon multiplied to well over one hundred of them.

With the organic chemistry revolution of the middle of the nineteenth century — born out of Kekule's vision of the benzene ring, in which tetravalent carbon atoms could be linked together to form carbon lattices — all sorts of new substances and products were manufactured, such as drugs, paints, petrochemicals, new kinds of food and food additives, plastics, etc. By the time of World War I, new and deadly forms of toxic gas — chlorine, mustard and phosgene — were being developed by Fritz Haber of the Kaiser Wilhelm Institute in Berlin, in collusion with German chemical corporations like Bayer and Höchst.

Now, the Union Carbide factory in Bhopal was basically an alchemist's laboratory blown up to macroscale as the result of the gigantism of what Zygmunt Bauman has termed "heavy modernity," which is the period extending from about 1800, with the rise of the first factories, down to about 1945, when the shift to "light modernity" began to take place. The main characteristic of heavy modernity, according to Bauman, is a tendency toward gigantism: this is the period when the largest ships, tallest buildings, biggest bridges and dams were constructed and it was also, not coincidentally, the time when the great nation state powers were claiming the largest swaths of the earth's surface as colonies. With light modernity, this epoch began to give way with the collapse of colonialism, and the technologies of the light and the small, microtechnologies, in other words, began to proliferate: the study of the atom that led to the detonation of the atom bomb; the rise of electronics, software and computers; and nanotech gadgets of all kinds.[12]

The Union Carbide factory in Bhopal was, then, in essence, a vestigial relic from another age, a fossilized holdover from the age of heavy modernity when the small technologies of previous ages began to give birth to the large and ever larger. Thus, the alchemist's laboratory, inserted into the epistemic framework of this age, looks as though it were a technology that had been built by a race of giants.

But whereas the alchemist had been concerned in his laboratory with manipulating matter in such a way as to produce epiphanies of the presence therein of the Spirit — consistent with the ontology of the metaphysical age — the Union Carbide factory was a machine for producing a chemistry of death designed to rupture and destroy the lifeworlds of living organisms. It was a machine, in other words, for producing a technically composed element for assaulting and destructuring the biosphere: not releasing the Spirit from its imprisonment in matter, but releasing living things from their envelopes of habitability.

If the elements of the chemosphere irrupt into the biosphere and there begin to dominate it, then life within the biosphere is no longer a possibility. Thus, in the Bhopal disaster, we have the chemical equivalent of a geological disaster, for just as when, in an earthquake, a tectonic plate subducts and pushes a chunk of the earth upward into a city — where the lithosphere does not belong and which threatens its very existence — so in the case of Bhopal, the chemosphere is pushed up into the world of the human biosphere and ruptures it in such a way that it deflates and collapses.

The Bhopal disaster, then, was an accident resulting from the collision of two spheres, the chemosphere and the human biosphere.

But the chemosphere does not normally collide at high speeds with the biosphere since, if left alone, as is usually the case, it moves at a slower pace than the metabolism of human culture. The temporal metabolism of the chemosphere is closer to that of the geosphere: the decay rate of Uranium 235, for instance, has a half-life of 700 million years; the corrosion of metal by rust is a slow and gradual process of oxidation; human teeth are worn away gradually through acidic erosion, and so forth.

So the chemosphere must be hurtled at high speeds in order to impact the human biosphere catastrophically. What is it then that could have set the toxic MIC gas in such rapid motion so that it could shatter a human biosphere?

Capitalism, of course.

It is the rapid flow of capitalism which picks up chemicals that are manufactured in the chemosphere and sets them going fast enough to crash into the human lifeworld at high speeds. There are, according to Fernand Braudel in his *Civilization and Capitalism*, three different strata of capitalism, each one moving financial flows and transactions through it faster than the one beneath: at the very bottom, there is the rural market, a ponderous and slow-moving economy based upon trade and barter, of ox-drawn carts, pulleys, wheels and ploughs; but above that, there exists the market economy of towns and cities, in which transactions take place at a much faster pace than they do in rural economies, for crowds now begin to assemble in market squares and, together with the rise of the merchant class, speed up the rate of flow of transactions; beyond that, there is the supra economy of international trade and finance which, today, at any rate, sends transactions racing around the globe at the speed of light.[13]

New and bizarre kinds of chemicals are daily manufactured by multinational corporations like Monsanto and Dow and, before they have time to be properly tested for their effects upon human lives, they are sent racing through the global economy at very high speeds. One chemical after the next is rapidly manufactured, put on the market with very little testing and quick approval by the FDA, and then set into the slower-moving metabolism of human and other biological life: growth hormones in cows; herbicides to be used on our crops; genetically modified organisms which replace traditional food supplies; perfumes, plastics, soaps, shampoos laden with phthalates; all of these chemistries are no sooner created than they are picked up out of the chemosphere by the multinationals and sent racing through the global economy.

The old-fashioned human body, meanwhile, like Grandpa crossing the street, does not move quite so fast. Biology proceeds on its own time scale, a scale that is more rapid than the lithosphere but less rapid than the human technosphere generally speaking. The body evolves defense mechanisms against new and dangerous chemicals which are thrown at it, but not nearly fast enough to keep up with the constant flood of such chemistries. The human body, biologically speaking, cannot evolve and mutate fast enough to adapt to this barrage of chemistries that are daily thrust upon it by the exigencies of a rapid metabolic economic system like

Part II: Disasters of Neomodernity

late capitalism, and consequently, cancers, neurological illnesses, endocrine disorders and weird illnesses are the result.

We see all of these processes brought to a focus before our mind's eye in the disaster at Bhopal, where the chemosphere is sent crashing into a human lifeworld as the result of the exigencies of capitalist profiteering. It is a crash which takes place at a speed that is slower than most dromospheric crashes, but the thoroughness of its devastation more than makes up for what it lacks in speed. Thousands and thousands of human beings are destroyed in this collision between two mutually incompatible spheres of technics.

Thus, the accident at Bhopal reveals to us how capitalism is gradually eroding the boundaries between lifeworlds, and driving them into one another at various deadly speeds. As it sends one sphere crashing into another — the chemosphere into the biosphere, the dromosphere into the polisphere, etc.— human civilization is slowly being ground up in a series of devastating lifeworld disruptions that are gradually adding up to a net effect of rendering life upon this tiny dirt clod very difficult.

Once all these spheres have collided and collapsed into one another — human lifeworlds with human technospheres, and human technospheres with non-human biospheres — the resulting scenario should look, if I am not mistaken, something like the ecological equivalent of the wreckage of a crash up derby. The landscape will be littered with the ruins of broken, half-functioning, malfunctioning and nonfunctioning systems. The bodies of living things will have become so interpenetrated by the chemosphere that the evolutionary separation between them — which made biospheric life possible in the first place — will be all but annihilated. The biosphere will become *part* of the chemosphere instead of the other way around.

At that point, the distinction between living and non-living systems may not be quite so evident to our eyes as it is today.

Five

Being-*Outside*-the World

Thoughts on the
Space Shuttle Disasters

Ascent to Heaven

The space shuttle *Challenger* disintegrated 73 seconds into its launch on January 28, 1986. It was carrying seven astronauts, including the school teacher Christa McAuliffe — who would have been the first civilian in space — and all were killed, not by the explosion, but when the shuttle's nose cone, which contained the seven crew members, separated from the craft and plunged for seven miles over the course of two and a half minutes, slamming into the Atlantic Ocean at a speed of over two hundred miles an hour. It is not known for certain whether the astronauts were conscious for this descent: experts have theorized that if the cabin had depressurized, they most likely would not have been conscious, but there is some uncertainty about this.

In any event, the accident, as is well known, was caused by the failure of the shuttle's O-rings to expand properly — O-rings are rubber seals designed to insulate the linkages between sections of the solid rocket boosters — which, when functioning properly, *should* expand to fill the joints between these segments when fuel and gas are firing through the rockets. But due to NASA's rescheduling of the launch to a day with frigid temperatures, the rings lost their necessary elasticity and failed to expand properly. However, tiny pieces of aluminum debris were jarred loose, and these acted as temporary filler while the rockets lifted the colossus into the air, thus preventing them from exploding on the launch pad, as the engineers who had designed the rockets at a firm called Morton Thiokol had prophesied would happen. These engineers, Roger Boisjoly chief among them, had voiced objections to NASA about the dangers of launching in cold weather, fearing that such weather would cause the rubber O-rings to freeze and therefore fail to expand properly.[1] But NASA, pressured by the media and public expectations to deliver a spectacle, overrode the warnings of the engineers and chose to go ahead with the launch anyway, reasoning that they had already been operating four years of shuttle missions with no problems from the O-rings.[2] Thiokol, the managers at NASA pointed out, had had six months to get their act together and yet they waited until the last moment to raise the issue about the O-rings. None of the engineers at the firm, however, had any idea that NASA was going to launch their 25th shuttle mission in the coldest weather ever attempted for such a launch.

At any rate, the aluminum debris that filled the gap that should have been filled by the O-rings was subsequently jarred loose by a massive wind shear that disturbed the shuttle's trajectory. With that debris knocked out of the way, the hot gases were enabled to escape, and they very quickly burned a hole in the side of the SRB that soon expanded and melted away the rocket attachment. This caused the rocket to tip loose and crash inward into the main fuel tank which was filled with explosive hydrogen and oxygen.[3] The shuttle, then, did not so much explode as rapidly consume all its fuel at once, burning a fireball onto the blue slate of the sky that terrified onlookers below. The two SRBs broke loose and, looking for a moment like the front claws of a scorpion, tore off into the sky in opposite directions.

The shuttle's nose cone, meanwhile, with all seven crew members alive and (theoretically, at least) aware inside of it, broke free, undamaged, and began a two and a half minute plunge to earth. It was later found that three of the astronauts had had time to activate their helmets' internal emergency air systems.

None survived the crash.

Descent to Earth

And it happened again seventeen years later when, on February 1, 2003, the space shuttle *Columbia* burned up on its reentry into the earth's atmosphere. This time the problem was caused not by O-rings, but by a piece of foam rubber insulation.

Whereas the *Challenger*'s mission had been undertaken largely to improve NASA's public image and to demonstrate the inevitability of civil-

Five. Space Shuttle Disasters

ian passenger space travel, *Columbia*'s mission was primarily a scientific one. The shuttle missions had, by 2003, devolved to merely ferrying parts to the international space station and, since NASA was pressed to account for the four billion a year it was spending on these launches, it decided to retrofit the *Columbia*, its oldest shuttle, with a new state of the art space laboratory.

The shuttle was then launched on January 16, 2003, and for sixteen days, it conducted experiments in space, such as studying the origins of dust storms and perceiving the effects of global warming. Its mission successfully completed, then, on February 1, at 8:40 A.M., the shuttle began its descent to earth. At 8:44, it entered the atmosphere traveling at the phenomenal speed of 17,500 miles per hour and was almost immediately enshrouded in temperatures nearing 3,000 degrees. The ship had been designed, of course, to withstand such temperatures by coating it with white and black ceramic tiles, yet at 8:54, when the craft was still two hundred thousand feet in the air, one of the astronauts radioed back to Mission Control that the shuttle had abruptly lost four temperature transducers on the left side of the craft. Mission Control confirmed, and then when it heard back no response, said: "Columbia — Houston, UHF com check." Then repeated it. And repeated it again. But there was no reply from the space shuttle.

By that point, the *Columbia* had burned up like a meteorite at 9:16, 38 miles above ground, killing all seven crew members. The pieces of the craft — like the ancient mythical body of Osiris — were scattered far and wide. Indeed, most of them have still never been found.

NASA investigators subsequently determined that the cause of the shuttle's crash was a two and a half pound piece of foam rubber insulation that had broken loose from the large orange tank and crashed into the shuttle's left wing at 81 seconds into its initial flight. By then, it was already doing 500 miles per hour, thus conferring on an otherwise harmless piece of foam rubber enormous kinetic energy, enough energy to punch a hole into the ultra-strong gray carbon panels lining the front edge of the ship's wing. Upon reentry into the earth's atmosphere, hot air rushed into this hole and damaged the shuttle's thermal protection system, melting the aluminum inside and consuming the shuttle from within. In moments, it was a mechanical fireball hurtling toward the earth at enormous speeds.

One of the spokesmen for NASA voiced his incredulity at a press conference given on February 5, 2003, when he held up a similar sized piece of foam and commented: "Today, I brought with me a piece of foam: it is very lightweight, and so it is designed to be resilient and be an insulating material to keep the tank cold. And it's easy to break, and it's easy to break up into particles. Right now, it just does not make sense to us that a piece of debris could be the root cause for the loss of *Columbia* and its crew. There's got to be another reason."[4]

But there wasn't. Subsequent tests proved that small pieces of foam rubber, when fired at very high speeds, can indeed punch holes through the kind of gray carbon panels lining the shuttle's outer wing edge.

The space shuttle, then, had been destroyed by a mythical entity — in accidentology, anyway — which I shall call the "One Small Thing," the very same Small Thing — whatever the particular circumstances might happen to be — that has brought down craft after craft throughout the history of aeronautics. Apparently, it only takes One Small Thing to bring hugely complex, and ultimately extremely fragile, mechanical systems crashing down into ruins.[5]

Above and Below

Every accident makes visible something that, had the accident never happened, would have remained obscured. This "something" that the accident brings with it into the light of day is inevitably ontological; that is to say, it tells us something about the status of the human Technological Project in terms of its implications for the human mode of being-in-the-world *as* human.

One of the things that the human being seems to have an innate talent for is the creation of cosmologies, especially since, as theoretician Peter Sloterdijk has pointed out, cosmologies are in reality extensions of the human immune system into public space.[6]

In the case of the two shuttle accidents, what is being made visible to us is the persistence — albeit hidden — of the ancient Two World cosmology: that is, the extremely archaic, and apparently outdated, cosmology in which Heaven and Earth exist in ancient dyadic opposition. In Chinese cosmology, for instance, the very geometry of the two spheres is opposed: the heavens are round and the earth is a square, the whole thing pictured as a macrocosmic chariot with an umbrella. And in *all* the ancient traditions, the Heavens are associated with Eternity, the realm of pure

Five. Space Shuttle Disasters

unchanging Forms, the abode of gods, spirits and the ancestral dead; while Earth is the realm of the changing, the ephemeral and the transient. The earthly world is a flowing river into which all forms inevitably dissolve and from out of which they rearise; the heavens, on the other hand, are an eternal slate into which the gods have inscribed their laws, to be valid for all time.

Indeed, Plato's divorce between Being and Becoming — in which the intelligible realm of the Forms translates the Homeric pantheon of gods into philosophical concepts, while things visible to the senses are condemned to the status of mere shadows without substance — replicates the same dichotomy. And Heidegger's critique of science as a process of deworlding the world, of removing objects from their lifeworld contexts by translating them into purely theoretical entities — *Vorhandenheit* as opposed to *Zuhandenheit* — is but a philosophical descendant of this ancient cosmological dyad.

The opposition itself, however, was reputedly put to rest by the achievements of Galileo, Kepler and Isaac Newton. Galileo, through the lens of his telescope, saw that Venus had phases like the Moon and that Jupiter had moons whirling round it like Earth. Kepler realized that the orbits of the planets were not purely circular, as Copernicus before him had insisted, but were rather squashed circles, or ellipses. The planets, furthermore, did not maintain uniform motion along these orbits, but sped up and slowed down, exactly like the motions of a machine. And Isaac Newton forged the heavens together with the earth into a single universally valid machine of falling bodies and inertial motion applicable to *all* objects in spacetime, not just earthly ones. The apple falls from the tree, just as the moon falls around the earth, in both cases as the result of precisely the *same* universal force of gravitation. Thus, the laws in the heavens are identical to those on the ground. The opposition which the ancients had imagined existing between them turned out to be false. The ancients were wrong. Q.E.D.

The space shuttle disasters, though, especially when considered from an ontological point of view, tell us otherwise. Upon closer examination, it becomes evident that the catastrophes reveal the presence of a *world ceiling* after all. There *is* a dome separating heaven from earth: *Columbia* crashed right into it. And the *Challenger* was ill prepared to exit through it. Thus we arrive, once again, at the very same boundary problem we already encountered in the *Hindenburg* chapter.

Part II: Disasters of Neomodernity

The ancient cosmology of the earth being encased inside of a macrosphere, or cosmic dome, which sealed it off from the realm of the heavens, was, it seems, correct after all. The cosmological truth of the woodcut associated with the tradition of Nicholas Oresme showing the Knower poking his head outside of this sphere in order to gaze at the cosmic machinery beyond it, is thus confirmed by these two accidents.

Because what the accidents reveal is that the human being cannot exist in the same way in outer space — in the space *beyond* the world dome — as he can down here on earth.

Different laws apply in both cases, exactly as the ancients had suspected.

Two Sets of Laws, Three Systems

But then: which laws are we talking about?

Newton, after all, proved that the *mechanical* laws are uniform throughout the cosmos. What he didn't prove, though, was that the *ontological* laws are the same, for the ontological laws of Being prescribe the way in which the human being behaves in different world systems. That is to say, the way in which he goes about the process of world-making, *inside* the two spheres, is not only entirely different, but inherently opposed.

If we go to the blackboard and draw this out, the resulting diagram looks something like this:

There are *three* primary systems of world-making upon the earth: natural systems; human cultural systems; and complex mechanical, or technological, systems. Different processes of world-making characterize all three.

As the earth's geological and biological history reveals, Nature (which the Greeks called *physis*) is a *self-making* system. To use the language of systems theory, it is "autopoietic," that is to say, it has created itself, by itself, with no help from outside. The ancient model of a human-inspired deity creating it was but a projection of world-making from the *second* system, that of human artifactual culture (what the Greeks called *techne*). Natural systems, it turns out, are self-made, self-making and self-regulating. In his essay "The Question Concerning Technology," Heidegger contrasts the differences between the Greek idea of *physis* and that of *poiesis* in the following manner:

Physis, also, the arising of something from out of itself, is a bringing-forth, *poiesis*. *Physis* is indeed *poiesis* in the highest sense. For what presences by means of *physis* has the irruption belonging to bringing-forth, e.g., the bursting of a blossom into bloom in itself (*en heautoi*). In contrast, what is brought forth by the artisan or the artist, e.g., the silver chalice, has the irruption belonging to bringing-forth, not in itself, but in another (*en alloi*), in the craftsman or artist.[7]

Human cultural systems (*poiesis*), furthermore, inevitably come into conflict with natural systems (*physis*) and *disrupt* their autopoietic abilities. Deforestation at Neolithic sites like Ain Ghazal, for example, destabilized the nearby ecosystem so badly that the village was eventually forced into becoming a ghost town. Salinization of the soil and the silting up of canals eventually rendered the irrigation systems of the Hohokam American Indians of the Southwestern United States — and also the hydraulic systems of the ancient Mesopotamians — unusable. So they abandoned the cultural landscapes which these technical systems had made possible. And "nature" then set itself back to repairing the damage.

Human cultural systems, on the other hand, are not autopoietic, or self-created, but made by human beings themselves. They are *created* as macro-scale works of art. Civilizations are works of art unto themselves. They have to be *made by* some other entity, in this case, human beings. And they fall apart when human beings, for one reason or another, lose the ability to reverse their entropy into systems of highly organized and beautifully made patterns of order.

Mechanical systems, though, are also *made by* human beings. They do not make themselves any more than do cultural systems. But they are made for entirely different purposes than cultural systems, for they are not constructed as works of art — in other words to realize some otherwise hidden aspect of Being — but rather to perform very specific, task-oriented functions. Machines are problem solving devices. Cultures, on the other hand, are realizations of Being that confer meaning and value upon human world systems of living. They are not at all the same thing.

But now there is a difference between the first two types of world systems and those of the third, or mechanical order: in the case of both natural and human cultural systems, the One Small Thing is averaged out. The systems, in other words, are flexible enough so that errors can be easily built into them, worked through them, or otherwise paved over without damage to the integrity of the systems as a whole. In an autopoietic system, such as a biological organism, error is a matter of course: these systems are filled with genetic errors that are simply averaged out. When the errors proliferate, they might eventually overwhelm the system, as when too many genetic errors lead to birth defects or life threatening diseases. But these are exceptions. The norm for such systems is to leave enough room for flexibility such that the errors are averaged out and the system functions smoothly for most of the time. The system, in other words, has built in enough redundancy to compensate for its own internal errors.

Human cultures are similar to biological systems in at least this one respect: they are imperfect and thrive on, or rather, in spite of, their imperfections. An error in a work of art is not necessarily detrimental to the artwork, as any admirer of the statues of Michelangelo well knows: the head of David, for instance, is too large in proportion to the rest of the body, and the hands are too big. Indeed, there is a certain awkwardness about Michelangelo's overall handling of the human form — this becomes even more evident in his frescoes — but the command and majesty of the performance is so astonishing that we are willing to look past such "errors."

With mechanical systems, though, the matter is otherwise. They can, indeed, as we have seen, be brought down by One Small Thing, a *single* error that can cause the system to come to a complete and catastrophic collapse. Thus, the failure of *Challenger*'s O-rings to expand at liftoff, an apparently minor flaw, is yet fatal to the entire system and causes it to come crashing back to earth. A tiny piece of foam rubber, in the case of *Columbia,* is enough to destroy one of the most complex and elaborate works of human technological mastery ever built.

The implications of this for the fragility of technological systems is overwhelming. They simply cannot withstand the kinds of catastrophic failures that natural and cultural systems routinely recover from. They are much, much more fragile than we are ordinarily accustomed to think.

World Islands

Now, in the world beyond the earth, *outside* the dome of the atmosphere, to be precise, there are natural, self-organizing systems of planets and stars and galaxies, but there are no biological systems (at least, none in our own solar system, anyway). And there are no biological systems out there because the world conditions do not exist in outer space to support such systems.

Consequently, when the human biological organism is transplanted into outer space, it is taken *outside* the dome of its world, where a living world is no longer provided for it, to nourish it and ensure that it can survive, and instead, it must provide for itself an entirely *artificial* world island. As Peter Sloterdijk puts it, a world island must be *transplanted* from the earth — or what he calls being-in-the-world 1— to outer space, in which the transplanted vessel becomes a being-in-the-world 2. However, I must disagree with Sloterdijk's conclusion when he says that this transplantation sets up an ontological *continuity* between the two worlds, for what Sloterdijk fails to take into account in his essay, is the degree to which the transplanted world island of the space vessel operates under *completely different* ontological circumstances, circumstances which, we need hardly point out, are entirely inimical not only to biological life, but also to complex, and yet very fragile, mechanical systems themselves.[8] The second, transplanted system — i.e., the space vessel — is in fact not a being-in-the-world at all, but rather a being-*outside*-the world.

The problem, then, is that in order for the human being to exist within this hostile environment, he must substitute a mechanical world island for the self-making, autopoietic world system of Nature *inside* which he has come to *be* over the course of millions of years. Such mechanical world islands, furthermore, must also function as replacements for those other world islands which Sloterdijk terms "macrospheres," i.e., the various architectural containers of our civilizations — houses, buildings, skyscrapers, etc.— which serve as what he calls Anthropogenic Islands inside of which human beings are enabled to come into existence as cultural entities. These containers are indeed, as Sloterdijk insists, attempts to replicate the uterine conditions by way of which the human animal first came into the world, and they serve to protect him against the ravages of Nature. They are cozy womb-spheres that he has erected around himself as prosthetic replacements for the womb.

But in the conditions of outer space, the mechanical world islands of our space stations and shuttles are *not* cozy womb spheres at all, but rather habitations subject to extreme conditions of stress in which the human occupants are in constant peril. They can never relax, but must be hypervigilant, lest that One Small Thing go wrong that may serve to bring down the entire system.

Part II: Disasters of Neomodernity

Nothing is provided for the human being in outer space: he must construct not only a substitute *physis* but a substitute *domus*, as well. He must make an artificial atmosphere to breathe the air; provide sufficient protection against solar and cosmic radiation; a means of eating, excreting and disposal of waste; he must exercise so that the body does not atrophy in a zero g environment, etc., etc. And, of course, this must all take place *inside* a container that must function for him as a substitute dwelling.

But notice that we are now asking for the human being to take over the autopoietic processes of the earth. In the sphere of the heavens, in order to survive and stay alive, the human being must take over the self-making processes by means of which the earth provides for it an already created container within which it can flourish. In outer space, the human being must create technologies that can imitate the biospheric conditions of the earth, which have *already been made for it* over billions of years.

The human intellect, in such a world order, is tasked to perform something that it was not designed to do: create and imitate a replica of the earth's very biosystems, the very systems which create for it a breathable atmosphere, an ozone layer to protect it from UV radiation, gravity by means of which its bones can form properly, etc. But in highly complex mechanical systems, as we have seen, *if one thing goes wrong, One Small Thing*, the entire system is in danger of catastrophic failure.

Imagine if the cultural worlds which human beings have built throughout history depended upon such One Small Thing never occurring. How long would we have survived if this had been the case?

Remember, in natural systems — riverine ecologies, animal herds, forested canopies — the One Small Thing is normally averaged out of the system, because the system has to be aware, at some level, of an entire panoply of variables, all of which it must take into account, *simultaneously* in order to self-organize. There is plenty of room for error in such systems. Indeed, error in an almost cosmic sense is built into these systems as a matter of course. Redundancy is what enables them to survive, adapt and shape the environing world to their own ends.

In the world order of the mechanical islands which we set drifting through outer space, however, there is not room for a *single* error. Otherwise, life within such systems becomes abruptly impossible, as the two space shuttle disasters so amply demonstrate.

The resiliency and toughness of our cultural macrospheres, on the other hand, is striking. Their ability to bounce back from cascades of error and catastrophe is astonishing. Consider the case of Hurricane Katrina, in which the destruction of the macrosphere of the polis of New Orleans was effectively shattered by the overflowing of the canals. The population subsequently found itself in one of Agamben's "states of exception" in which the juridical order that normally protects them was withdrawn and the population could, therefore, be treated like wild animals and killed with impunity, just like refugees in a camp situation. But even after a literal flood of many, many things going wrong the polisphere reconstituted itself and New Orleans soon emerged as a functioning macrosphere once again. In ancient history, we find the same phenomenon reiterated over and over again with places like Mohenjo-daro, which endured flood after flood and was rebuilt each time with shoddier and shoddier architecture. Çatalhöyük, too, was destroyed numerous times by fire, but it recovered each time until after a certain point, like Mohenjo-daro, it succumbed to desolation and had to be abandoned. Such Anthropogenic world islands are extremely tough and can endure disaster after disaster.

But this is not so for the *absolute* world islands which we put up into outer space, for, despite their complexity, they are brittle constructions that cannot withstand much stress and do not, therefore, serve very well as uterine containers to protect their human occupants. If houses are extensions of the human immune system, then the vessels which we put up into outer space are immunologically weak and cannot therefore serve as incubators for *any* kind of livable human societies. They are in no way, then, valid ontological extensions of the human being-in-the-world into outer space, but rather flimsy space islands on which their human occupants may cling as so much flotsam from their shipwrecked earthly worlds down below. They are a being-*outside*-the world.

Thus, it appears that the ancients were correct after all: there *does* exist an invisible boundary — a sort of ecological limes — that demarcates the realm of biological habitability on the earth below from that of biological hostility in the world above.

Above and below: the realm of gods, Heidegger's *Vorhandenheit* in which objects exist *outside* the bounds of world containers; and the curved blue and green geosphere of men engaged in their various lifeworld tasks down below.

Two worlds, then, after all.

Six

Back from History
Some Implications Regarding the the Accident at Chernobyl

The Explosion

The worst nuclear accident in history[1] — an accident which took place early on the morning of April 26, 1986, at 1:24 in a part of the Soviet Union known as the Ukraine — was actually the result of an attempt to *simulate* an accident. Just a few years earlier, a Soviet built nuclear reactor in Iraq had been bombed by the Israeli air force and the Soviets wanted to find out what would happen in the event of an attack and a loss of power to the plant. It was important to establish, in the event of such a power cut, how long it would take the two backup generators to kick in and thus, whether the turbines, while waiting for the generators to begin functioning, would have continued to provide the necessary electricity to operate the cooling pumps and the motors for the reactor's control rods. (Control rods are the brakes of a nuclear reactor. Inserting them into the core slows down the process of uranium fission, while lifting them out speeds it up).

The Chernobyl power plant had been built during the 1970s at the small twelfth century town of Chernobyl in order to provide energy to the city of Kiev (with a population of 2 million) and its surrounding towns and villages. An entirely new town, called Pripyat, had to be constructed two kilometers away to the north in order to house all the plant's workers. One thinks of the special cities built for the tomb workers of the time of Rameses III at places like Deir el–Medina.

The accident occurred in the plant's reactor no. 4, which had just recently become operational on December 21, 1983. Two more reactors were in process of being constructed at the plant, and if those reactors, nos. 5 and 6, had been completed, Chernobyl would have been the world's

Six. The Accident at Chernobyl

largest nuclear power plant. All four reactors thus far were producing 4000 megawatts of electricity between them.

The test on reactor no. 4 that led to the accident was supposed to have been conducted *before* the reactor ever went online in the first place, although a similar test had already been conducted the previous year on reactor no. 3. There had, furthermore, already been an accident at Chernobyl in September of 1982, when reactor no. 1 was shut down for maintenance and then restarted. The valves controlling the flow of water into that reactor were momentarily closed, and, as a result, some of the fuel assemblies overheated, the uranium melted, and there was an explosion in the core with a release of radioactivity into the power station, although no one was killed at that time.[2]

The test was initially supposed to have been conducted earlier in the day on April 25, but because of a shortage of power, the city of Kiev required reactor no. 4 to stay powered up until 11 P.M. that night. At midnight, there was a shift change, with a new crew coming on, a crew which included one Alexander Akimov, the shift foreman, and Leonid Toptunov, one of the chief operators in the reactor's control room.

The whole operation was under the supervision of chief engineer Anatoli Dyatlov, who had been advised not to perform the test with power levels below 700 megawatts. However, Dyatlov wanted to perform the test at 200 megawatts in order to preserve the cooling water that stops the reactor from overheating.

Toptunov thus set about reducing the reactor's power further — it had been running at half power all day — by inserting the boron control rods into the reactor's core. His partner, Akimov, had also instructed him to shut off the plant's emergency core cooling system so that it could not override their test, but this also meant that in the event of an emergency, the operators would have to act fast to prevent a catastrophe.

When Toptunov set about inserting the control rods to lower the power, however, he brought the reactor to an unintended near shutdown state, lowering its power level to only 30 megawatts, a very difficult level to bring it back from safely. Dyatlov ordered him to remove control rods quickly, and Toptunov did so, stabilizing the power at around 200 megawatts. But the initial shutdown had led to a poisoning of the reactor's core as the result of the accumulation of Xenon-135, a gas by-product of the radioactive decay of the uranium absorbed neutrons. The operation of the reactor at low power with high xenon poisoning of its core was accompanied by an unstable core temperature (a hidden hot spot began to form in the reactor) and coolant flow.[3]

Inside the reactor core were 1,661 uranium-filled fuel rods. The splitting of the uranium atoms inside them releases enormous heat from the fuel rods, heat which turns water into steam which then drives the giant turbines to generate electricity. To harness this power, 211 boron control rods are spread throughout the core. If they're raised, power accelerates, but if they're taken out altogether, then the engineers lose their ability to apply the brakes.[4] Dyatlov ordered the operators to pull the control rods out in order to bring the power back up, although this left the reactor working with a dangerously small number of rods in the core.

Somewhere around 1 A.M., with the reactor thus operating at a more or less stable power level of 200 megawatts, the operators proceeded with the test, which was supposed to shut down power to the massive turbines, while back-up diesel generators would then take over; the only catch was that there was a forty second delay before they kicked in. The question, then, became how effectively the slowing turbines would keep the water pumps going until the diesel generators took over, since with the control rods out, the only thing to cool the reactor was the water flowing around it.

The power to the turbines was then shut down at 1:23:09 A.M.. As they powered down, the pumps pushed less water through the reactor core and so more and more steam was produced from less and less water. Steam pressure was now building up at the hot spot forming at the reactor's core.

In the control room, meanwhile, Toptunov saw the temperatures rising in the core as warning alarms began blaring. He hit the reactor's emergency shut down button, but this meant that the boron control rods were automatically lowered into the reactor core to reduce power. However, there is a fatal flaw in this particular reactor's design such that when the boron rods are lowered, instead of immediately slowing power, the power momentarily surges. Imagine slamming on the brakes of a speeding car only to watch it shoot forward before slowing. Thus, the reactor heated up very, very quickly.

The result: an enormous explosion which blew the reactor's 2000-ton steel roof sideways. Eight tons of highly radioactive fuel blasted into the night sky. A cloud rose and drifted away, sprinkling graphite and radioactive fuel across the countryside.

The amount of radiation released was 200 times greater than the atomic bomb at Hiroshima.

Six. The Accident at Chernobyl

After the Explosion

For 10 days, the burning reactor continued to spew forth radioactivity into the lifeworld of Europe. A radioactive cloud with Strontium 90, Caesium 137, Iodine 131 and both Plutonium 239 and 240 rained down on Eastern Europe, the south of France and Corsica, travelled north to Sweden and eventually drifted as far as the eastern shores of North America.

These radioactive elements, called radionuclides, have some interesting properties that are worth taking a moment to consider:

Strontium 90, for instance, has a 29-year half-life, which means that it requires 290 years for it to disappear from the environment that it has contaminated. Strontium has a chemical structure that is similar to calcium and our bodies mistake it for such, so that it accumulates in teeth, bone marrow and bones, eventually causing cancers such osteosarcomas and leukemias.

Caesium 137 has a 30-year half-life, taking 300 years to disappear. It has a chemical structure similar to potassium and when it enters the body, it causes genetic mutations, tumors and pathologies in various organs.

Iodine 131 has only an 8-day half-life, causing it to disappear in 80 years. Its structure, though, is similar to the iodine which the thyroid gland uses in order to function. It therefore accumulates in the thyroid, where it can cause tumors.

But the real monster is Plutonium 239, which has a half-life of 24,000 years, which means that it requires *240,000 years* for it to melt away. A single particle of plutonium that is inhaled into the body is enough to cause a lung tumor.

Finally, Uranium 235, with a *700-million-year half-life, requires 7 billion years to disappear.* It too, by the way, causes cancer.[5]

Thus, Chernobyl, and the land around it for many miles, will continue being radioactive for hundreds of thousands of years to come. The initial danger to the population after the plant ceased being radioactive was the ingestion of Iodine 131 through milk from cows pastured on contaminated grass. About 25,000 square kilometers of land were contaminated beyond five curies per square kilometer. Three months after that, the danger came from Caesium 137, also ingested through milk. Over 86,000 cattle had to be evacuated from the zone.[6]

The flames burning in the reactor core, meanwhile, were eventually put out by helicopters dropping bags of sand, boron carbide and melted lead from above; while from below, the possibility of a second, much more dangerous explosion (equivalent to a 3 — 5 megaton bomb that would have rendered Europe uninhabitable) was averted only by sending a team of miners to tunnel beneath the reactor and set up a liquid nitrogen refrigeration unit beneath it.

Thirty-six hours after the accident, the inhabitants of the town of Pripyat — who had already been exposed to doses of radiation high enough to alter the composition of their blood and later induce cancers — were told that they needed to leave their things and march down to the 1,000 buses that the Soviet government had sent to carry them away. The population of roughly 43,000 people was told that it would be gone for three days, and that no one was allowed to leave the city on their own, so as to avoid clogging the roads with traffic. By 5:30 on the afternoon of April 27, Pripyat was a ghost town, its single ferris wheel creaking in the wind.[7]

By May 2, all people living within a 30-kilometer radius of the plant were evacuated from their towns and villages, many of whom had already received dangerously high doses of radiation. 130,000 people were thus displaced. A 300,000 hectare area, straddling the Ukraine and Belarus, was isolated and evacuated. Soon, it, too, was full of empty, silent shacks and rotting, abandoned farm houses.

The next task for the Soviet authorities, then, after the fire in the core was put out, was to build a giant steel and concrete sarcophagus over reactor no. 4 to seal it off from leaking radioactive particles. A sarcophagus of steel and concrete 170 meters long and 66 meters high was built by a team of "liquidators" under incredibly adverse conditions, since the site was thoroughly saturated with high levels of radioactivity. The roof of the reactor was found to contain highly radioactive pieces of graphite that had to be cleared away, first by remote controlled robots and then later, when these ceased functioning due to the radioactivity, by humans. Each worker, heavily suited up, was only allowed on the roof for 45 seconds at a time. For ten days, a new crew climbed up on the roof every ten minutes. A total of 3,500 people participated in the clean up. The level of radioactivity on the roof was about 7000 roentgens. A human being can absorb 2 roentgens a year without being affected, but a lethal dose is an exposure of over 400 roentgens.

The sarcophagus was eventually completed in October of 1986, but it was only built to stand for thirty years and more than two-thirds of that time has already gone by. It is in danger of collapsing from storms and rain erosion, and if such a collapse should occur, Europe would have another nuclear disaster on its hands. There are currently plans to build a gigantic, movable steel structure that would cover the sarcophagus and the reactor entirely, but the budget for such a structure is estimated to cost over one billion dollars and the Ukraine does not have sufficient funds for this.

The magma inside the reactor—14 meters underground—*still* remains a threat. If the sarcophagus should ever collapse, there are 100 kilograms of plutonium inside waiting to seed the earth with more devastation.

Today radioactive particles continue to poison the land. Eight million people live in contaminated areas of the Ukraine, Russia and Belorussia. They live off of contaminated food, and as a result, cancers in the region are very high, as are deformities in both animals and human embryos. In Belorussia alone, 300,000 children are currently suffering from radiation contamination.

After the accident, Russia stopped building nuclear reactors, and by the year 2001, the other three reactors at Chernobyl had been shut down.

The death toll is still a matter of controversy. According to one report, delivered by the United Nations Scientific Committee on the Effects of Atomic Radiation, the official number of deaths from radiation is only 64. But the World Health Organization suggests something closer to 4,000, while a report made by Greenpeace advances this drastically to 200,000. But according to the recent book *Chernobyl* by Pierpaolo Mittica, the number in reality will come somewhere closer to one million people.[8]

Most of the alarming data, though, has been downplayed by the authorities, especially those associated with the International Atomic Energy Agency. Its then-general director, Hans Blix, was reported to have stated, giddily: "The world could tolerate a nuclear accident as serious as Chernobyl every year."[9]

Anti-spheric Technology

Looking through a volume of color photographs of the ruins left behind by the disaster, Robert Polidori's *Zones of Exclusion: Pripyat and Chernobyl,* and especially at the large photograph on page 9 of this book, detailing a shot from above looking down on the Pripyat city center, one notices something interesting: the photograph shows a collection of bone-

Part II: Disasters of Neomodernity

white multi-story buildings, apartment complexes arranged around a concrete city square from which grass and weeds are now poking through cracks; in the background sits the rusting hulk of the abandoned ferris wheel; while an army of trees is slowly, inexorably, marching in toward the city and surrounding it on all sides, as though to reclaim the land that rightfully belongs to them. Another page shows a similar scene, closer in, of apartment high rises with row upon row of yawning, gaping black windows void of human habitation, windows that had once provided people with world island habitations to call "home," habitations where no human presence will ever return.[10]

Shells, in other words.

The empty streets and ghostly buildings in these pictures show us, very clearly, what radiation does to human worlds when considered ontologically: that is to say, it cleans human beings out of the exoskeletal shells of their polispheric habitations as though it were an enzyme that had been chemically engineered specifically to go into these shells and, while leaving the shells themselves intact, to scrape out the human biological matter inside them. What's left behind are empty cities, houses and dwellings that are the human equivalent of the seashells found scattered along the beaches of the world's oceans, shells from which all signs of biological life have long since vanished. Radiation, in other words, attacks human polispheres and leaves them void of occupants.

Nuclear technology is, therefore, in essence an *anti*-spheric technology: that is to say, a type of technology that is completely inimical to human civilization, for it is a technology that empties out such spheres, separating the human inhabitant (along with its logosphere, or realm of meaning) from the exoskeleton of the polisphere that shelters it and brings it into formation. Nuclear technology, then, actually has a *fissioning* effect at the larger ontological level of the human world, where it cleanly and neatly shears the sociosphere away from the polisphere like a butcher cutting meat away from the bone.

In fact, never in human history has there been a technology so powerful as to be capable of actually assaulting an entire human *cosmology* by separating world spheres from one another, i.e., fissioning the sociosphere from its particular polisphere. It is a technology that is therefore completely at odds with the human way of living-in-spheres, or the construction of those cultural envelopes that we have called "cities." There is, therefore, no more certain method of *ending* such human living in spheres

Six. The Accident at Chernobyl

than by unleashing radiation through accidents at nuclear power plants, accidents which will inevitably increase as these plants age and crumble (they are only designed to produce power for about thirty years, after which time they must be disassembled and their radioactive waste buried in the earth somewhere, where it will remain radioactive for thousands of years).

Such a technology that is so inimical to the human way of building habitations in polispheres may be called "Shaivite" in nature after the Hindu god Shiva, a god who is also similarly antipathetic to the human mode of being in cities, for Shiva is a god of mountains and the wilderness and a patron of yogis who have left civilization far behind, as they sit, locked into the trance states of *samadhi*.

In my previous book *The New Media Invasion*, I termed the new technologies of self-luminous video screens and monitors "*sukshma* technologies," meaning that they are self-luminous and therefore imitate the structural pattern of light-*through* in the form of myth and dream.[11] But electronic technologies so named may also be called "Vaishnava technologies," after the god Vishnu, the god who sleeps and dreams the nightmare of world history that composes the fabric of our lives. In contrast to such subtle technologies, nuclear physics is a technology not of *light* but of *matter*, of manipulating dark, heavy matter, cutting it apart and releasing enormous amounts of energy. It is, then, a Shaivite form of technology, especially since Shiva — one of the three gods of the Hindu Trimurti — is known as the Destroyer, for he is the god of destruction and death and of sublime, awesome power that shatters tiny human lives into fragments.

In Indian mythology, the three great gods, Brahma, Vishnu and Shiva are known respectively, as the Creator, the Preserver and the Destroyer. In the West, therefore, we have created technologies whose essence mimics this structural trichotomy: our Vaishnava technologies are electronic; our nuclear technologies are Shaivite; and our biotechnologies of genetic engineering are Brahmic in character, since Brahma is the god who creates forms simply by thinking about them and then realizing them in some kind of material substrate, whether subtle or concrete.

Our Western technologies, then, actually mimic and replicate the structures of religious ideas. This might be a fairly trivial observation on the surface were it not for the fact that the Shaivite nature of one of these technologies has the potential to render human civilization obsolete.

Part II: Disasters of Neomodernity

The Poisoning of the Logosphere

One of the main problems with nuclear technologies is that they threaten to dissolve and permanently erode the boundary separating civilization from the wilderness. If Shiva is allowed to have his way, such a boundary will cease to exist and nature will be impossible to distinguish from culture. Nuclear technologies, as we have seen, separate human society from polispheres and in doing so, threaten to banish — completely, once and for all — the membrane that emerged and was built up, very gradually, during the long, long stretches of the Neolithic, in which our polispheres first took shape as tiny towns and villages with mud walls. Such walls, usually constructed out of mud-brick or lime plaster, were erected in the ancient Near East — the earliest one is from Jericho circa 9500 B.C. — but they began to become common right around 6000 B.C. at sites like Tell es Sawwan on the Tigris River in Iraq, or later, during the Chinese Neolithic amongst the Lungshan peoples of the Yellow River civilization around 3000 B.C.

Such walls are not just architectural monuments but actually markers indicating the advent of a new ontological separation in human consciousness that took place in the Neolithic, in which small cultural microcosms began to demarcate themselves and break off from the background of Nature in a new and significant way. They point to a singularity — in the sense of the philosopher Alain Badiou's use of this word[12] — the singularity of the World Event in which a human terrarium was created and set apart, like nests of eggs in which culture is thus enabled to incubate and come into being. A tiny world, a "*not*-wilderness" is separated by these walls from *the* Wilderness, and as a result, human History begins to come into being as an ontological Event with its own unique structural characteristics. History is coterminous with life inside the boundaries of walled cities, for what is *beyond* the walls takes place out in the wilderness of *a*-history, an eternal realm of dusty, shambling Martu without culture, of Enkidus lacking refinement, of ibn Khaldun's Bedouins — held together only by the mystical *asabiyyah* of descent from a common ancestor — wandering across vast surfaces of eventless planes of smooth space.[13]

It is very possible that a nostalgia for this realm of Nature and eventlessness, of nomads and tribes and wild animals, lies somehow behind our use of nuclear technologies as an unconscious driving force — a sort of civilizational death wish — since the use of these technologies, especially as they age and begin to crumble, is an almost certain means of separating the entirety of human society from the polisphere; of moving the human mode of being-in-the-world-inside-spheres *back* to the state in which he existed prior to the advent of History, that is to say, the mode of being-in-the-world-unprotected-by-spheres. Human culture is almost impossible to separate from the polisphere *without* devolving back to a state of historical insignificance and cultural eventlessness. Life in cities, with monumental art and architecture, writing and painting and sculpture, *is* human history, even if we expand the word "city" to mean only a local town or village. It is *inside* such containers, protected from the entropic forces of the wilderness, that the experiment of Civilization takes place. *Outside* them, nothing much happens beyond endless tribal wars where refugee populations which, because they are no longer protected by such bounding walls, are also, existentially considered, *outside* of History proper.

Nuclear technologies threaten to disrupt this distinction between World and Nature, or historical-being-in-the-world vs. *a*-historical-being-in-the-world, for once the separating boundary is removed, human life will devolve and blend back into the landscapes of the earth. His mode of living will fade back into the wilderness in just the way that this was demonstrated for us in the ruins of Pripyat, where the forests and vegetation are slowly moving in to reclaim the ruins of the town in the same way in which the jungles of the Yucatan peninsula eventually swallowed up the temple cities of the Maya. On a topographical map, or a satellite view from outer space, the distinction between the human mode of living in cultural containers and that of living like animals in the wilderness will no longer be evident, since his existential mode of being will have become indistinguishable from the surrounding terrain.

It is of the essence of nuclear technologies to destroy boundaries and membranes of all kinds: they remove the boundary, for instance, that separates complex biological systems from inanimate non-living systems, for radioactive contamination is essentially tantamount to a poisoning of the biosphere by atomic elements from the realm of pure matter. Nuclear technology fatally confuses the two orders of being, and it does the same thing to human cosmologies, eroding and effacing the cultural boundary separating nature from culture.

In other words, what I am getting at here is that nuclear technology is a kind of technology which not only contains the potential to undo our way of living in cities and thus bring on a new Dark Age — that point seems fairly obvious — but it also has the potential to actually *reverse* and destructure the entire human logosphere. It is *so* antipathetic, in essence, to what characterizes the human being as an existential entity, that it may actually discompose the very fabric of that logosphere itself.

For with the dissolution of the historical mode of being back into the wilderness, the very ontological level of the constructed human logosphere — built up over thousands of years — will collapse in on itself. The erection of temples, skyscrapers and monumental art is a negentropic task that involves an uphill push against the forces of chaos and entropy that perpetually threaten to undo such brittle achievements. But the sum total of these achievements, from the caves of Chauvet to our cities of steel and concrete, actually demarcates an entire level of Being from *inside* the evolutionary arc that moves from subatomic particles to atoms to molecular combinations to plants to animals to humans. The top of this arc is the human logosphere: and though the Derridas of the world may deconstruct this logosphere all they want, the very fact that they are enabled to do so presupposes their embeddedness *within* it, just as the existence of a fish presupposes the water that it lives in. Nuclear technology is a *deconstructive* technology.

Once you remove the human being from the polispheric greenhouse inside which he is enabled to create history, then there will be some serious consequences, for it is like taking the fish out of water and throwing it alive onto the bank: for a time, it will flap and squirm and writhe about as the existential envelope that it has been unplugged from exerts the disastrous consequences of its sudden *absence* upon him. Death is not only imminent in such circumstances, it is certain.

It is therefore possible that the human logosphere itself will become poisoned by radioactivity and, just as in the case of the body which breaks down in stages as a direct result of radioactive poisoning, so too, there exists a danger that the human logosphere will become radioactive and itself break down in stages, slowly, over time. Just as the bones and cells of the body are attacked by radioactive isotopes, so too, the skeletal structure that makes the logosphere possible, namely, the polisphere, will be made uninhabitable.

The German mystic Rudolf Steiner has remarked somewhere that the human skull is a sort of vestigial survival of an exoskeleton. Likewise, the logosphere exists *inside* the polisphere which protects it exactly like an exoskeleton protects the soft tissues of an organism such as an insect or a

Six. The Accident at Chernobyl

crustacean. As the polisphere dissolves and becomes uninhabitable, so too, the potentialities of the logosphere that it had been protecting inside of it will vanish to zero.

All the great higher religions and thought systems — yoga, Taoism, the works of Plato and Plotinus, Buddhism — were produced *inside* the polisphere. The very existence of these higher thought forms was made possible by the development of the human psyche as it has passed *through* the evolutionary incarnation of life in cities. The Buddha may have become the Buddha by walking away from palace life in the city of Kapilavastu, but his entire religion depends upon, and is, to a large degree, a response to, the mode of human existence in cities. The same goes for Yajnvalkya's discovery and introduction of yoga as a system of individual self-salvation designed to free the individual from the dharmic commitments imposed upon him by his existence in the all-surrounding network of life in the city. Yoga could never have been invented by cave men with no experience of higher forms of media and civic life and neither would any of the other great world religions, *all* of which are products of the greenhouse environment created for them by cities designed to protect and house the human logosphere.

So, with the inevitable proliferation of radioactive landscapes ahead of us — Chernobyl and Fukushima are only the prelude — what we are confronted with is the gradual increase of topographies rendered inherently hostile to the human project of cultural efflorescence. And with the increase of such exclusion zones around the world — for this is the type of world, ontologically speaking, that the technology of nuclear physics makes possible: a world wholly opposed in type and substance to that of the human cultural project — the protective exoskeleton inside which that exotic human activity known as signification will gradually, slowly, inevitably crumble and begin, bit by bit, to slide into cessation. This is precisely what I mean by the radioactive contamination of the logosphere.

So, now we are faced with the triumph of the small over the large; of atoms over complex, advanced organisms; and of the irony of one of the end products of the human logosphere itself as a technology that is capable of actually effacing its existence altogether.

There will *be* no more Buddhas, no more Mohammads, no more Lao Tzus on the road ahead of us, since the very existential conditions of the human-mode-of-being-in-spheres that is necessary to produce them will have long since ceased to exist. The Axial Age is long behind us; now, we are preparing to move into the Age of Vanishing, and of the *dis*-evolution of human consciousness, for now we have actually created the tools for bringing this about.

Such a reversion back from history to living in the wilderness in the form of human wolf packs roving across the countryside in search of food would, of course, be tantamount to an abrogation of the great human experiment of creating cities and living in History in the larger sense. The Human Project would have to be chalked up as a failure; an abortive experiment in attaining civic life that led to a catastrophic collapse of such polispheres, with an attendant exit back to an Eden-like existence in which neither history nor culture in any higher sense exists any longer.

The great human experiment would then be written off as a failure, and the gods would shift their interest and attention to other worlds with other potentialities, leaving the pathetic human-monkeys behind as a fascinating but ultimately tragic failure in the experiment of the evolution of consciousness.

Then history really *will* be over.

Seven

The Amsterdam Cargo Plane Crash and the Derailment at Eschede
Parallel Accidents

Bolt Out of the Blue

El Al Flight 1862 crashed into an eleven-story apartment high-rise on October 4, 1992, in Amsterdam in the Netherlands. Surprisingly, the crash killed only 43 people, including four people on the plane — a cargo flight carrying supplies and consumer products to Tel Aviv — and 39 people on the ground. This occurred at 6:30 in the evening, and the weather was nice, so most people, fortunately, were out doing other things.

The cargo plane had been traveling from New York City on its way to Tel Aviv, and at 2:31 P.M., it stopped over at Amsterdam Schiphol Airport for refueling and to take on more cargo. The plane's captain was one Yitzhak Fuchs, an experienced aviation pilot who had flown in the Israeli air force, and whose crew consisted of First Officer Arnon Ohad, who had only been flying for about a year, and Flight Engineer Gedalya Sofer. There was also a passenger, Anat Solomon, who was on his way to Tel Aviv in order to marry an El Al employee.

Flight 1862 departed at 6:20 P.M. from runway 01L, traveling north. Shortly after it was airborne, the craft made a right turn to follow the Pampus departure route, a straight line that heads east over the Amsterdam suburb of Bijlmer, located to the south-east of the city center. Bijlmer was a troubled area with a high crime rate and had been designed as a single project laid out along a grid with large high rise apartment buildings arranged into hexagonal blocks. Much of the area was given over to illegal immigrants from Suriname, and was generally regarded as "black Amsterdam."

Part II: Disasters of Neomodernity

The El Al flight, meanwhile, was climbing to 6,500 feet inside of an orange evening sky. Captain Fuchs had turned the controls over to Arnon so that he could get some more flight time. They would be in Tel Aviv in about five hours. Everything was going smoothly.

But at that very moment, there was a loud bang: Fuchs, noticing that the plane was starting to lose altitude and tilting sharply to the right, took the controls back from Arnon and wrestled with the plane for about thirty seconds before he could get it to stabilize. They had just lost both engines on the right wing of the aircraft. Later, investigators would discover that the inner engine had simply snapped off, the fuse pins holding it to the wing having suddenly given way due to metal fatigue. Upon breaking away, furthermore, it had smashed back into the outer engine on that same wing, shearing it away cleanly while both engines plummeted into Lake Gooimer on the ground below. Fuchs radioed in to the ATC at Schiphol that they would be returning for an emergency landing and had just lost engines three and four.

For the next few minutes, the captain managed to keep the plane stable as he turned it around and headed back over the Bijlmer suburb. But as he lifted the nose to slow the plane in preparation for landing, it rolled once again sharply to the right. For 90 more seconds, Fuchs fought to control it, but the tilt continued to worsen until the plane rolled onto its side at a 90 degree angle, and then curved and plunged like an arrowhead toward the city below. Slowing down the plane for landing, as it turned out, actually failed to provide enough lift to the right wing, which caused it to roll and spiral out of control.

At 6:35:25 P.M., the first officer radioed to ATC: "Going down, 1862, going down, going down, copied, going down." With its right wing pointing directly at the ground, the aircraft smashed into the Groeneveen and Klein-Kruitberg apartment buildings at the sixth floor where the angle of the two buildings met at the corner of a hexagon. A huge portion of the building exploded and collapsed inward. The cockpit separated from the plane and came to rest on the ground somewhere east of the buildings. Flames engulfed the complex with temperatures approaching 1,100 degrees Celsius.

Amazingly, only 43 people, total, were killed, including all four people on the plane. It is possible that there were actually more than 39 people killed on the ground, however, since many of the illegal immigrants living in the apartment high rise were undocumented and may not have turned up in the official count of the missing.

Now, it is standard engineering practice to design wing engines in such a way that the fuse pins attaching them to the wing will fail if there is a problem with the engine, for example, if it is hit by a bird and starts vibrating violently. Since it can do a great deal more damage to the plane if it remains attached, the bolts are supposed to break loose so that the engine falls cleanly away, but in this case, there *was* no crisis to the engines. Rather, it was later found out that the fuse pins had simply given way due to metal fatigue.[1]

Loud Crash in a Quiet Town

The train derailment at Eschede forms an interesting counterpoint to this crash.

This wreck took place on June 3, 1998, at 10:59 A.M. near the German village of Eschede, located about 80 miles from Hamburg. The train had been nearing completion of its 530-mile journey from Munich to Hamburg, a south to north jaunt with seven stops along the way. The train was a high speed ICE, or InterCityExpress, operated by Deutsche Bahn AG, and the accident was the worst high speed train accident ever. The ICE had been inaugurated on June 2, 1991, and it crashed exactly seven years later on June 3, 1998. In the years between, there had never been a single fatality. The ICE is a luxury train specifically designed to compete with air travel: its coaches are designed like the first class sections of airplanes, with air-conditioning, televisions embedded in seats, and plugs for laptops and earphones. It is capable of traveling up to 155 mph. At the time of the accident, it was doing 125 mph.

Passengers had boarded that morning in Munich at 5:45. Its twelve coaches could carry up to 400 people, but on the day of the accident, there were 287 passengers onboard. After stopping at Hanover at 10:30, the train continued northwards. A passenger who had boarded at Nuremberg, one Jörg Dittmann, was sitting with his family in coach 1 when, at precisely 10:56 a sudden steel rod punctured through the floor between his and his wife's seats. It was actually the metal rim of the coach's third axle, which had split apart due to metal fatigue — the equivalent of a car's blowout — and the rim had gone straight up through the floor of the train. Dittmann told his family to follow him and ran to find the conductor who insisted upon seeing the damage before he would use the emergency brake to stop the train. This was company policy.

Part II: Disasters of Neomodernity

But it took the conductor a full minute to wend his way back to the seat Dittmann had been sitting in and meanwhile a series of mechanical failures were piling up, failures that caused the train to crash and kill 101 people.

Traveling at 125 mph, with the lower end of the straightened wheel rim hanging loose below coach 1, the train was fast approaching a double lane 300-ton road bridge near the town of Eschede. At this point, there were three separate tracks going beneath the bridge, where the local line branched off to the main line. Apparently, the hanging end of the wheel rim, as it approached the switch point, scooped up a piece of the rail — which also punched up through the floor of coach 1 — and caused two of the wheels at the rear of the coach to derail. When the train passed over the second set of checkpoints, one of the derailed wheels smashed into them and forced them open, causing the subsequent carriages behind coach 1 to shift onto another track, so that the train was actually traveling on two tracks simultaneously.

The approaching bridge was supported by concrete pillars standing about six feet away from the track when the train derailed about 650 feet in front of it. The power car and the first two coach cars managed to clear the bridge, but the momentum caused coach 3 to swing out and slam into the pillar. Coach 4 managed to clear the bridge but was flung off the track into a copse of nearby trees. Coach 5, as it passed under the road bridge, was partially crushed by the falling concrete, but coach 6 was completely flattened by it. The remaining cars slammed into the wreck, accordion style, folding in on itself. The quarter-mile-long train folded up into a wreck that was about the length of a single carriage.

Two Deutsche Bahn railway workers standing near the bridge were killed instantly. A car found in the wreckage and later assumed to have caused the crash by falling off the bridge into the path of the train turned out to belong to the workers and simply came down into the wreck with the collapse of the bridge. One hundred one people in all were killed in the crash.

ICE 1 trains had been equipped originally with what are known as single-cast, or monobloc wheels. These caused such a vibration in the restaurant car, however, that when passengers complained that their drinks and plates were creeping across surfaces, Deutsche Bahn's engineers then substituted the monobloc wheels for duobloc wheels, which are wheels in which an outer steel tire is separated from the inner rim by a 20 mm thick rubber damper. The new design was never tested at high speed, however, but it solved the vibration problem and for seven years, there were no other problems with the wheels.

But the wheels revolve approximately 500,000 times in a day of typical service, causing the tire rims to flex and unflex into the shape of an ellipse. This flexing and unflexing gradually created metal fatigue that caused cracks to appear in the tire rim. The cracks were never detected, though, because routine inspections were carried out with flashlights which could only illuminate larger, more obvious cracks. The engineers at Deutsche Bahn had stopped using their sophisticated metal fatigue detection equipment because it kept coming up with error messages and was therefore thought to be unreliable. But it was later found out that in the week just prior to the crash, the very wheel on coach 1 that had snapped had been highlighted as defective in three separate automated checks, but was not replaced.[2]

In a subsequent trial, nobody at Deutsche Bahn was found guilty of any wrongdoing and the company was instructed to pay out a mere 30,000 Deutsche marks — the equivalent of 19,000 American dollars — to those who had lost loved ones in the accident.[3]

The Dromosphere

Now, of course, the first point to remark about the two accidents is that they are morphological equivalents of each other. Not only did they have the same cause — metal fatigue in the fuse pins and in the duobloc wheels — but they are earthly and heavenly versions of the same accident. The El Al cargo plane's loss of its two engines caused it to veer from its flight vector and crash into the city down below; in other words, it was derailed, since a flight vector is simply a non-physical equivalent of a train track. A grid of invisible flight vectors radiate from the Schiphol Airport like train tracks in the sky: if planes deviate from these vectors, as with trains from their tracks, disaster results.

And these two accidents are morphologically the same because they operate in the same technoscape which Paul Virilio terms the *dromosphere* (from Greek *dromos* meaning "speed").[4] The dromosphere has very specific properties: its existence, for one thing, is entirely metaphysical, for it is an imagined plane of smooth space in which objects can travel with rectilinear motion at high speeds. Every engineer, when designing his aircraft or automobile engines, presupposes its existence within his imagination as an ideal space within which his machines may travel with unimpeded motion, *forever*. It is, in fact, the same space which Newton presupposed when he formulated his inertial law of motion in which an object is imagined as travelling with no friction or air resistance in a straight line to infinity. In physical reality, there is no such thing as a literal smooth space, for all objects in motion must, sooner or later encounter friction and resistance that dissipates their motion. But nevertheless, the ideal plane exists — even if only in the mind — as the metaphysical plane of smooth space within which all machines, especially machines of transportation, exist and move about.

The airplane, following its invisible vectors through aerospace, travels through this dromosphere, as does the high speed train, following its thin, narrow strip of smooth space along the ground; and so too, the automobile; indeed, any machine or transport vehicle whatsoever that is in motion through space. The goal of the dromosphere is for the engineer to eliminate all obstacles to his imagined machine's motion through this space, to make the space, that is, *as smooth as possible*.

But then, is this not Deleuze and Guattari's nomadic space, that smooth space across which nomads — usually mounted upon horseback or camels — travel and exist? The nomad, according to them, wishes only to hold and occupy this flat smooth plane of space, be it desert or steppe. The nomad is always *moving through* space. He is never at rest in it, never in one spot for very long. He moves from one point to the next in this space: from this watering well to that desert oasis. In between, there is nothing.[5]

Air travel is a type of technology which attempts to reconstitute this nomadic space, this dromosphere of smooth space in the air above our cities, where the planes can move about unencumbered by the striations of such cities. Aviation technologies, then, are an attempt to overlay a strata of smooth space above the striated space constituted by cities. They recreate and reenvision the ancient, archaic world of the timeless nomad, who exists outside of history because he is forever drifting beyond the bounds of the contained walls and battlements of cities. The city, to riff on the title of Lewis Mumford's famous book, is not *in* history, the city *is* history. What happens outside of its walls is of no significance for historical and cultural processes. In the event ontology of Alain Badiou, events have consequence only for the dwellers within the cultural containers of the polis; beyond them, there is nothing but an endless, featureless landscape of non-events.[6] The world of the nomad is *a*-historical.

The high speed train, too, attempts to reconstitute the smooth space of the dromosphere, only it does so as a narrow strip of horizontality that moves sometimes *within* and *through* the city. The faster the train, the more satisfied the engineer who has designed it. The railroad was not originally called an Iron Horse for nothing. It is, indeed, mechanized man's equivalent of the old nomadic horse captured and constrained to run along straight lines within, through and around modern cities, connecting one city to another just as the Bedouin moves from one watering hole to another. Virilio's transport revolution is thus a retrieval by mechanical man of the ancient attempts of the nomad to maximize his speed.

The Polisphere

The city, of course, is something else altogether: it is a machine, as Deleuze and Guattari put it, for coding flows of all kinds. It is composed of *striated space*, and these striations are, of course, erected specifically for the purpose of stopping, checking, freezing and arresting motion and speed of all kinds. The city is a dromospheric impediment. It opposes the striated space of the city dweller to the smooth space of the nomad. Water, electricity, immigrants, machines of transport: everything that flows through it must be coded, slowed down, branded, tattooed, inscribed. It is an entirely different type of technology than the dromosphere, as all nomads who hate cities know. It is a polisphere in which segments are connected, built up, arranged and rearranged like the components of the buildings in a Paul Klee painting; segments designed for capturing and bonding in place the human organism. The city *fixes* in place; the transport machine *liberates*. They are mutually opposed technologies.

Hence, when the El Al cargo plane is derailed from its flight vector and crashes into the Groeneveen apartment building, it is enacting a very ancient scenario in modern guise. It is the ancient collision between two different and mutually opposed technospheres: the dromosphere and the polisphere. One sphere maximizes the movement of the human body about through space; the other freezes and arrests it.

The Groeneveen apartment building is a type of architecture which

Part II: Disasters of Neomodernity

we may call *cellular architecture*. It is designed to capture and arrest human beings by connecting them together in a rectilinear grid of segmentation that has the effect of locking them in place: a chain of world islands or cells which are stacked up in a vertical grid of human occupants who can go nowhere, like the cellular architecture ascribed by Foucault to the disciplinary society. The human occupants exchange this freedom of physical motility for the vantage point that is afforded them by the view which surveys the earth from high up. They cannot move very far, but they can *see* far, and indeed, several of them saw the El Al cargo plane coming toward the building from a long way off.

A subtle web of cavities and walls, this kind of architecture arranges human bodies together to form a kind of multicellular organism in which all the flows of biological material — urine, feces, menstrual blood — are locked into place and can do nothing but cycle vertically up and down from heaven to earth and back again, exactly like the juices moving through the vascular system of a plant. Hence, the crime rate tends to be so high in these living apparatuses because their occupants can go nowhere and do nothing. So they slam into each other, each attempting to steal the other's space. There is not much space in such a situation to go around.

The cargo plane comes like a giant mechanical arrow out of nowhere and inflicts a rupture in this huge system of cellular segmentation, a flaming rupture that recalls the holes punched into the walls and battlements of ancient cities by armies using siege engines like trebuchets.

And indeed, in the ancient world, the collision between the dromosphere and the polisphere normally took the form of technologies of ballistics coming up against technologies of obstruction, as Paul Virilio has often remarked in his books.[7]

Historically, cities are the ultimate technology of obstruction: they erect walls, battlements and bridges; they fix archers and warriors in strategically advantageous places; they dig ditches and moats; they are built atop hills so that they can see armies, with their ballistic missiles of various kinds, coming from a long way off.[8]

Besieging armies, on the other hand, are a form of the ancient dromosphere: men mounted upon horseback with swords, compound bows and spears; riding camels over the arcs of wind-cut polished dunes; even infantry, on foot — the common dromospheric ancestor of both the polispheric pedestrian and dromospheric mounted army — moving over muddy earth and across fields cut with canals like dendrites in a nervous system, chiseling away at cities with battering rams, catapults and siege engines.

If such imagery, conjured and overlaid upon the strata of the Amsterdam plane crash, makes it sound like I am suggesting that a sort of hidden modern war is going on, then that is exactly what I am after here, for a war *is* going on in our civilization between mutually incompatible forms of technology. Such technologies do not just crash into each other for no reason, but precisely because they *are* incompatible technologies. They are designed to carry out different, mutually opposed, tasks. To try to cross the dromosphere with the polisphere, to combine them in the reckless manner we have done, results only in the proliferation of catastrophes. In the ancient world, such collisions between these two spheres appeared in the form of wars and world destruction. Should we expect any other kind of result when the same two spheres are crossed under the circumstances of today's technologies?

From Gods to Machines

For the ancient Greeks, the central conflict or agon that gave to the Greek psyche its peculiar tension was that between the claims made upon the human being by mutually opposed orders of gods. Today, on the other hand, the human being's agon is to be ground up in the friction generated by mutually opposed *technologies*.

The Greeks, of course, were polytheistic, and each of their gods represented a different order of claims and made different demands upon the human being. One god demanded this; another god demanded that. The human being was torn asunder as a result. Thus, in the *Oresteia* of Aeschylus, Orestes is torn to pieces by the conflicting demands made upon him by the gods of the chthonic matriarchy, who insist that a mother's murder must be punished, and those of the sphere of Father Right, who demand that the son must avenge his father's murder, even if the murder has been committed by the son's mother. Apollo insists that Orestes must avenge his father's murder; but according to the gods of the matriarchate, thou shalt not kill thy mother. Orestes is not a happy man.

In antiquity, the gods of the dromosphere, furthermore, were opposed to those of the polisphere. Gods of speed, that is, were often in conflict with sedentary gods; thus Apollo, who is always depicted with his sun chariot, slays the Delphic serpent, the god tied to a specific geographical place. Zeus, the god of the ballistical thunderbolt, together with his swift eagle, goes to war against the gods of the soil and the farmer, the brood of Gaia herself, the Titans and giants. The contrast between Homer, the sea-going island-dweller, and the farmer, land-locked Hesiod, is exemplary. Shiva, the lord of yoga, is a god of absolute stasis; Indra, the fearful god on horseback, rains destruction down upon the cities of the Sapta Sindu. The gods of the nomads, one and all, are thunderhurlers: Indra, Thor, Baal, Teshub, Set; the gods of the soil and the garden, the Neolithic crops and the ramified dendrites of their nourishing river networks, are often their victims: Osiris, the Midgard Serpent, Yam, Typhon.

Pushing further back down into the archaeological stratum, we find the fat, rotund mother goddesses of Neolithic towns and villages: Halafian figurines of fat women with no faces; rotund goddesses of Starčevo and other villages; the enormously fat goddesses of megalithic Malta.[9]

Opposed to them are the gods of motion and speed: the Indo-Aryan Asvins who ride in a swift golden car drawn by horses; Ganesha, the elephant headed man who crushes everything in his path; Thor with his hammer; and the warrior with his bronze axe and spear.[10]

Sometimes it is the dromospheric gods who are victorious, as in the case of Indra's slaying of three-headed Trisiras; sometimes, the victory lies with the gods of obstruction and stasis, as in the case of the yogic sage Dirgha-tamas, who cursed the flying elephants to forever walk the earth when one of them landed, bird-like on a nearby tree branch and disturbed his meditation.

In ancient Sumer, it is interesting to note that whereas Gilgamesh, the warrior hero of the city of Uruk, is associated with building the walls of that city, his father Lugalbanda was a man given the power to run faster than any human being by the Anzu bird who confers this ability upon him. Lugalbanda runs all the way back to Uruk to deliver the messages from the besieged army that he has left behind on the battlefield. Gilgamesh, on the other hand, makes his slow, meandering, lumbering journey through the cosmos. Lugalbanda is a hero of the army; Gilgamesh of the city.[11]

James Hillman, in his book *Revisioning Psychology*, said that there are gods in our ideas.[12] But here we have stumbled across gods in our machines.

Thus, the technologies of rapid transport and those of the city-as-obstruction and impediment to speed conceal ancient archetypal scenarios in which gods of speed conflict with those of soil and field and battlement. Hence, we should not be at all surprised when they collide on the modern asphalt streets of our cities.

Collateral Damage

In the case of the El Al cargo plane crash, we have an example of a vehicle from the dromosphere dropping down and crashing into the polisphere. It is an incursion into the polisphere which does not belong there. Airports are smooth spaces which are often built well away from cities, or at their peripheries, for precisely this reason.

The city, traditionally speaking, is the domain of the pedestrian. Its streets have been full of walkers, flaneurs and strollers ever since there have been cities. But with the intrusion of the dromosphere, we notice that the pedestrian disappears. With the coming of the automobile, highways and roads obtrude, cities expand with elastic force and the distances become too vast for walking. Pedestrians are collateral damage in the crossing of the polisphere with the dromosphere.

In the case of the ICE derailment, we have an incursion into the dromosphere of an object from the polisphere, for the bridge with its concrete pillars, a striation, appears in the path of the train and causes its narrow strip of smooth space to smash up into a broken, disorderly wreck. Smooth space disappears; striation, with its corrugations and serrations, supervenes. And destruction ensues.

As long as we moderns are going to insist on trying to combine the two spheres, human beings will continue to be ground up in the catastrophes generated by their friction. Our cities are becoming disaster zones in which it is a hazardous undertaking just to go about the business of being human. City dwellers living amongst rapid forms of transportation are now constant targets of dromospheric misalignments.

Foucault has pointed out that the origin of the police in the sixteenth and seventeenth centuries was connected almost exclusively with towns and not with the countryside at all. Specifically, they emerged at precisely those nexus points where towns crossed with roads and highways, for one of their main functions was to regulate the circulations of goods through market economies. Although they had other functions as well, Foucault makes very clear that one of their main purposes was to monitor traffic of all kinds: "Thus police will be concerned," he says, "with the condition and development of roads, and with the navigability of rivers and canals, etcetera... So the space of circulation is a privileged object for police."[13]

The police, then (as the word indicates, which comes from *polis*) are a sort of polispheric immune system, an immune system that develops as the result of the internalization and "folding inward" (in Deleuze's sense)[14] of what used to be the externally aggressive realm of the dromosphere. Once the walls of Medieval cities were brought down by the advent of gunpowder, cities could no longer keep the dromosphere out, and so the emergence of the police in the sixteenth century, we note, coincides with the (eventual) fall of the walls surrounding Western towns. The walls come down; the dromosphere enters; the city's immune system responds with the invention of the police.

But now the dromosphere has simply grown too large for the police to control or contain. The police are of little use anymore in dromospheric sieges (witness their almost complete uselessness at Columbine) and so the human inhabitant of our cities is now under constant threat from dromospheric assaults. (Indeed, every 110th person will die in a car crash).

For the first time in history then, cities have become unsafe places for human beings to live in. It was once the case — very long ago — that the threat came from *outside* the walls of the city. The city, traditionally, was a sanctuary for human beings, a safe place where he could come to do business, trade, transact, sell his wares, make things, etc. The threat from the dromosphere of mounted warriors approaching the city always lay *out there* somewhere beyond its walls. That, in fact, was why walls were built in the first place: to keep the dromosphere *out* and render the city a safe haven within which the human being could exist.

But ever since the advent of gunpowder and the rise of ballistic weaponry like canons, the walls of our cities have been coming down. Now they are gone, and so the dromosphere, with its roads and highways, aerial vectors and rapid transport, is enabled to cross through cities and dice them up. Now the dromosphere is *inside* the city and the hapless human being has nowhere to run.

Indeed, as the El Al plane crash illustrates, he is no longer safe even inside his own home.

Eight

The Aum Shinrikyo Nerve Gas Attacks As an Attempt to Recode Japanese Society

Underground

On March 20, 1995, between 7:00—8:10 A.M., the world's first assault on a major urban transit system unfolded when the Tokyo Metro was attacked with sarin nerve gas by the Japanese religious cult known as Aum Shinrikyo. Five men, together with their drivers, were sent down into the Tokyo underground, where each man boarded a different train, leaving two sarin packets on their floors which had been punctured by the men with the tips of their umbrellas. Then, as the liquid evaporated into gas, the men left their trains and exited their stations, where each was picked up by a different driver and escorted back to Aum's Satyam 7 compound located at the foot of Mount Fuji to the north of the city.

These five assassins, moreover, were no ordinary thugs: they were physicists and engineers with very high level achievements at major Japanese institutions.

Ikuo Hayashi, for instance, who had been assigned to train A725K on the Chiyoda Line, had been a heart and artery specialist at Keio Hospital and subsequently became head of Circulatory Medicine at the National Sanatorium Hospital in Tokai, Ibaraki, before joining Aum in 1990. He took his family to live with him in the cult, where he became one of Shoko Asahara's favorites and was appointed Minister of Healing. When Hayashi got onto his train, he placed the package of sarin at his right foot and poked it with his umbrella, although he was only able to puncture one of the bags, later claiming that his heart wasn't really in the deed.[1] At Kasumigaseki Station, two attendants were killed while trying to dispose of the leaking bag. Two hundred thirty-one other people were injured.

Kenichi Hirose, who had graduated at the top of his class in Applied

Part II: Disasters of Neomodernity

Physics at Waseda University, was assigned train A777 on the Marunouchi Line. In 1989, he had rejected many offers of employment in order to join Aum, where he became a key figure in their Automatic Light Weapon Development Scheme. At Ochanomizu Station, Hirose had difficulty getting the package out due to the dense number of people on the train, and dropped it on the floor, while kicking it away. He pierced it with his umbrella, however, and got off the train, and then, while driving back to the compound, realized that he was exhibiting the effects of sarin poisoning, since his breathing was difficult and he couldn't speak properly. He injected himself with atropine sulphate, the antidote for sarin. On his line, only one person died, but 538 were injured.

Also on the Marunouchi Line, but assigned to train B801, was Masato Yokoyama, 31 years old and a graduate of Applied Physics from Tokai University Applied Engineering Department. He had taken employment at an electronics firm, only to leave after three years in order to join Aum, where he belonged to Aum's Ministry of Science and Technology. Yokoyama had boarded the 7:39 Ikebukoro-bound Marunouchi Line departing from Shinjuku, and as it approached Yotsuya Station, he poked his bags several times, only managing, however, to puncture one of them. As a result, no one died on his line, although 200 people were seriously injured.

Toru Toyoda, assigned to B711 on the Hibiya Line, had also studied applied physics, in his case, at the Tokyo University Science Department. He had just completed his Master's degree and was about to proceed with his doctorate, when he dropped everything and took vows with Aum, where he belonged to the Chemical Brigade under the Ministry of Science and Technology. At 8:01 A.M., Toyoda placed his package of liquid sarin on the floor, poked it with his umbrella, and then exited the train as the liquid began to rapidly evaporate and turn to gas. Only one person died in the scramble to get off the train, but 532 were injured.

Yasuo Hayashi, also on the Hibiya Line, but assigned to train A720S, had entered Kogakuin University to study artificial intelligence, but while in India, he awoke to religion, encountered Aum and took their vows in 1988. He was the only one of the five who had taken three packets of sarin with him, which he placed on the floor of his train, and punctured zealously with many holes (he was known for his sadistic tendencies within the cult) and then, at Akihabara Station, got off and returned to his driver's car. A total of 8 people on his train died, the most out of all five trains, while 275 were injured.

98

Eight. The Aum Shinrikyo Nerve Gas Attacks

In all, thirteen people were killed in the attack, while over 6,000 were injured, many of them seriously. Sarin is the most volatile of the nerve gases, but it is short-lived. All it takes is a pinhead drop to kill a human being. At first, the afflicted person notices a runny nose, drooling and tightness in the chest. The field of vision narrows as pupils contract to pinpoints, and muscle spasms, sweating, nausea and vomiting follow. Then come convulsions and seizures and eventually, coma and death.[2]

Origins and Evolution of a Cult

Aum was founded in Japan in 1984 by Chizuo Matsumoto as a company called Aum Inc. Back then, it was a one-room yoga school, with a profitable sideline in health drinks. On a beach on Japan's coast, while meditating one day, Matsumoto heard God's voice telling him that he was to lead God's army. With an impending vision of the coming end of the world, Matsumoto believed he had been singled out to save it, so he changed his name to Shoko Asahara, wore a beard and began dressing in white clothing. He had been born blind in the left eye and had only partial vision in the right. Asahara claimed, furthermore, to have attained the same level of enlightenment as the Buddha, and insisted to his followers that he was a god, endowed with special magical abilities.

Later, he changed the cult's name to Aum Supreme Truth and began distributing leaflets that promoted him as its guru. The Hindu god Shiva became its patron deity, and Asahara began prophesying to his followers that the end of the world was coming. By 1996, he said, Japan would sink into the ocean and by 2003, the world would be destroyed by a nuclear war.

He established Aum headquarters at the base of Mount Fuji and in 1989, registered Aum with the Japanese government as an official religion, thus giving him tax breaks. Soon, Aum had over 3 million dollars in assets, and membership surged to 4,000 as the cult began buying up real estate in Japan.[3]

Aum, as we have seen, attracted highly intelligent, professional people: physicists, engineers, chemists, etc. These people formed the upper ranks of the Aum hierarchy, and they spent much of their time working for Asahara to invent and perfect weapons of mass destruction: lasers, nuclear bombs, chemical and biological weapons. Such weapons would hasten the coming apocalypse, which Aum saw itself as the only group destined to survive. Their elite core of scientists would live through the subsequent Dark Age by centralizing the world's remaining knowledge and using it to rebuild society along the lines of a hierarchical spiritual state.

They sold bizarre devices to their followers, such as the PSI (Perfect Salvation Initiation), which was a cap with electrodes that would deliver electric shocks to the initiate. They sold these for about $7,000 per month. They claimed, furthermore, that the master's DNA had magical properties, which they offered in the form of blood to drink and sold for $7,000. They also sold Astral Teleporters, which were supposed to faithfully reproduce the master's vibrations of his mantra through electric signals that would cleanse one's astral body.

Then, in the spring of 1988, they started killing people. One cult member who asked Asahara if he could leave the cult was dunked in freezing water in order to cleanse the "heat" out of his aura, but the man went into hypothermic shock and died.[4] The cult had the body cremated so that no one would ever find him. Other members who wanted to leave met with similar fates and were also cremated.

In October of 1989, when an attorney named Tsutsumi Sakamoto, representing the parents of children who had become cult members and disappeared from their parents' lives, confronted the group, Asahara sent his henchman to kill the lawyer, along with his wife and one year old son, in their own house in the middle of the night. The bodies were disposed of, their sudden disappearance from society puzzling the Japanese police. Other murders, over the years, followed.

Life inside the cult, for the average member was, needless to say, severe. Each member had to subsist on a daily diet of rice, bean curd and something called "Aum soup." They had to drink water out of containers with moss growing inside them, and drinking coffee, tea or alcohol was forbidden. Sexual relations, too — except for Asahara, of course — were likewise forbidden. Aum members, in addition, were allowed very little in the way of sleep and were forced to work long hours. They were also given drugs to pacify them, such as LSD. Believers needed permission to leave their compounds, and access to friends and family was absolutely not allowed.

In 1993, Aum bought Okamura Ironworks, a company that was going bankrupt and whose president had joined Aum, for 2 million dollars. They pulled out all the manufacturing tools from the plant and moved them to

Eight. The Aum Shinrikyo Nerve Gas Attacks

a private warehouse, and then used these machines to mass produce weapons, such as knives and AK 74s.

After experimenting, unsuccessfully, with botulin — which they had tried out on some of their own members — they began to manufacture sarin nerve gas in very large quantities. Later, police would find enough at their compound to kill four million people. After testing sarin on a flock of sheep at a compound in Australia, Aum targeted three judges in Matsumoto who were giving them a hard time about purchasing a building in that city. On June 27, 1994, they parked a refrigerated truck leaking sarin in a supermarket parking lot at 10 p.m., hoping the easterly winds would blow the gas toward the dorm where the judges lived. The attack killed 7 people and poisoned 200 others, but the judges were not killed, though they were temporarily hospitalized.

By that point, at least 12 people had already died at the hands of Aum: 7 in Matsumoto and the rest were either cult members who had tried to escape or the lawyer Sakamoto and his family.

At this time, its membership was over 10,000, about 10 percent of which lived in various cult compounds.

In that same year, Aum planned an attack on the Japanese government in Tokyo, the Diet, which it called "X-Day," a *coup d'etat* in which Aum would assume control of the government and install Asahara as Japan's new emperor.

The subway attacks at Kasumigaseki, where the Tokyo government was located, was to be but the first stage of this larger, longer, more sustained attack.

Question Number One

The first question to ask, then, about the Aum attacks, is Why would such individuals — i.e., the five men who carried out the attacks — with such prestigious and respectable career achievements, abruptly leave those careers to join what, to the outsider anyway, appears to be a bizarre and perverse doomsday cult?

Haruki Murakami, who interviewed a number of Aum cult members, provides us with a hint of an answer, for the cult members that he interviewed said that they joined Aum because it gave meaning, values and purpose to their lives, a significance which a career inside the Japanese

Part II: Disasters of Neomodernity

megamachine would simply have averaged out. The goal of working to realize a utopian cosmic state, to rebuild, that is, a society based upon spiritual values that gave the individual a place of worth and esteem, was a much more attractive life path to them than simply becoming another cog in the Japanese social machine, where the individual would be condemned to a small role serving the global capitalist economy and its shallow consumer values.

Aum, in other words, took its followers and placed them *inside* a cosmotopic enclosure, that is to say, a bounded and isolated world with a spiritual center and a tiered hierarchy. The Japanese mind, with its penchant for miniaturization, had, in the case of Aum, miniaturized the type of ancient cosmotopia which once upon a time bounded, enclosed and built *all* the world's great civilizations.

A cosmotopia is a kind of gigantic glass dome that revolves about a central axis which functions as the backbone of a tiered and multi-leveled cosmos. A particular city is often located at the center of such a cosmotopia, while all around it, the world is sealed off and enclosed.

Take, for example, the ancient Buddhist cosmotopia, in which the world revolves about a central axial mountain called Sumeru, which is located at the top of a multi-leveled world island in the center of a cosmic ocean. At the four quarters of this surrounding ocean, there lie four continents: Jambudvipa in the south (our world); Purvavideha in the east; Aparagodaniya in the west; and Uttarakuru in the north. Beneath this world, there lay the realm of the dead, Naraka, stratified into eight distinct levels. At each of these levels, the dead suffered a different form of punishment, such as trees with leaves made out of razor blades that sliced them up, or demons who diced them into pieces or birds with iron beaks that pecked at them, and so forth. Above this world, there was a stratified series of ascending levels mounting up to 23 different heavens, with different gods located in each one.[5]

The stratified roofs of Japanese pagodas and buildings are meant to exemplify the structure of this tiered and enclosed cosmos. Tokyo itself, moreover, in the days of the Tokugawa Shogunate, was thought to embody the center of this cosmos, as indeed, were all the cities of the ancient world. On the oldest cosmic map that we possess, a piece of clay from Mesopotamia with a circle drawn upon it, the city of Babylon as a world island in the shape of a rectangle occupies the center of the map.[6] On the so-called Medieval "T and O" maps, Jerusalem occupied the bull's eye center of such maps.[7]

Modernity, however — meaning Western Industrial capitalism together with its political component, the democratic nation state — flattens and destroys such cosmotopias by shearing off their worlds above and their worlds below, leaving the individual naked and exposed beneath a sky under which absolutely *anything* could befall him, while his city — hitherto the center of a cosmotopia — is now reduced to a mere cosmopolis, a provincial world-island floating in the sea of an international ecumene. With the city now unplugged from a cosmotopia, it is placed as a mere component — like an integrated chip — into the larger machine of global electronic capitalism, in which no city is peripheral anymore, since all are equally centers unto themselves. It is part of a World Order — a technological and economic one — but not a cosmotopic one which takes the heavens, together with its gods, and the Underworld, together with its ancestral dead, into account. The individual's life, accordingly, is reduced to the level of a biological accident. The world, in other words, is completely indifferent to his existence and has no need whatsoever for him. If he wants to exist, fine: there are machines that need tending to. But if he doesn't, that's ok, too. After all, who needs him?

The modern world ecumene, needless to say, is absolutely shorn of spiritual values, and the individual of today finds himself in a world of nihilism and meaninglessness. But the human psyche isn't built to accept Nothing. It is specifically designed to engage with a larger spiritual world of meaning and purpose, and if those needs aren't met by the social order that it finds itself in, then it turns to the nearest available substitute, a shabby, dirty little cult, say, like Aum.

Today, the human psyche, everywhere on the planet, is faced with this decision: to choose between meaninglessness and pointlessness in service to a life of consumerism, or else to turn to some type of cosmotopic system that takes him into account as an individual and puts him to work in service toward realizing a world order of meaning and value upon the earth.

Which answers our first question: Why?

But now comes the second: How?

Question Number Two

A Boundary Act is an act of violence that takes place when one culture, society, or ethnic group finds itself threatened by another, and seeks to draw a distinct dividing line between itself and that other group. If, as Marshall McLuhan said, violence is a quest for identity,[8] then we can say that a Boundary Act is a means of inscribing a line into the socius using pain as its mnemonic device, just as a tattoo is inscribed into a physical body, where it leaves a defining — often ethnically inclusive — trace.[9]

The Maccabean Revolt of the second century B.C. is an example of such a Boundary Act. When the Jews of Palestine, under their Greek Seleucid rulers, refused to worship the god Zeus in the temple, Mattathias the Hasmonean stepped forward to kill a Hellenizing Jew who was preparing to make his offering to the idol. He and his sons then fled to the wilderness of Judaea, where a revolt led by Judas Maccabeus made use of guerrilla tactics to overthrow their Greek rulers and establish a Jewish state.

The Battle of Marathon was another such Boundary Act: when in 490 B.C., the Persian king Darius attempted to subjugate Greece by landing an army in Attica, it was met by the fierce resistance of the Athenians who, though outnumbered, were able with the strength of their hoplites to turn the more lightly armored Persian infantry away. The Greeks thus successfully evaded being consumed within the Achaemenid Universal State.

The Battle of Tours in A.D. 732 is yet another example: in this case, the Franks led by Charles Martel successfully stopped an invasion into France of the Umayyad Caliphate led by Abdul Rahman Al Ghafiqi, who was killed in the battle. Charles was nicknamed "Martellus," meaning "the Hammer" as a direct allusion to the name of Judas Maccabeus (since Maccabeus also means "the Hammerer").

Thus, Boundary Acts are culturally defining moments when one society successfully resists assimilation by another. In the case of the Aum Shinrikyo gas attacks, something similar is involved, for the attacks were specifically designed to reject the modern democratic Japanese nation state and to inscribe into the Japanese socius the memory of an atrocity that would form a dividing line in the Japanese psyche as a kind of etheric scar forcing them to recognize the friction between the Aum cosmotopia and the Japanese cosmopolis.

The difference, of course, between the Aum attacks and these other historical examples is that Aum itself was part of the same ethnic society that it was reacting against. It is, therefore, an example of the secession of an *internal* cosmotopia from the mother body of the Japanese society. It is, as it were, an attempt at slaying the Mother and, as in the Babylonian myth of the slaying of Tiamat in order to make the cosmos out of her body, using her parts to reconstruct a new cosmic order. If Aum had been successful in its attack, it would then have moved on to its planned *coup d'etat*, and it would have had to cut the Japanese state apparatus up into pieces and make a new cosmos out of it.

As Toynbee long ago pointed out, an internal proletariat only secedes from the body social of its parent society when the creative minority of that society fails in its task of inspiring the uncreative majority with models for them to imitate.[10] If the Japanese state apparatus is producing discontented stateless social formations like those of Aum as a new internal opposition, then it is because the Japanese state is failing to address the needs of a significant part of the psyche of its population. The suspicion then becomes that further internal proletariats will eventually splinter off from the Japanese state until it is ultimately overthrown.

Aum may be the wave of the future.

Recoding the Flows

Once a discontented social formation seizes power in a society, it must proceed to *recode* that society by overlaying upon it a fresh stratum of signs, a new sign regime, to use the language of Deleuze and Guattari.[11] And though Aum's revolt was not a successful one, we can begin to guess what it might have then set about to achieve in the event that it had been successful by examining hints from the structure of the attack itself.

It is not, for instance, an accident that Asahara sent precisely *five* men to perpetrate the attack, since five is a constitutive number in the differing religious sign regimes of both Hinduism and Buddhism. In the *Mahabharata*, there are *five* main heroes, the Pandava brothers, because they are meant to embody the cosmic structure of the five elements: earth, wind, fire, water, and aether.[12] Japanese tombstones have five component parts, and each different geometric shape refers to one of these elements, ascending upwards from earth, water, fire, wind and space.[13]

The phrase "Aum" itself, taken from the Hindu *Upanishads*, can be analyzed out as the sound made when all five vowels of Sanskrit — the same as in English — are run together to make the sound "OM."[14]

The five perpetrators, then, were sent out as avatars of Asahara. It was Asahara himself, not the men, who performed the deed, *through* them. As the despotic ruler of Aum, Asahara was the mystical body of the cult, and all the cult members were inscribed onto him as organs of his full body. Their mouths, their lips, their wills, their hands, all belonged to him and all were but extensions of his will.

Thus, though Aum was a stateless social formation, it was also a miniaturization of the Bronze Age despotic state, with its central ruler, its inner elite and its peripheral population of peasants. Such was the world order of Japanese society down to the end of the Tokugawa Shogunate in 1868.

The structure of the attack itself also realizes the ancient trichilocosm of the Buddhist and Indian sign regimes: with their headquarters at Mount Fuji, a stand in for Mount Sumeru, the attackers came down from the World Above as avatars of the Master, and entered Tokyo, the flat mid-world of the earthly plane, with a mission. The Tokyo underground subway constitutes a mechanization of the ancient Underworld — as Murakami points out — and so it is precisely that mechanized Underworld that Aum sought to overlay with the ancient Buddhist codes, for the Underworld in Buddhist cosmology is the place of suffering and torment. The sarin gas attacks were an attempt, then, to transform the modern Tokyo underworld into a place of suffering, where punishment is meted out upon a society of consumers and materialists for failing to heed the values of the spirit world.

Thus, whereas modern industrial society has overlain the semiotics of the ancient world with a new set of codes by building mechanized equivalents of its spiritual cartographies — the Eye in the sky of God becomes the satellites of the Thermosphere; the Underworld becomes the subway which moves the physical body about through space instead of punishing the subtle body — so discontented social formations like Aum seek to reclaim modernity by overlaying it with a fresh set of signs from an archaic sign regime. New societies, when they come to power inside of or against old ones, overlay new codes.

Japan itself has already undergone two such phases of recoding: in the shift from the Tokugawa Shogunate to the Meiji Restoration of 1868 – 1912, the ancient cosmotopia of the Japanese social order was flattened out and overlaid with the semiotic codes of Western industrial society. The samurai were put out of work, absorbed into the creation of a new administrative army, and their swords and robes were traded in for Western military dress. In the new sign regime, the samurai becomes illegal, for he belongs to an outdated set of codes. Factories are built; railroads are built;

Eight. The Aum Shinrikyo Nerve Gas Attacks

the telegraph is instituted; compulsory education for children is established; and the megamachine is set in motion, structurally redesigned to compete on the world stage with Western colonial powers. Indeed, the stress of the overcoding process is such as to inflate and disequilibrate the Japanese psyche which, now armed with the Machine, goes on a rampage of colonial conquests in Taiwan, Korea and Manchuria.[15]

The second phase of recoding, then, took place after the Japanese lost World War II: for though the society had been united with the global international ecumene during the Meiji Restoration on the technological and economic plane, it had proceeded on the political plane along the lines of an authoritarian state. But in the new postwar regime, a fresh set of codes is overlaid once again, this time aligning the Japanese state apparatus with the democratic nation state on the Western model. New signs mean new codes: the Emperor is forced to go on the radio and renounce his divinity. In the new regime, he is no longer a god, just a man. Parliamentary democracy is instituted; political figures, even provincial ones, are elected to their offices; and a whole new series of economic codes comes into place. To compete on the new global stage of Late Capitalism, one must not acquire land and colonies, one must amass capital, and so the Japanese state becomes a new economic superpower by pouring its colonial energies into conquering vast sums of money.

But certain elements of the Japanese psyche remain fixated on its ancient imperial past and refuse to come along with Modernity. Thus, the appeal of Aum, which promised to restore the authoritarian order of the past to many Japanese. If its coup had been successful, Japan would have undergone yet another recoding, this time along the lines of a mixed Buddhist—Hindu sign regime in which the subway, for instance, is aligned with the ancient realm of the dead, and Tokyo breaks away from the global ecumene to exist in its own isolated world space once again as it was in the days of its Tokugawa isolation when contact with the rest of the world was largely eschewed.

Thus, discontented social formations—and there are many of them in the world today—are always waiting in the wings with a new sign regime that will overcode the semiotics of the old order with a new set of signs.

In the event of Aum's victory, Tokyo would have been restored to the center of a cosmotopia once again, and would have broken off, like North Korea, into a state of isolation and authoritarianism, in which the international world ecumene of capitalism would simply have had to flow *around* it, without including it.

But in the actual outcome, Tokyo will continue for now as a cosmopolis, as one world island floating in a sea of other world islands, none of them privileged to set itself up as the Center any longer.

Inside the global Crystal Palace of capitalism and Free Trade, there is no center, only aisles of booths where merchants hawk their wares.

But note the metaphor: the walls *are* made of glass, and stones *can* be thrown at them.

Eventually, one day, they might even break.

Nine

The Columbine Shootings and the Absence of Meaning

The Plan

The massacre at Columbine High School — located near Littleton, Colorado — took place on a Tuesday — the 20th of April, to be exact — in the year 1999. Columbine is a very large high school, with a total of about 2,000 students normally attending. In the massacre, thirteen people were killed — twelve students and one teacher — over the course of nearly an hour by two students: Eric Harris (who had just turned eighteen) and his sidekick, seventeen-year-old Dylan Klebold. Twenty-three other students were injured, many of them seriously.

The original plan, though, as conceived by Harris and Klebold, had been far larger and more ambitious in scope: with the Oklahoma City bombing in mind as their model (that event had occurred on April 19, 1995) Eric Harris — the main architect of the plot — had intended to destroy the entire high school by igniting two propane fuel tank bombs in the school cafeteria where 500 students gather daily. Then the two boys would wait outside the cafeteria doors as the survivors of the bombs fled, shooting at them as they came out. But since the bombs never detonated, Harris and Klebold had to settle for a shooting spree instead.

The first order of business, then, is a brief recap of the course of that spree.

The Spree

At 11:10 on the morning of the 20th, Eric and Dylan drove separate cars to the Columbine High School parking lot: Eric parked in the junior lot directly facing the student entrance, while Dylan parked his 1982 BMW in the senior lot in front of the cafeteria. As Eric was unloading a duffel

Part II: Disasters of Neomodernity

bag, he was approached by an old friend of his, one Brooks Brown, who admonished him for missing a psych test earlier that morning.

"It doesn't matter anymore," Eric told him. "Brooks, I like you now. Get out of here. Go home."

Brooks did as he was told and has lived to tell the tale.

At 11:14, the boys enter the commons (i.e., the cafeteria), where they leave two duffel bags containing the propane tank bombs on the floor. No one notices them. The timers are set for 11:17, when the cafeteria is at the peak of its traffic. Eric has studied this phenomenon carefully, for he and Dylan have been planning their attack for over a year: on the day of the 20th, there are, at this time, about 480 students in the cafeteria.

The boys, then, head back out to their cars, where they wait for the bombs to go off. When they don't, they know something is wrong, and instead proceed to arm themselves with two sawed-off shotguns and two semiautomatic weapons, together with various crickets (miniature explosives) and pipe bombs. They are garbed nearly identically in black combat boots, black jeans and long black trenchcoats, but asymmetrically: Eric wears a white T-shirt with the words "Natural Selection" printed on it, while Dylan wears a black T-shirt with the word "Wrath" emblazoned upon it. Oddly, they share a single pair of black gloves, Dylan wearing the left glove and Eric the right, as though to connote that they are a single, two-headed creature of wrath, like something out of Hindu mythology.

They immediately proceed up to the external stairway of the building's west exit, near the green-tinted windows of the cafeteria, the highest vantage point on the campus. Surveying the terrain below, they begin firing randomly and hurling pipe bombs at pedestrians. Nearby, students Rachel Scott, 17, and Richard Castaldo, also 17, are eating their lunch, when a pipe bomb explodes, with little effect, in their general direction. The gunmen shoot Rachel in the head and chest: she dies instantly, but Richard, though shot eight times, lies on the grass and will manage to survive the ordeal (although he will never walk again).[1]

Three students, Danny Rohrbough, 15, and Sean Graves, also 15, together with Lance Kirklin, 16, are ascending the steps, thinking that a paintball game is in progress, when they are all shot: Danny dies on the spot and though Lance is shot in the face at point blank range, he lives.

At 11:23, just as the first cell phone call to 911 is being made by a student, the police officer assigned to the school, Neil Gardner, eating lunch in his squad car, is contacted by the school custodian, who tells him that

Nine. The Columbine Shootings

an emergency situation is developing. When Gardner pulls up in the parking lot and sees the shooters at the top of the stairs, he fires at Eric over the roof of his car, and for a moment, suspects that he might actually have hit him. Eric wheels, though, firing back, and then heads through the west exit with Dylan.

Inside the school, at about 11:25, a part-time art teacher named Patti Nielson hears the shots coming from the top of the stairs at the west exit and heads out to reprimand what she supposes are students filming an action-oriented video. Through the glass exit doors, however, she sees Eric turn to face her and smile before shooting at her through a hole in the doors. Having sustained an injury to the back of her right shoulder, she turns and runs into the library, where she yells at all the students to get under the tables, while calling 911.

Coach Dave Sanders, meanwhile, having herded the kids out of the cafeteria and into various classrooms for safety, happens at that moment to hear the shots fired at Patti Nielson and heads off down the hallway in their direction to find out what's happening. He passes the library door just after Patti has vanished inside it, and sees the killers coming up the hallway at exactly the same time as the school's principal, Frank DeAngelis, sees them from a different hallway. But the killers are distracted by Dave and shoot him twice in the back as he turns to flee their advance. Dave goes down, and after the killers have entered the library, two teachers spot him and drag him inside a science classroom where they try to help him stay alive by distracting him from his wounds with pictures of his family taken out of his wallet.[2] Eventually, he will bleed to death, but not for another three hours, for by the time SWAT team members find him, he will have expired.

By now, six police units have arrived at the school, a couple of them parked just below the shattered windows of the library, where they clearly hear the massacre that then proceeds to take place inside. But they do nothing to stop it.

In the library, meanwhile, at 11:29, the horrible centerpiece of the attack begins to unfold. Fifty-two students, two teachers and two library assistants are hiding under various tables and niches in the library as Harris and Klebold proceed, one by one, to execute ten students and wound 12 others. They are heard to laugh and mock at the students before killing them; several beg for their lives, but for most, this does little good. Dylan and Eric simply lean under the tables and fire at them, point blank range, killing some, wounding others. The screams are terrible. It is a bloodbath, one which Dylan, in particular, is reported to have enjoyed thoroughly. One or two kids are allowed to escape, but for the rest, the killers show little mercy. This goes on for seven and a half minutes, by which time, Harris and Klebold have begun to tire.

They wander from the library, bored, at about 11:44 and drift down the empty hallways back toward the cafeteria, where Eric makes his first attempt at suicide by trying to detonate one of his failed propane tank bombs. He has, by this point, broken his nose as the result of a recoil from his shotgun while executing a student in the library. He fires his weapon at the tank, but it refuses to explode. The cafeteria surveillance video shows Dylan, in grainy black and white, hurling a Molotov cocktail into the commons as they leave it behind, while a flock of students, who have been hiding under the tables, scramble out away from the flames. The fire alarm and the sprinklers go off at this point.

At 12:02, the boys have returned to the library, which is now mostly vacant — with the exception of the dead and wounded — where they fire off a few half-hearted shots out the broken windows at the cops gathering on the ground below. The cops fire back at them, but no one is injured during this altercation.

At 12:06, a SWAT team has finally entered the school building from the opposite side, at the east entrance. On the west side, near the cafeteria, another SWAT team, hiding behind a yellow fire engine, slowly approaches the school.[3]

But by 12:08, it is all over. Lying on the floor of the library with their backs against the wall, the two boys have put their guns to their heads and taken their own lives. The police — having traipsed in slow, cautious single file throughout the hallways — find their bodies on the blood-soaked floor three hours and fifteen minutes later.

The "wrath" of Eric Harris and Dylan Klebold has transpired over the course of 49 minutes.

The Structure of Suburban Cosmology

The first point to note about *any* terrorist attack is the target: in this case, Harris and Klebold were shooting at high school students, but that is only because the bombs in the cafeteria failed to detonate. The attack,

Nine. The Columbine Shootings

then, was aimed at the cafeteria, rather than, say, a sporting event or the prom or any particular social group. It is not the exceptional event, then, that these boys were after, but just the opposite: the daily, banal, quotidian center of the high school world; its repetitive and monotonous, machine-like behavior. It is high school life at its most boring and typical moments that they are wishing away. The cafeteria, in many respects, is the dead center bull's eye of a high school, for it is the place where *all* the students, from whatever clique or social group whatsoever, have gathered together as a single group, mixed indiscriminately. It is not this or that social group—jocks, stoners, etc.—that the boys were attacking, then, but the *high school apparatus as such.* For the student is the main product which the high school as an institution is designed to manufacture.

Indeed, it is the task of the high school to mass produce its students just like products on an assembly line. For eventually, they will become the next generation of inhabitants of the very suburbs the high school has been outfitted to service. Indeed, a high school does not just exist by itself as a separate entity, but is, in fact, part of a *system*, a social apparatus which we normally call "the suburbs." The high school is embedded within a larger social machine that encompasses and surrounds it: a suburban machine that has a very particular kind of structure that is designed and built to facilitate a very particular world view.

Jürgen Habermas, in his *Structural Transformation of the Public Sphere*, pointed out how the bourgeois public sphere—i.e., the realm of public, reasoned discourse and debate on political, cultural and social issues—had its origins in the private domestic sphere of the bourgeois family which, in the days when the public sphere was born somewhere in the middle of the seventeenth century, had an active and involved interest in its formation. The coffee houses that came into being at this time, and the salons which were hosted in the front rooms of the bourgeois home, provided the public sphere with its forums. But long about 1850, the public sphere underwent a structural transformation when, with the rise of the new mass media—advertising, telegraphy, mass circulation newspapers and popular periodicals targeted at the bourgeois family—the middle class family became divorced from the sphere of letters and reasoned discourse, while their former role was taken over by the cultural avant garde. The bourgeois public sphere then became a mass public sphere, in which reasoned discourse and literacy gave way to the passive consumer who was no longer capable, because he did not read, of responding to the culture industry in

Part II: Disasters of Neomodernity

a critical manner. But the middle class family never again became the center of cultural values and in fact, ever since this structural transformation, it has normally been thought of as being *opposed* to such values.[4]

Indeed, while the public sphere has gone one way, the Intimate Sphere of the bourgeois family mutated into that of the suburban cosmos, a realm with its own distinct structural attributes. And it is this suburban cosmos itself which Harris and Klebold were attacking and attempting to dismantle and restructure in their own terms. This social machine not only has a very distinct structure, but even comes equipped with its very own cosmology, as well, and it is this cosmology, in particular, that the boys were attempting to reshape.

Let's take a look, then, in cross-section, at the structure of this suburban cosmology.

Every cosmology, to begin with, whether ancient or modern, comes equipped with a central principle of iteration that guides how things *within* that cosmology come to be. For example, the arithmetical principle of iteration in which the One becomes the Two, the Two becomes the Four, and so on.[5] In suburban cosmology, the equivalent principle of iteration by means of which things appear is that of Seriality and Repetition: nothing appears within the suburban world as a singularity. Everything appears rather in *series*: multiple houses, multiple cars, multiple streets, etc. Each thing or entity which appears, furthermore, does so in accordance with the principle of Repetition, for nothing is allowed to be unique in such a cosmos. Rows of houses of identical architecture, with only subtle differentiations between them; entire streets that look so completely alike that one can easily get lost driving around their neighborhoods.[6]

The same principle applies to the inhabitants: they are mass produced clones of one another with lives which, though on the surface may differ in circumstance, are in essence structurally identical: this person may be a doctor; his neighbor may be a mortgage consultant and his neighbor may be an electrician. But they are all equally engaged in *selling their labor* so that they can pay off mortgages, car loans, student loans, etc. They are, in other words, cogs of the capitalist megamachine, which demands their servitude for its smooth functioning. Anyone who deviates from this principle of servitude is an anomaly and must be treated accordingly. Such an anomaly, the One Who Does Not Conform, will find himself punished for his lack of conformity to the principle of Seriality and Repetition by not being invited to social events, such as the backyard barbecue, the block

Nine. The Columbine Shootings

party, the Neighborly Visit, etc. He will be regarded with precisely the same scorn and suspicion once directed at communist sympathizers in the 1950s.

No one can be allowed to be an exception to this overall background of Same: everyone must do the same thing, not because of anything so clichéd as social pressure or some kind of system of non-existent ethics — for there is no longer any such thing — but simply because the structure of the suburban cosmology demands that for anything to appear within it, it must do so in the form of identical series. It cannot be allowed to appear singly, otherwise, this would be a violation of the rules of the game.

Part of the motivation for Harris's and Klebold's attacks, then, lies in a resistance to the two-dimensionalization of life imposed upon the human mode of being-in-the-world by the strictures of suburban cosmology. If you want to stop a machine from mass producing its goods, you break up the machine in order to make room for the Individual-as-Singularity, the unprecedented individual who disrupts the smooth flowing of Seriality and Repetition by interjecting Difference into the system.[7]

Either that or you create a Singular Event, something so unprecedented that the machine's efficiency cannot encompass or consume it, an *a*-rhythmic event that throws everything out of alignment. Such events, in ancient history, tended to be violent foundational acts, such as Cain's murder of Abel, or the crucifixion of Christ, or even the Non-Event of Abraham's sacrifice of his son that institutes the disruption in the serial repetition of the production of human sacrifice. Such events become religious singularities — that is to say, are non-repeatable — and are foundational of human culture, becoming institutionalized in the form of myth and ritual.

Heiner Mühlmann, in his Maximal Stress Cooperation theory, articulates how such founding events imprint upon the episodic memory of those who experience them — such as Mary and John, who were present at the Crucifixion — acute stimuli as stressors which are then handed down vertically through the generations via written media — such as the Gospels — which encode the event as latent stimuli. But it is only the practice of liturgy and ritual that reactivates the original acute stressors of the founding event as enculturating traits which build cultural memory.[8] If there is no founding event of maximal stress, we might add, then there is no culture and hence, we are left with a semiotic vacancy.

René Girard, meanwhile, in his book *Violence and the Sacred* elaborates an alternate theory on how violence is transmuted into culture by means of ritual. In his case, cultures attain solidarity through participation in a unanimous act of violence *against a scapegoat*, an act of violence that deflects further violence — aleatory, non-patterned, and hence, wayward violence — from spreading throughout the community. When, however, a sacrificial crisis occurs and the rites break down or are no longer practiced, culture decays into a state of reciprocal violence that tears the community apart.[9] Girard thus sees religion as a kind of social immune system that keeps violence directed *out* of the society, as a form of cultural entropy, by directing it towards an Other.

In so doing, of course, it functions as the very opposite of Levinas's compassion for the Other which breaks down the individual's own private sense of Self, causing a traumatic rupture in the flow of his sense of stable self-identity. But it is precisely the irruption of the human face into one's own world order that becomes the occasion for this compassion: "The presence of the face," Levinas writes, "thus signifies an irrecusable order, a command, which puts a stop to the availability of consciousness. Consciousness is called into question by the face... The I loses its sovereign self-coincidence, its identification, in which consciousness returns triumphantly to itself to rest on itself. Before the exigency of the Other (*Autrui*), the I is expelled from this rest..."[10]

This *perhaps* sheds some light on the killings in the library: with the students under the desks, and their faces mostly hidden, was it easier for Harris and Klebold to kill them? There is, of course, no way of knowing, but in any event, Harris and Klebold were apparently incapable of such Levinasian compassion for the Other, and instead perfectly exemplify Girard's idea of what happens to a community when the myth and ritual of the violently sacrificed Other disappears from the civilization as a whole. With the disappearance of the myth of the Sacrificed Redeemer from our current episteme, Western society no longer has a single overarching Scapegoat image that acts as a magnet to draw violence *away* from its communities and sublimate it into ritually reenacted form. As a result, we are plagued with outbreaks of real and terrible violence which spread throughout our communities as attempts to fill the semiotic vacancy once occupied by the signifier of the Crucified One.

Thus, at least part of the architecture of Harris's and Klebold's act of terrorism has to do with an attempt to fill in this missing X, this Void in our culture once occupied by the central Image of the Crucified One. Violence, whether ritualized or real, can never be done away with completely: but ritual, symbol and myth *can* be used to build constructive (virtual) channels which harness and catalyze such violence into cultural outlets that serve the purpose of keeping the community alive and thriving. Those theoreticians, like Christopher Hitchens or Sam Harris,[11] who think religion is an archaic holdover from the days of superstitious humanity, simply don't understand how religion works to stabilize and hold society together precisely by ejecting violence from it as a form of cultural entropy.

Thus considered, violence resembles the entropy that is ejected from a dissipative structure, for in order for such a structure to function properly, the entropy has to be ejected outside it, otherwise it gums up the works from within.

Suburban Cosmology Continued

So much for the principle, then, of iteration by means of which things *appear*. Now for the *structure* of suburban cosmology: what does the world look like from inside it?

It is, like many ancient cosmologies, an image of the world as a flat, two-dimensional circle that closes back in upon itself. Thus, one can drive from one end of a suburb to another and find that one has only ended up in the precise spot where one began. This is not an accident, but a principle of enclosure that is inherent to the design of the suburban world horizon. There is a gate of entrance at every suburban housing community, usually with words printed upon it like "Crestwood Estates" or "Rocky Horizons" and this is usually paired up with a twin exit. But both entrance and exit can be used interchangeably, for in reality, they are connected and enclosed by an imaginary circle that walls the suburb off inside a horizon of false security. For living inside of a suburb, one has the distinct feeling — which is, of course, as are all things today, fake — of being secure and protected from social Chaos. The entrance and exit gates, together with the usually walled backyards, give one the same sense of enclosure that used to be the *raison d'etre* of cities during the Medieval period when they were all enclosed by walls with gates that shut down at night and refused to allow entrance or egress to anyone after sunset. Thus, like the imaginary community in Shyamalan's film *The Village*—which perfectly exemplifies this new sense of community construction through exclusion — suburbs are bounded by a principle of social enclosure: We live here; the Others live out There.

The Others are, of course, those who do not qualify to live within the enclosed world of the suburban community: the poor, the homeless, the sick, the indigent, the insane, the diseased, etc. Traditionally, these others also included non-white ethnicities, but that is no longer the case, for nowadays, racial exclusion has given way to financial and economic exclusion. Economic prejudice is the new racism.

In reality, though, this is not community at all, but rather the *absence* of community, as the sociologist Zygmunt Bauman perceptively writes:

> The heavily guarded, electronically surveyed "gated communities" into which the moment they [i.e., the successful] get enough money or credit they buy themselves to keep their distance from the "messy intimacy" of ordinary city life are "communities" in name only. What their residents are prepared to pay an arm and a leg for is the right to stay aloof and be free from intruders. "Intruders" are all other people guilty of having their own agendas and of living their lives in their own ways. The nearness of other agendas and alternative ways of life undermines the comforts of "finishing quickly and beginning from the beginning" and for this reason "intruders" are resented as obtrusive and vexing ... it is freedom from such characters, promised by the heavily armed guards constantly on the beat and a dense network of electronic spy cameras, that makes "gated communities" so alluring and avidly sought after and becomes a point which the developers and estate agents of such communities emphasize much more than any other feature in their commercial handouts and advertising leaflets.[12]

One's bank account, then, must wind up, at the end of every month, exactly where it started. This is another instance of the principle of circularity, for if an asymmetry appears in the bank account that disrupts it, this must be made up for by the end of the month so that all accounts come back to zero, where they started. Asymmetry is another threat from the Cosmic World Out There: for if it appears in one's bank account, it can cause a destabilization that disrupts the principle of circularity and brings the whole thing crashing down into Difference. But it is precisely Difference that the suburbs have been constructed to exclude.

So much, then, for the main structuring principle of the suburban cosmos. Next, we have to consider topography: the world of the suburbs, as we have seen, is a flat enclosed circle bounded by the suburban enclosure walls, and the invisible boundaries of the minimum financial limits demanded by the right to live in them, but yet, there exists, beyond these

Nine. The Columbine Shootings

circular worlds, Another World that is annexed to them: the Circle is connected to a series of Rectangles that touch it at certain tangential points. These Rectangular annexes consist of shopping malls, golf courses, gas stations, supermarkets and strip malls. And these annexes are so essential to the functioning of the suburb that it actually cannot exist in isolation without them. They are the modern equivalent of the Markets and Town Squares that kept the cities of the Middle Ages thriving. No suburb fails to come equipped with its corner grocery and convenience and drug stores: Safeway, Walgreens, 7 Eleven and Chevron. These stores also appear phenomenologically in strict accordance with the iterative principle of Seriality and Repetition, for they are all identical and usually come in clusters separated from each other by just a few blocks. Where there is one Walmart, another will surely be found only a few miles away. No anomalies or singularities are allowed: local merchants, with their idiosyncratic pricing and wares, disappear, for there is no such thing anymore as the corner butcher shop, toy store, tailor or bakery. They have all been swallowed up by chain grocery stores, each one structurally identical to the next, just like the houses, and the people living in them.

Then there are the ubiquitous golf courses, which are miniaturizations of the pastoral hills and green dales that once existed before the coming of the suburbs displaced them. Their memory is preserved in the fake hills and ponds of the golf course, which reiterates the principle of social exclusion that the suburbs themselves are based upon. And in the game itself, it is not so much getting the ball into each hole that matters, as the symbolism of conquering large swaths of territory: with each hole conquered, the entire greenery surrounding it has been made one's own. This is why golf is so popular — indeed, almost exclusively so — with wealthy, upper class whites: it is a self-congratulatory reenactment of the conquest of North America and displacement of its native inhabitants that the very existence of the suburbs is based upon. Golf provides the suburbs with its central myth of Exclusion and Conquest.

And so, with suburban cosmology, we are presented with a series of topological surfaces without depth, a two-dimensional universe of enclosed circles, adjacent rectangles, excluded Others and protected inhabitants who differ from each other just about as much as each house differs from the one beside it. It is a world of lies and self deceptions, in which one can maintain one's place within this cosmos only so long as one's bank account is guided by the principle of circularity. If that circle fails to meet itself at the end of the month, then the individual is ejected from the system like so much corporate effluvia going down the rivers and valleys of the earth. He falls into the role of Suburban Entropy and soon finds himself ejected back into the very city, with its decaying homeless shelters and crumbling social infrastructures, that the suburbs were designed to protect the individual from in the first place.

It is, to say the least, a precarious existence.

Semiotic Vacancies

Now that we have some familiarity with the structure of suburban cosmology, we are prepared to take a look at what is *missing* from this cosmology: namely, the world-structuring principles of Death, Chaos and Violence which, in traditional thought systems, are always entangled with *meaning*. But these principles have been carefully walled out of the *a*-signifying suburban universe. Their existence is not only completely unacknowledged — with few exceptions, such as the occasional suicide or episode of domestic violence — but their ontological status is similar to that of the creatures in Shyamalan's film, *The Village*, i.e., they are the One Thing of Which We Do Not Speak. In the suburbs, Death is elsewhere. Try looking around for the cemeteries and graveyards in which the suburban dead are buried and you will have to squint very hard to find them. They are usually hidden somewhere out of the way: in difficult to access parts of the city, where they are inconspicuous and generally avoided. Indeed, they are as much avoided as are the elderly in general, who are disposed of when they become a burden the same way in which we dispose of our trash: by simply ejecting it from the system.

Death, that ultimate signifier, is not to be spoken of in the suburbs. Mention it in a conversation at a dinner party or a backyard barbecue and you will find yourself immediately unpopular. No one will sit next to you, talk to you or indeed even look your way. Once the taboo of Death is breached, the individual is relegated to the status of Impure and Unclean and is treated accordingly.

Suburban cosmology differs from the traditional cosmologies of the past of human history, then, in that it assigns no place in its semiotics for Death: it features no Underworld, and gives the Dead almost no role to play — with the exception of a couple of hours after dark on Halloween,

Nine. The Columbine Shootings

the world's shortest and briefest Day of the Dead ever. It is a two dimensional cosmology composed only of surfaces without depth. The Underworld does not exist and Death and Violence, because they are loaded with *significance*, are unwelcome.

But death and violence can no more be evaded than sex or the act of birth itself. As biologically incarnate Beings, death is an inevitability: and the human psyche being what it is, violence will not — ever — go away simply by closing one's eyes and flipping a few more hamburgers over the grill.

Far from being a meaningless act of violence, then, Eric Harris's and Dylan Klebold's attack on Columbine High School was an attempt — albeit unconsciously — at a structural transformation of the suburban sociosphere. By bringing violence and death out into the open, they were attempting to transform the *a*-signifying cosmology of the suburbs by opening up a portal of meaning at Columbine High School, a connecting portal between this world and the next, a sort of corridor connecting being-in-the-world (this world) with a being-*beneath*-the-world. Their act of terrorism was an attempt, in other words, to bring depth to the two-dimensional suburban sociosphere.

By building a semiotic world of violence *into* the suburban sociosphere, Harris and Klebold were attempting to complete what was left incomplete at the time of its creation, for all ancient cosmologies, without exception, have had Meaning woven into them. Thus, the cardboard and plastic universe of Walmarts, chain stores and gas stations becomes at once stained with something like the aura of Truth: for the very cosmos of Death and Violence which the suburbs have attempted to exclude from their purview has left them insufficient and semiotically incomplete. They are, in other words, semiotic vacancies built out of houses and high schools and strip malls. But it is the traumatic impact of the world of the Real — a Real that lies somewhere Out There beyond the enclosed membranous walls of the suburbs — that these two troubled teenagers were attempting to inflict on the suburbs in order to transform their shallow world into something a *little* closer to Reality.

Something, in other words, with Meaning; for violence, wherever it occurs, always *signifies*. Violence is a quest for meaning: the Islamic terrorist crashing his plane into a building; the criminal who robs, rapes and kills; the nation state intervention in a humanitarian crisis. All are attempts to find and create meaning in a world in which meaning has been increasingly stripped away, deconstructed into insignificance or, as in the suburbs, denied altogether. In a world in which Meaning has become an endangered species, ever more atrocious acts of genocide, violence and terrorism are in full bloom as the peoples of this planet scramble to find narratives that will make sense out of their lives.

For Harris and Klebold, then, the necessity to construct an order of being-*beneath*-the-world, i.e., an Underworld, through inflicting an atrocious act of violence was the result of the fact that, for them, the suburbs meant Nothing, for they saw them as simply void of significance in the larger sense. (Hence, Eric Harris's interest in Nazi semiotics can be read as a desperate attempt to find a system of meaning that was for him simply *missing* from the suburbs).

Whatever else remains uncertain in this uncertain world, there *is* one thing that we can be sure of: wherever nihilism reigns — and such nihilism is pervasive in American society — violence will be sure to follow.

Psychopaths?

The transformation of Columbine into a portal to the Underworld is based upon an attempt to bring meaning and depth to a two-dimensional sociosphere that believes it has successfully isolated itself from the kinds of tragedy — together with its semiotic struggles for meaning — with which the rest of the world has had to deal nearly every day. This is not to sympathize with the position of the killers, but merely to understand them correctly. They *must* be understood, for the absurd levels of horror to which the tragedy accelerated are simply too terrible to be ignored.

But the essence of the tragedy, as we have seen, is that it was propelled by an attempt to confer systems of meaning onto a suburban universe where such forms of meaning have been largely disallowed.

As Dave Cullen documents in his book on the tragedy, though, the investigators who were hired to create psychological profiles of Eric and Dylan, in their attempts to arrive at an official "understanding" of the tragedy came to the rather simplistic conclusion that it happened because Eric Harris was a "psychopath."[13] Dylan Klebold, his sidekick, was merely a suicidally depressed teenager suffering from love angst who had the misfortune to hook up with an innate sadist. It was Eric, the sadistic and manipulative con man, who was the real culprit, for it was decided by

Nine. The Columbine Shootings

these investigators that he was a textbook psychopath who might have gone on, had Columbine never happened, to kill other people in other ways. Case closed.

But once again, we have here yet another semiotic failure, for branding Eric Harris as a psychopath is really a *non*-explanation, a confession that experts are not semiotically trained enough to actually explain what happened on a cognitive level. Such experts, knowing little about cosmology, religion, mythology or philosophy, do not have the necessary tools that are required to make sense out of the disaster — and Columbine *was* a type of catastrophe, a sociological one — and consequently have only their conceptually thin, and philosophically shallow, DSM Manual with which to resort.

Columbine — like the Aum Shinrikyo attacks in Tokyo — is about the failure of consumer society to produce a world that *matters*. A suburban cosmology of consumer nihilism is a poor substitute for a cosmology. The failure to provide our children with a world that includes them as part of a larger cognitive map is instead producing a world in which they are seen, and are taught to see themselves, as insignificant by-standers of a meaningless landscape which they had nothing to do with building and does not need them, or their contributions, in any fundamental way.

Thus, Columbine is an example of the type of sociological disaster that results when the logosphere fails to build Death, Violence and Last Things into the map of its World Picture. When such a lacuna in the cosmological map governing a society exists, the resulting disorientation that it causes ignites anger, and such anger becomes fuel for a quest of violence that will lead to an attempt at *filling in* the missing gap of the World Picture. But in order to fill in this semiotic vacancy, *another world*, an Underworld, a being-*beneath*-the-world, must be constructed as a new annex located vertically *below* the flat two-dimensional disc that the suburbs have retained from ancient circular cosmologies while simultaneously shearing away their vertical depth dimensions of worlds above and worlds below.

Thus, we have in Columbine yet another example of a catastrophe made possible by a flaw in the cosmological map of our society. Our children should not be blamed for taking it upon themselves to revise this map.

The map should have been complete to begin with, for its completion would have prevented the catastrophe from ever occurring in the first place.

Part III: Planetary Scale Disasters

The new millennium has brought with it new disasters of unprecedented scale and scope. These disasters have not only grown larger than they were in Neomodernity, but they are now coterminous with the sphere of the entire globe. There is now nowhere where disaster is *not*. The days of peering safely over the fence at the catastrophes which have befallen the misfortunate Other are over with, for no matter who we are, or where we find ourselves on the map — First World or Third World no longer makes any difference since, as Hurricane Katrina demonstrated, these two worlds have now become tightly intermeshed — disaster, sooner or later, is going to find us.

The third and final part of this book, then, proceeds to analyze a series of disasters of planetary scale: the September 11 terrorist attacks upon New York City; the devastations wrought by Hurricane Katrina on New Orleans; the 2008 Sichuan earthquake in China; an obscure and little known disaster that took place in the Exosphere above the earth in 2009, when two orbiting satellites, for the first time ever, crashed into each other; the BP oil spill; and the 2011 Tohoku earthquake, tsunami and Fukushima meltdown.

The 9/11 terrorist attacks, though they were localized to New York and Washington, D.C., were nonetheless global precisely because they were inflicted by a global terrorist network, an example of what Arjun Appadurai has termed diasporic public spheres. These are groups of people living in exile from their home states who are able, nonetheless, to connect with each other via the use of globalized technologies like cell phones and the Internet.[1] Al-Qaeda, and other terrorist groups affiliated with it, such as the Islamic Group or al-Jihad, represent a new kind of enemy to the nation state, one that is diffuse, non-localized and stateless. As a result, it is a near impossibility to eradicate such social formations brought into being by global technologies, for they are like cancer in the sense that in order to get rid of them, you would have to attack the entire global system, which would have to be shut down and unplugged. At that point, they would cease to exist, but so, unfortunately, would everything else. Al-Qaeda and groups like them compose the shadow side of globalization, for with global technology comes global terrorism.[2]

The attacks themselves — and those that followed in Madrid and Britain in the subsequent years — are also planetary in another sense, one specified by Ulrich Beck, in which he pointed out that such attacks demonstrate that there is no longer any safe place anywhere on the planet that is *not* under threat by terrorist attack. The apparent randomness of the attacks points up the fact that the *entire planet* is now their target, for there is no longer a battlefield of any sort.[3] In traditional wars, the front was where the tanks were,[4] but today there *is* no front precisely because the front is right where you and I are standing. Anyone, anywhere could be hit: that subway, this bus, that building over there, this train station over here. No place is safe, and the entire planet, therefore, is now, for the first time, under military threat (before that, nuclear threat was planetary, too, but not a particularly credible one).

This, of course, thrusts the contemporary human being into a new existential situation in the world in which, far worse than Heidegger's *Angst*, the individual as a member of a molar population, now finds himself a potential target. *We are all targets today.* The disintegration of the polarity of battlefield vs. domus — together with so many other such traditional philosophical polarities as nature vs. culture, inside vs. outside — is now upon us.

September 11 also replays the Amsterdam cargo plane crash of 1992, but on a higher, much more complex turn of the spiral. Whereas that accident was a strictly local affair, global terrorist threats are specifically non-local in nature.

In the case of Hurricane Katrina, another apparently localized catastrophe, the "natural" catastrophe of a hurricane that nearly wiped out an entire metropolis, we find ourselves facing the results of another planetary catastrophe, in this case, that of global warming. As many of our climate scientists have demonstrated, 2005 was the hottest year on record, with a record number of named storms.[5] A warmed planet means warming oceans, and that means more energy in the atmosphere. Global warming is an ongoing planetary catastrophe that is happening, in slow motion, all around us right this very moment. As you read these words, CO2 levels continue to rise; Greenland and West Antarctic ice sheets continue to melt; and sea levels continue to elevate. In one hundred years, most climate scientists are now saying, we will be living in a *very* different, indeed, scarcely recognizable, world.[6]

Hurricane Katrina also replays the sinking of the *Titanic* on a higher turn of the spiral, in this case, with the roles of the respective players reversed: the speeding object of the dromosphere is now a "natural" threat, while the man-made industrial artifact is stationary. But the collision and subsequent drowning are equally severe.

With the 2008 earthquake that took place in the Sichuan Province of China, we are dealing with the world's first man-made earthquake (or at least, the first that we know of). As the result of the pressure and weight of the reservoir at Zipingpu Dam, which sits right on a fault line, the tectonic plates were disrupted and loosed enormous amounts of energy in the form of a 7.9 earthquake.[7] This, too, is a global problem, since massive industrial engineering projects have been built everywhere on the planet, and it is within the bounds of possibility that such projects are somehow destabilizing the lithosphere beneath our feet. Geologists have suggested recently that earthquakes are on the rise and getting bigger, and more of them may be man-made than we care to want to realize. Our technologies have taken on a truly vast, gargantuan nature, and now they seem to be disrupting the very cosmic forces that hold the planet together.

The 2009 crash of two orbiting satellites in the Exosphere above the earth is the first dromspheric accident to take place in orbit. The implications of this accident, as the essay explores, are that the entire planet is now surrounded by a thermo- and exospheric envelope of crashes and collisions which, according to the Kessler Syndrome, are waiting to unfold over the next few decades.

So, consistent with the planetary scale of our industrial undertakings, the accidents and disasters that such projects inevitably bring along with them have now been scaled up in magnitude to the size of the entire planet. Indeed, the value of this technological experiment undertaken by Western civilization has never seemed to be more in question than it is now.

In attempting to surround himself with a technospheric exoskeleton in order to compensate for the loss of the ancient planetary spheres that once protected him from the impact of "too much reality," the human being has now walled himself *inside* of a metallic shell in which catastrophes have become a daily occurrence. Indeed, the belt of satellites in the Thermosphere have now become the modern equivalent of the ancient Roman limes, that ancient wall stretching across the middle of Europe that demarcated the civilized world of the Romans from the lawless and chaotic wilderness of the Germanic barbarians. It is only in the Exosphere above and beyond the satellized Thermosphere where today the artifacts of human technological civilization begin to thin out and shade off into the chaotic wildernesses of outer space.

And now, the option of escape from this techno-shell has vanished, for there is no longer any such thing as an "outside" of civilization to escape *to*. In the cosmologies of the ancient Gnostics, the cosmos was a sort of prison constructed by evil cosmic architects known as Archons, who built it as a machine for trapping and confining human souls into physical bodies. The only way out of such confinement was to attain, through gnosis, an escape of the soul from the body, which could then ascend out beyond the whirling spheres governed by the Archons to the cosmic Plenum that lay beyond them. Today, such an outside would exist only somewhere beyond the pale above the Exosphere, but then, that is a realm that is inherently hostile to biological life and no place for man to build space rafts for himself as substitute vehicles of ascension with which to escape from a decimated earth and its techno-polluted solar system.

Like it or not, the earth is an orb upon which we find ourselves stranded for the foreseeable future.

Ten

On the September 11 Terrorist Attacks

Simulated Accident

At 8 on the morning of September 11, 2001, American Airlines Flight 11 took off from Boston Logan International Airport, headed for Los Angeles. About fifteen minutes into its flight, the plane was hijacked by five members of al–Qaeda, including Mohammad Atta, a man with college degrees in urban planning who believed that the building of skyscrapers in Middle Eastern cities like Cairo and Aleppo had ruined those cities by taking away privacy and dignity from its inhabitants and creating unattractive skylines. At precisely 8:46, Atta crashed the plane into the north face of the World Trade Center's North Tower between the 93rd and the 99th floors. Everyone above the 92nd floor, a total of 1,344 people (658 of them employed by Cantor Fitzgerald) was killed.

At 8:14, meanwhile, United Airlines Flight 175, also bound for Los Angeles, took off from Logan Airport just a few minutes after Flight 11. Carrying 56 passengers and 9 crewmembers, it too, was hijacked by five members of al–Qaeda approximately 30 minutes into its flight. Making a U-turn over New Jersey, the hijackers then crashed the plane into the South Tower of the World Trade Center at 9:03 between the 77th and 85th floors. Of the 7,000 or so people working in this tower, approximately 6,000 of them had evacuated the building safely by 9:30, and of the one thousand or so who remained, about 600 of those would perish.

At 8:20, American Airlines Flight 77 took off from Washington Dulles Airport in Virginia. It, too, was bound for Los Angeles, and was hijacked by five al–Qaeda members approximately 35 minutes into its flight. Carrying 58 passengers, the plane crashed into the west side of the Pentagon at 9:37, traveling at 530 mph and laden with 5,300 gallons of fuel. 189 people were killed, 64 on the plane and 125 inside the Pentagon.

At 9:59, in Manhattan, meanwhile, the South Tower, rendered unstable by fires burning from 10,000 gallons of jet fuel — fires which were hot enough to weaken the columns and cause the floors to sag, pulling the perimeter columns inward — collapsed in on itself in a cloud of gray dust and ash composed of asbestos, lead, glass fibers, dioxin, PCBs and toxins from thousands of vaporized computers. The collapse occurred in a mere 20 seconds.

Earlier that morning, United Flight 93 had taken off at 8:42 from Newark International Airport in New Jersey, bound for San Francisco with only 37 passengers and 7 crewmembers. At 9:28, it was hijacked by four al-Qaeda members; however, during a wrestle with a group of passengers, the plane was wrenched to the ground in Shanksville, Pennsylvania, at 10:03. Its likely target was the United States Capitol building.

Then, at 10:28, in New York City, the North Tower collapsed, killing 624 more people, 343 of them New York firefighters.

The number of fatalities in New York was 2,763 people: this comprised 1,466 in the North Tower and 624 in the South.[1] One hundred fifty-seven people died onboard the two planes. The total number of people who died at the hands of al-Qaeda terrorists on that day was just under 3,000.

The whole ordeal had transpired over the course of a mere hour and forty-two minutes.

Inside or Out?

The first thing to notice about the attacks — and it is a point that seems almost too obvious to mention — is the degree to which they reveal the vulnerability of the modern city dweller to a sudden surprise attack from out of the blue. No one saw the planes coming — not the aviation authorities, not the military, not air traffic control — until it was too late. The nakedness and exposure of the modern city dweller to catastrophe that is here revealed is almost unbearable, so unbearable, in fact, that it spawns conspiracy theories as a means of erecting defense mechanisms against the cosmology of randomness that it implies. September 11 conspiracy theories are *hugely* popular, more so than perhaps any other conspiracy theory ever, and that is because they disguise the ontological terror that lies hidden beneath them: if the attacks were an inside job, then at least they weren't random. *Somebody* was in control of them, even if their intent was malicious.

Ten. The September 11 Terrorist Attacks

The reality, though, is much harder to bear, for it is tantamount to admitting that we moderns stand naked beneath a world that is open and unprotected — both ontologically and cosmologically — all around us. *Anything* can fall out of the sky and come crashing into our cities at any time. The truth is that we simply have no means of defending ourselves against this possibility.

And, in fact, cosmologically speaking, we have been living under the absence of a protective world ceiling ever since the natural scientists of the seventeenth century dismantled the outer spheres-within-spheres apparatus turned by the angels which had been in place since the days of the Greeks, protecting, surrounding and enclosing the human being in a comforting universe of limited and very narrowly defined dimensions.

But when that cosmic immune system was shattered about the year 1600, our cities were still protected — militarily speaking — by walls. Cities, since the earliest days of their inception in ancient Mesopotamia, had always been surrounded by walls which demarcated them cosmologically from the world of nature "out there." This nature / civilization dichotomy ran parallel to an ontology of interiors vs. exteriors for thousands of years, years in which the human being was always *inside* something somewhere and hence, protected.[2]

But with the advent of gunpowder and cannons in the fifteenth century, first used extensively by the French on their rampages through Italy, the ancient curvilinear walls of Medieval cities had to undergo a structural transformation with the advent of the star-shaped city: the rounded turrets at the corners of the battlements had diamond points added to them, and these triangular points soon grew into arrow-shaped bastions that the city thrust out to protect itself from cannonfire in a 360 radius. Cannons could be loaded onto these bastions and a ditch dug around the city made it very difficult of approach for sieging infantry.

The success of the star-shaped city spread from Italy throughout Europe and it became a basic staple in the designs of all utopian architecture until the nineteenth century when, with the advent of high explosive shells, such urban geometries were rendered obsolete. From henceforth, Europeans and Americans lived in cities without walls, and their vulnerability to attack from the air was demonstrated copiously by the aerial bombardments of two world wars.

It was the Germans who, with their rigid airships, were the first to begin to drop bombs on cities from the air during World War I. On August

Part III: Planetary Scale Disasters

25, 1914, they bombed the city of Antwerp from the air, killing or wounding some 26 people. On September 8, 1915, London itself was bombed during the night by three zeppelin airships under the command of one Heinrich Mathy. Twenty-two people were killed and five hundred thousand pounds worth of property damage was inflicted. Mathy's enthusiasm over the results are evident in his comments, recorded later: "'The explosive effect of the 300 kilogram bomb must be very great since a whole cluster of lights vanished in its crater.'"[3]

But the Germans paid for the invention of their atmoterrorist strategy when, during World War II, their cities became the targets for firebombing projects initiated by the Allies. The novelist W.G. Sebald provides us with a particularly harrowing description of the firebombing of Hamburg in the summer of 1943:

> The aim of Operation Gomorrah, as it was called, was to destroy the city and reduce it as completely as possible to ashes. In a raid early in the morning of July 27, beginning at one A.M., ten thousand tons of high explosive and incendiary bombs were dropped on the densely populated residential area east of the Elbe, comprising the districts of Hammerbrook, Hamm-Nord and Hamm-Süd, Billwerder Ausschlag and parts of St. Georg, Eilbek, Barmbek, and Wandsbek. A now familiar sequence of events occurred: first all the doors and windows were torn from their frames and smashed by high-explosive bombs weighing four thousand pounds, then the attic floors of the buildings were ignited by lightweight incendiary mixtures, and at the same time firebombs weighing up to fifteen kilograms fell into the lower stories. Within a few minutes, huge fires were burning all over the target area, which covered some twenty square kilometers, and they merged so rapidly that only a quarter of an hour after the first bombs had dropped the whole airspace was a sea of flames as far as the eye could see. Another five minutes later, at one-twenty A.M., a firestorm of an intensity that no one would ever before have thought possible arose. The fire, now rising two thousand meters into the sky, snatched oxygen to itself so violently that the air currents reached hurricane force, resonating like mighty organs with all their stops pulled out at once. The fire burned like this for three hours. At its height, the storm lifted gables and roofs from buildings, flung rafters and entire advertising billboards through the air, tore trees from the ground, and drove human beings before it like living torches. Behind collapsing facades, the flames shot up as high as houses, rolled like tidal waves through the streets at a speed of over a hundred and fifty kilometers an hour, spun across open squares in strange rhythms like rolling cylinders of fire. The water in some of the canals was ablaze. The glass in the tram car windows melted; stocks of sugar boiled in the bakery cellars. Those who had fled from the air-raid shelters sank, with grotesque contortions, in the thick bubbles thrown up by melting asphalt. No one knows for certain how many lost their

Ten. The September 11 Terrorist Attacks

lives that night, or how many went mad before they died. When day broke, the summer dawn could not penetrate the leaden gloom above the city. The smoke had risen to a height of eight thousand meters, where it spread like a vast, anvil-shaped cumulonimbus cloud. A wavering heat, which the bomber pilots said they had felt through the sides of their planes, continued to rise from the smoking, glowing mounds of stone. Residential districts so large that their total street length amounted to two hundred kilometers were utterly destroyed. Horribly disfigured corpses lay everywhere. Bluish little phosphorous flames still flickered around many of them; others had been roasted brown or purple and reduced to a third of their normal size. They lay doubled up in pools of their own melted fat, which had sometimes already congealed. The central death zone was declared off-limits in the next few days. When punishment labor gangs and camp inmates could begin clearing it in August, after the rubble had cooled down, they found people still sitting at tables or up against walls where they had been overcome by monoxide gas. Elsewhere, clumps of flesh and bone or whole heaps of bodies had cooked in the water gushing from bursting boilers. Other victims had been so badly charred and reduced to ashes by the heat, which had risen to a thousand degrees or more, that the remains of families consisting of several people could be carried away in a single laundry basket.[4]

Thus, with the coming down of the walls of the city, the dromosphere shifted to the smooth spaces of the skies above them and moved from a sphere of geostrategic operations to one of aerostrategic tactics.

However, with the launching of Sputnik in 1957, something else happened, a singularity that restructured the world society in a novel way. With the cluttering up of the Thermosphere by geosynchronous telecommunications satellites in the ensuing decades, the archaic world ceiling of the ancients — dismantled and scrapped around 1600[5] — was retrieved, plugged in and turned on. The world ceiling was reconstituted this time by currents of electricity which were shot through it in the form of electric pulse signals beaming from satellite to satellite in a complex grid that ensheathed and enclosed the earth inside a new electrosphere.

In the ancient world, each city, isolated from the others by the presence of a wall, was a kind of hermetically sealed terrarium with its own world ceiling invisibly cast over it, a ceiling that was contiguous with the architecture of its walls. Nowadays, however, our cities no longer have walls and stand unprotected beneath the sky, but they all share the same roof: *all* of our cities are protected and enclosed *inside* a gigantic world dome that has been rendered possible by satellite technologies.

Thus, the old cosmological dichotomy of interior vs. exterior has been rendered obsolete, for there is now no longer any place on the planet that can be considered to be *outside* this world dome of globalization. We are all on the *inside* of a vast world sphere composed of digital information sent beaming around the globe in the air above us and around us at the speed of light. The realm of 1's and 0's, of high finance, of capital and information, has captured us and taken us prisoner. We all dwell inside the belly of the whale of global digital capitalism.

But it turns out that not everyone is happy with this situation ontologically speaking. Islamic fundamentalists — Islamists — to name one group, wish to be on the *outside* of this world dome.

The World in Between

In the ancient world, each city was its own polisphere, bounded by its own wall, encompassed and contained inside of its own world ceiling. Indeed, there were as many world ceilings as there were cities. But the spaces *in between* these cities was another matter: that was the realm of the smooth space of the nomad, the Bedouin, the Berber, the Arab and his camel, a realm beyond the reach of the laws of the cities or its taxes or its complicated, anti-tribal system of social machinery. The world of the nomad is *un*-bounded and it is not contained by any world ceiling whatsoever, except, of course, the dome with the stars written upon it. The smooth spaces of the nomad in his primitive dromosphere — be it desert dune or Asiatic steppe — is a world that is beyond the codes and coding processes of the cities. It is a realm, as Deleuze and Guattari would put it, of decoded flows.[6] Cities are striations in the midst of these smooth landscapes of the Midworld, striations that code, check, freeze, capture and arrest the motions of the dromosphere through all manners and means.[7]

Now, there have been two formative divisions of Arabian society since the days of its founding. Indeed, the great philosopher ibn Khaldun built an entire philosophy of history out of the opposition between what he called the Bedouin and the sedentary societies.[8] The Bedouin tribe — including under this term the Arab nomad — is bound together by what ibn Khaldun terms "*asabiyyah*," a sort of mystical social glue shared by people of a tribe descended from a common ancestor. But with the formation of sedentary societies by such nomads, this *asabiyyah* is gradually

Ten. The September 11 Terrorist Attacks

depleted and wiped out by new social configurations which are hostile to tribal formations. Eventually, sedentary societies are inevitably ruined by vices, greed, the taste for luxuries and social laxity, etc, and are soon conquered once again by other nomadic societies.

These two social formations — the stateless society of the nomad and the sedentary world of the city dweller — comprise the structural history of Arabian civilization down to the coming of Western modernity in the 20th century. The pastoral nomad, according to Albert Hourani, disappeared from Arabic society in the 1920s with the coming of the automobile, the paving of new roads and the expansion of cities like Cairo with new quarters to accomodate a wealthy new middle class bourgeoisie.[9] At just about the same time, however, the first of the Islamist societies was formed in Cairo by Hasan al–Banna who, in 1928, created the Muslim Brotherhood. Al-Banna's friend and rival Sayyid Qutb, meanwhile, upon returning from a visit to America in the 1940s, created the basic ideology of the Islamist world view in a series of books and essays, an ideology which perceives the West — with its loose ways, its immorality, sexual concupiscence, equal rights for women, and especially its separation of church and state — as a corrupting influence upon Islam.[10]

Thus, not only do the Islamists represent the Muslim counter-culture — a culture that counters the too secular and modernizing ways of Egyptian and even Saudi ruling regimes — but it also retrieves and reconfigures the ancient Arabic social formation of the nomad who exists *outside* the state apparatus as such. Osama bin Laden, Ayman al Zawahiri, Sheikh Abdul Rahman: *all* of these men led nomadic existences outside the confining boundaries of their own native born states, drifting hither and yon throughout the Middle East and back and forth across state lines. The mujahideen, as a classic example, at the end of the war with the Soviets in Afghanistan, found themselves a more or less stateless people, since none of their original countries, perceiving them largely as social rejects to begin with, wanted them back.

But of course, these Islamists do not want to be on the *inside* of anything. They are a neo-nomadic social formation and they thrive on existing in the interstices *between* cities, worlds and states. The whole problem, and the basis of their whole rejection of Western modernity, is one of exteriors: they wish to be *outside* the world dome of global digital capitalism. This was the basis of Osama bin Laden's wish to have the Americans withdraw their military presence from Saudi Arabia after the First Gulf War, for with them *out* of the Holy Land, a step could be taken toward existence *outside* this world dome.

But, of course, on a planet in which there is no longer any such thing as a world exterior (one would have to go beyond the satellized thermo- and exospheres for that, since these now constitute our modern limes) we are all equally encompassed by the world dome of capitalism, and so the question then becomes, how to get out of the belly of the beast.

And amongst all the various Islamist factions, it was al-Qaeda alone which came up with the answer.

Cosmic Axis

But to understand the nature of this answer, we have to look back for a moment at ancient cosmology. All the traditional societies envisioned the heavens in one way or another as a lid or a roof or a ceiling—whether analogized to a tent or a temple—which, like the pillars of a temple, had to be supported by something. The Egyptians imagined the sky being held up at the four quarters by the four sons of Horus, and the Scandinavians by four dwarves. But in some cases, the world ceiling was held up by a single pillar, known to comparative mythologists as the *axis mundi*, a pillar which was variously depicted as either a tent-pole, central column, pyramid or cosmic mountain. Sometimes in these ancient myths an assault upon this central axis took place as a means of knocking the world out of order and off its axis.[11]

In the *Epic of Gilgamesh*, for instance, there is the episode when Gilgamesh and his hairy companion Enkidu chop down the Sacred Cedar tree in the forest. As scholars point out, though, this is no ordinary tree, but a cosmic one, for as the result of cutting it down, a cosmic catastrophe results in an earthquake which forms the Beqaa Valley in central Palestine as a ridge that runs right on down through the Rift Valley in East Africa.[12] In Chinese myth, likewise, there is the story of the war between the god of fire, Zhu Rong, and the god of water, Gong Gong, in which the water god hurls himself at Mount Buzhou, the cosmic pillar, and knocks it down. As a result, he tears a hole into the world ceiling through which demons and monsters from the world beyond begin streaming through.[13]

The Twin Towers of the World Trade Center thus become, as reimaged in the archaic imagination of al-Qaeda, modern equivalents of this

Ten. The September 11 Terrorist Attacks

celestial cosmic axis holding up the world ceiling. Thus, if you want to bring down the world ceiling—like Samson pushing out the twin pillars that brings down the roof of the temple on the Philistines—then you have to assault the pillar(s) that support it. In doing so, you will cause the capitalist world dome of digitized information speeding around us to collapse. Once this collapse has taken place, you can then find the hole in the sky and make your way to the outside. And it is, of course, precisely on the *outside* where al–Qaeda wants to be.

In the ancient world, when armies attacked a fortress, they mounted up into the dromosphere on the backs of their horses and camels and hurled at the city different kinds of siege engines: catapults, trebuchets, onagers, testudos, galleries, etc. But with the now vanished world of the nomad, substitutes for this dromosphere must be found, and the nearest equivalent are airplanes which do indeed reconfigure the nomadic plane of smooth space, free of striations, around the world. (One cannot, after all, assault a modern city with camels and donkeys.) Thus, the hijacked airliner is immediately transformed into a dromospheric weapon of ballistics, a missile which can be hurled at the fortified city in a manner that will effectively break it to pieces. To a city of colossal dimensions, one must respond by scaling up the ballistical weapon to the size of a gigantic arrow.

Ancient cities, on the other hand, were fortresses based upon technologies of obstruction designed to freeze and arrest such dromospheric assaults with battlements, turrets, archers, moats, parapets, bastions, etc.[14] Nowadays, these technologies of obstruction have disappeared from our cities in physical form but they have reappeared as electronic obstructions in the form of computer profiling, X-rays, baggage searches, identification, passports, etc. To the modern wall-less city, one responds with electronic pulse signals which saturate the entire space of the city with security apparatuses, as Heiner Mühlmann has pointed out.[15] Al-Qaeda's genius lay in its ability to move through this new world of spatial striations using simple, mechanical means: box cutter knives, convincing white collar clothes, proper IDs, etc. No one suspected them because they were effectively invisible, concealed in plain sight.

This even extended to the realm of images, for the attacks, as played on CNN, had the look of an accident of some wayward, catastrophic kind. Indeed, most people assumed the first plane to hit the North Tower to be an accident; after all, a B-25 bomber had once collided with the Empire

State Building.[16] Thus, al-Qaeda very cleverly made use of the semiotics of an aviation accident as a means of disguising their attack. Images, nowadays, have to be taken into account as a basic part of the strategy of *any* attack, since the mediascape is ubiquitous. No attack can afford to take place without first calculating what semiotics the image will initially convey.

So, in reconstructing the Prophet Mohammad's attack using siege engines on the city of Ta'if in A.D. 630[17] as an attack on a modern global cosmopolis like New York, al-Qaeda's intent was to bring down the world ceiling of capitalism by destroying the twin axial pillars which held it up. In doing so, they could then find the hole and climb out, where they would be, at last, on the *outside* of the world dome. There, they would be free to live, like Osama bin Laden often did, in ramshackle farm houses and compounds with no running water or electricity, but at least they would be beyond the reach of the juridical — and very secular — order of the polisphere.

It is the *pace* of modernity, then, which al-Qaeda was trying to slow down, paradoxically by hurtling the fastest moving objects in the contemporary dromosphere at the rapidly streaming realm of global high finance incarnated in its modern architectural temple. Beneath this modern catastrophe, and organizing it as though by a palimpsest, there exist some *very* ancient civilizational structures.

Of course, al-Qaeda's plan backfired, since the world dome is now in process of tightening down all the more securely around them. Indeed, the global hypersphere of capitalism has swallowed up *all* other societies, whether they like it or not. They all now find themselves on the *inside* of capitalism's worldspace.

The question now before us, then, is: How long will the dome hold?

Eleven

Hurricane Katrina and the Flooding of New Orleans

The Flood

On August 29, 2005 — a year which tied with 2010 for the hottest ever on record — the city of New Orleans, Louisiana, was nearly destroyed by a Category 5 hurricane named Katrina. By the time it made landfall at about 6:10 A.M., however, the hurricane had weakened to a Category 3, and at the last moment its path swerved slightly to the east, missing New Orleans and hitting Buras, Louisiana, instead. But the counter-clockwise rotation of its winds swept the waters of Lake Pontchartrain to the north of the city down onto its levees, undermining their weak foundations and causing them to burst asunder in several places, while a 15-foot storm surge up the city's Intercoastal Waterway caused the Industrial Canal to overtop and spill forth its waters, creating an 800-foot-long breach near the Lower Ninth Ward, an area of working class blacks, which was flooded catastrophically.

The city's population of 480,000 people had been mostly evacuated by that point, but since approximately 100,000 of its poorest (mostly black) citizens did not have access to cars or public transportation, they remained behind, stranded in their homes, many of them, especially the elderly, drowning in their attics as the floodwaters rose above their heads. The city's mayor, Ray Nagin, did not have a competent evacuation plan in place to accommodate these people, offering them instead the option of fleeing — on their own and without buses — to the city's gigantic sports arena, the Superdome. Some 12,000 of these people managed to find their way to the arena before the storm hit on Monday morning, but by Monday evening, their numbers had swollen to about 25,000. Sometime earlier that morning, however, the dome's electricity had gone out, taking the air conditioning along with it and as a result, temperatures inside the arena subsequently rose to over 90 degrees. Supplies of food and water were limited and ran out very quickly, while the arena's plumbing system failed and backed up, causing most people to have to relieve themselves in the corridors and stairwells.

By 9 o'clock Monday morning, six feet of water from the large breach at the Industrial Canal had flooded both the Upper and Lower Ninth Wards. By noon, Lake Pontchartrain was flowing into the city at three breaches, flooding Lakeview — a posh area with expensive million dollar homes — the downtown civic area and New Orleans East. By nightfall, the waters were still rising and since communications systems had gone out along with the city's electricity, most of the population had no way of knowing that floodwaters were headed their way. Indeed, many people in the south of the city went to bed that night with dry houses, only to be woken up in the middle of the night with floodwaters up to their waists. Of the 200,000 or so houses in New Orleans, approximately 120,000 were destroyed or damaged beyond repair by the floodwaters.

The U.S. government's response to the plight of the victims was (in)famously slow. Most of them went without food and water for five or six days. As a result, many turned to looting in order to acquire provisions for their families, although of course, many of these poor people also took advantage of the situation to steal plasma TVs and DVD players. The New Orleans Police Department, however, was given permission by their superiors — illegally and unconstitutionally — to shoot looters on sight. Many of these cops from a notoriously corrupt police department put the hunting of looters first as their main priority above rescuing those in need. Indeed, a few police officers even participated in the looting themselves. The shootings of the looters also resulted in several murders of New Orleans citizens by police officers, some of whom tried to cover them up. The episode of the Danziger Bridge stands out in this respect.[1]

Ultimately, over 1,500 people — most of them poor, black and elderly — died in Louisiana during the fourth largest hurricane ever to make landfall in the United States.

The City

New Orleans is a city that sits in a bowl whose terrain varies at points anywhere from 6 to 15 feet below sea level. It is surrounded on all sides

Eleven. Hurricane Katrina and New Orleans

by water: the Mississippi River to the south and west; Lake Pontchartrain to the north; and Lake Borgne to the east. When it was founded in 1718, it was actually several feet *above* sea level, but due to geological subsidence and coastal erosion (all man made) the city is actually sinking at a rate of about three feet per year. Indeed, many experts believe that, entirely apart from the problem of hurricanes, the city will be under water within 80—90 years. Consider the following exchange on the television program *60 Minutes* between the interviewer and one Tim Kusky, professor of Earth Sciences at Saint Louis University, who gives the following prophecy of the city's future:

> "New Orleans is going to be an island?" [the interviewer asks].
> "I wouldn't exactly call it an island. I would call it a fishbowl because New Orleans is going to be 15 to 18 feet below sea level, sitting *off* the coast of North America, surrounded by a 50 to 100 foot tall levee system to protect the city."
> "And completely surrounded by the Gulf of Mexico?"
> "Completely surrounded."
> "And you're talking about just 90 years from now?"
> "That's the projection. Because we're losing land in the Mississippi delta at a rate of 25 or 30 square miles per year. That's two acres per hour that are sinking below sea level."

So Professor Kusky predicts that by 2095, New Orleans *will* be under water. It is a mathematical certainty.[2]

Unless, of course, Congress is willing to authorize the use of billions and billions of dollars to build 100 foot tall levees surrounding the city. The U.S. Army Corps of Engineers, whose shoddy construction work on the levees was what caused them to breach in the first place, has completed the process of rebuilding the breached levees, but only to withstand a Category 3 hurricane, just as they were before. The city would *not* be able to withstand a direct hit from a Category 4 or 5, which would require 30-foot levee walls which, as Colonel Waggoner of the Army Corps points out, would require billions of dollars, and also many years of construction work, to build.

But New Orleans has neither the money nor the time for this. In an age in which the dollar bill is the overriding factor in all decision making, the sad reality is that nobody is going to authorize billions and billions of dollars to rebuild a city that only features *one* Fortune 500 company as a resident. New Orleans is not a businessman's city and never has been. Its primary economy is fueled by shipping, which brings in 13 billion dollars a year, followed by tourism, which pulls in an additional 5 billion.[3] It is a cultural capital, the birthplace of jazz, the blues, gospel and early forms of rock and roll. It is a city where people like to go to party and hear, and create music, *not* to make business deals.

So not only are 100 foot levees out of the question, but even the 30-foot levees that would protect the city from a direct hit by a Category 4 hurricane. The city's future, in an age of global warming, rising sea levels and corporate greed, seems rather grim.

Over 70 percent of the population *has* returned to the city, though, and much progress has been made towards rebuilding it. However, the resulting city, in which most of the poor black neighborhoods are being bulldozed to make room for expensive white real estate, will resemble pre-Katrina New Orleans only vaguely. Thirty percent of the black population, in a city which had been 67 percent black before the storm, did not return.

It is unlikely, therefore, that the city will ever approximate anything like its former cultural creativity again. Poor blacks, and the ragged, mournful, angry music that they produced, were essential to the city's vibrant culture. Once they are swept out of the city, the culture will go right along with them, a fact that is apparently neither well understood, nor appreciated, by the city's council members. A gentrified New Orleans is no longer New Orleans.

So between gentrification, global warming and coastal erosion, it does not appear that the city has much in the way of a future in store for it.

Record Warming

The year 2005 — up until 2010, that is — was the hottest on record, and also, probably not coincidentally, featured the most active hurricane season ever. There were over 30 named storms that year, three times the national average.[4] Indeed, since the 1990s, there has been a *doubling* of Category 4 and 5 hurricanes, and an overall worsening of the intensity of these storms. It is therefore no surprise that the hottest years on record all date from this period as well, since global warming produces warmer seas, and warm seas, as everybody knows, are the engine that drives hurricanes. As Douglas Brinkley puts it, a hurricane is a machine for sucking energy and heat out of the ocean and putting it into the atmosphere. The hurricane vacuums up water from the ocean and when it makes landfall, lets all that water loose as a storm surge.[5]

The temperatures in the world's oceans have increased by about 1 degree since the 1990s. In 2005, the Gulf of Mexico was actually five degrees Fahrenheit warmer than usual. Part of the problem was that the cold waters normally dumped by the Mississippi into the Gulf were lower than normal, since a severe drought in the Midwest—its worst in 20 years—had reduced the Mississippi's water levels. And not only was the Gulf water hot, but the hot water ran deep, 200 feet deep in places as the result of the presence of a loop that had broken away from the warming Gulf Stream and was rotating around the Gulf of Mexico.[6]

The years 2004 and 2005 produced some interesting weather anomalies, as well. For the first time ever, in 2004 a hurricane appeared in the South Atlantic off the coast of Brazil, where no hurricane had ever been recorded. It had 95 mph winds and swept ashore near the town of Torres, damaging 30,000 houses and killing several people. In 2005, a hurricane, also for the first time ever, approached Europe. Hurricane Vince, as it was called, fortunately weakened before making landfall near Huelva, Spain. Indeed, it is very possible, according to Mark Lynas, that as global warming advances over the next few years, we may even begin to see hurricanes entering into the Mediterranean where they have never ventured before.[7]

Although hurricanes are a natural occurrence, it seems very likely that global warming is exacerbating them. The year 2005 was a record year, both for number of hurricanes and for warming sea temperatures. According to Lynas, furthermore, two climate scientists who decided to use complex math in order to find out how much of the warming during that year was natural and how much contributed by man-made global warming, found that "at least half of the extra warmth had come from human-caused global warming."[8]

So the phrase "natural disaster" does not quite seem to fit comfortably when applied to Hurricane Katrina and its devastations.

Exospheric Population

Hurricane Katrina—on one level, anyway—seems to be a replay of the sinking of the *Titanic*, only on a much larger, more complex, planetary scale. Whereas in the case of the *Titanic*, industrial civilization had transferred a piece of its polisphere into the dromosphere and sent it hurtling at breakneck speed into a natural object, in the case of Katrina, the scenario was the other way about: it is the natural object that comes hurtling out of the planetary dromosphere and slams into the stationary polisphere of New Orleans, ripping an 800-foot gash into its side (the breach at the Industrial Street Canal) and causing it to sink. The impact is forceful enough to shatter the city's protective macrosphere, or the invisible dome of civilization erected by the city to protect and shelter its inhabitants inside a kind of man-made immune system.

Cities erect invisible tensor fields around them — like Buckminster Fuller's tensegrities — which function by pushing against the natural entropic tendencies of a particular environment, actually *reversing* or at least *suspending* them so that the city can function as a protective vessel for its inhabitants. As theoretician Peter Sloterdijk has remarked, man is never just camped out *in* nature, but rather — at least since the days of the mammoth bone houses at Dolní Věstonice — has always distanced himself *from* it by creating uterine vessels.[9] But such vessels can only function so long as they resist the entropic conditions of the natural landscapes surrounding them: hence, Venice and Amsterdam must resist the tendency to subside into the sea; the cities of ancient Mesopotamia must resist the salinization of their soils and the sedimentation of their canals; the cities of the modern American Southwest must resist the tendency to *use up* all their water supplies, and so on.

But the real danger to the human being is more subtle than just the disruptive nature of the entropic force that irrupts into the city and interferes with its metabolism. That seems fairly obvious. The *real* harm in such situations is how the natural forces *bring with them inside the city* a corrosive force that actually erodes and changes the ontological status of the human being who calls the disrupted vessel his "home."

Human beings living *inside* such cities are not just walking around, existing and breathing in safety from natural threats. They are actually cocooned like mummies inside a whole web of subtle relations called "laws" and "rights" which guarantee his ontological status as a citizen of a polis. As such a citizen, he is not just physically protected, but his whole well-being is provided for: he has a social security number, for instance, which entitles him to collect social security and Medicaid upon retirement; he has the right to social services such as the use of libraries and medical facilities or, if he is less fortunate, unemployment and welfare; he has the right to protection provided by a police force whose job is not only to enforce the law but actually to guarantee the safety of the citizen. And so on.

But Katrina reveals just how fragile this macrosphere that surrounds and protects the citizen really is, for with its sudden and catastrophic dissolution at the moment of impact, the individual's ontological status as a "citizen" is abruptly changed and transformed into something *else*, something more like the status of a wild animal. The individual becomes suddenly *suspect* and cannot be trusted. His freedom to move about through the city is now limited and constrained by force tactics and he must be corralled into certain slots like cattle. Congealed and aggregated into a molar mass along with other fellow refugees, he is now an entirely *different* phenomenon than he was before, when the functioning macrosphere protected him and guaranteed his rights. Now he is potentially dangerous, reduced to the random and unpredictable behavior of an animal, and must be treated accordingly.

Thus, under these changed circumstances, those who resort to looting and thievery can now be shot and killed with impunity. They are no longer "citizens," for the juridical order has been withdrawn from them, like Agamben's *homo sacer*, and consequently, they can be disposed of at will.[10] They are regarded, and treated, just as if they were wild animals which had suddenly broken loose from the zoo and irrupted into the civic order, where their erratic motion through the polisphere — which demands precise and logical right-angled lines of trajectory from its citizens' peregrinations — must be seized and arrested at once.

Thus, the police force which, as Michel Foucault has shown,[11] originated in the sixteenth century precisely to protect the pedestrian from the rapidly moving dromosphere accelerating through the streets and rivers all around him, now undergoes a change in *their* ontological status, too, shifting from the city's immune system to a kind of autoimmune disorder which treats its former citizens as antigens which must be destroyed at all costs. They even place this urge for destruction as a higher priority than assisting those in need of help, who, meanwhile, are still busy waving pieces of tattered clothing and sheets from flooded rooftops to be rescued. (This latter task is a job for the Coast Guard and also average citizens, who perform it admirably in the absence of the police who are otherwise occupied in shooting looters).

As the floodwaters come pouring across the ruptured membrane, the city-as-organism begins to lose its immunological ability to differentiate "self" from "other." In the ensuing collapse and submergence by natural forces, it begins to lose its capacity to self-organize as an autopoietic structure. The entropy which it had formerly *ejected* from the system is now mistaken for *part* of the system and begins to be symbiotically built into the city's new, chaotic structure. Thus, citizens are mistaken for wild animals, and destructive behavior is accepted and integrated as a new norm. Looting and murder, for the ontologically confused cops, now open up as new behavioral pathways for them to adopt and follow. Even illogic now has its own intrinsic logic.

The population of the poor and the immobilized, meanwhile, who were either unable or unwilling to evacuate, is drawn to the Superdome as a kind of gigantic lifeboat which will enable them to remain afloat just a little while longer. The dome functions magnetically as a kind of technologized substitute for the invisible macrosphere that has just collapsed all around them, drawing those whom the dromosphere has left behind from all directions simultaneously. Inside the dome, these misfortunates are physically protected, but they are no longer citizens with rights, for they have entered a zone of exclusion inside which their rights and liberties, like concentration camp victims, are now forfeit. They have attained the status of a refugee population and so can now be dispensed with as far as immediate needs go. Once they have been corralled and immobilized like a single dangerous gigantic animal, locked up inside the circus hippodrome, they can proceed to be forgotten about.

But what the episode of the Superdome now makes visible for the first time in the eyes of the global media is the presence of a hitherto obscured Third World population *within* North America. This population, previously tucked away in the shanties and shotgun shacks of the Lower Ninth Ward and in its public housing projects, now surfaces into view for the first time, and America's image as a clean First World country, with the world's highest standard of living, begins to disintegrate under the impact of these mediatized images which now begin to circulate and proliferate like viruses. The hidden obscene underside of America — like the Victorian lady's pudenda — suddenly comes shockingly into view and now it can never be seen the same way again. This population, no longer protected by the city's macrosphere, now finds itself in an *exospheric* mode. That is to say, though they are still *physically* within the city, they are no longer *of* the city ontologically speaking and can now, therefore, be gathered up into buses and exported to other cities.

Slowly — and yet inevitably — the catastrophe also reveals America's hidden fascism coming into view: looters are shot with impunity; bodies are hidden and crimes covered up; refugees are gathered into buses and shipped off elsewhere. It is a glimpse of a strange and unfamiliar America — one that, in the course of my entire lifetime living in this country I have never seen — an America that is still to come, perhaps, but whose approaching outlines are beginning to be seen like a dim landscape glimpsed through a distant fog. As the occurrence of catastrophes on American soil pile up, this hidden fascism, I suspect, will become more and more conspicuous until it becomes America's new political norm.

With the city's cognitive and immunological ability to discern self from other now compromised, the city, through the ethnic cleansing of its poor — still ongoing in the gentrification of the city — begins not only to eject floodwaters as part of its entropy, but now it also ejects *people* as part of its entropy. People, mostly poor and black, are ejected from the city right along with the floodwaters that were pumped out during the weeks following the breaching of the levees. The population of New Orleans, as a result, has been diminished by about 30 percent, and it is doubtful that it will ever fully return to what it once was.

Diasporic Societies

History, however, shows us that it is not necessary for a people to have a uterine polisphere within which to exist, as the exospheric status of many populations, the Jews, in particular, demonstrates. A population *can* exist outside of a polisphere in diasporic mode.

When the macrosphere protecting Jerusalem, for instance, was destroyed by the Romans in the Jewish Wars of A.D. 70, and the Jews then found themselves in an exospheric mode of existence, what followed was the decoupling of culture from polispheric monumentality. With the destruction of the Temple, that is to say, the early Jewish Christians began to write down the Gospels on parchment codices, so that the Word could now be made portable by writing. They could take it with them wherever they went. And likewise with the Pharisaic Jews who then proceeded to create the rabbinical traditions of textual exegesis of the Torah, a cultural act which could also be made highly portable and taken anywhere. Indeed, the Jews have managed to survive in an exospheric mode since the formation of the state of Israel in 1948.

Likewise, with the inevitable sinking of New Orleans below the waves

Part III: Planetary Scale Disasters

of the Gulf of Mexico, the black culture of New Orleans will be forced to exist in diaspora. With the city gone, and its population exiled to nearby Houston, Austin, Memphis and Lafayette, its traditions will have to become highly portable and decoupled from the physicality of the French Quarter. Mardi gras, in fact, is already being practiced for the first time in Houston, a city with an otherwise incompatible cowboy culture mentality, and so too, the musicians of Bourbon Street now find themselves playing gigs in these other cities as their new polispheric abodes.

Indeed, the electronic revolution of translating texts into tablets with iPads, Kindles and iPhones may turn out to be a boon as our cities melt down and culture becomes decoupled from locality. The writers, poets and musicians of our sinking coastal cities will be able to leave their heavy books and instruments behind as, one by one, our cities become uninhabitable, and their culture is replaced with portable electronic substitutes.

Sooner or later, though, New Orleans *will* have to be abandoned. For now, it is being rebuilt, just as similar towns and cities throughout history, under persistent siege by the elements, were tirelessly rebuilt before finally being abandoned. Neolithic Çatalhöyük, for example, was destroyed by great fires time and time again, and each time it was rebuilt, but with a diminished culture.[12] Mohenjo daro, likewise, situated in the middle of the Indus River, suffered catastrophic floods which periodically destroyed the city, and the archaeological strata show that it was rebuilt several times, although each level reveals the architecture to be shoddier and shoddier as the war with the elements gradually sapped the strength and enthusiasm of the rebuilders with every new flood that came along

Transforming New Orleans, as some have suggested, into an American Venice is simply dreamy and impractical, for any waters that are floating about in its streets will be magnified into catastrophic floods when more Category 4 and 5 hurricanes come hurtling out of the planetary dromosphere to crash into the city.[13] At that point, *all* the city's rooftops, save those of its skyscrapers, would disappear beneath the floodwaters.

It is painful to let go of a great city, especially a cultural metropolis like New Orleans, which has functioned as the Great Ear of American culture for three centuries. American pop music would simply not exist in its present configuration without the city's original inventions of jazz, gospel, the blues and rock.

But fortunately, as has been amply demonstrated since at least the turn of 1900, this is the type of culture that *can* function well in diaspora, since its music can be played or listened to live or on CD or iPod anywhere. At least it is not a culture of the Eye, like Venice or Florence, cities which, once lost, will take their whole cultural heritage along with them, glued to its walls.

The inevitable sinking of New Orleans sometime later this century, however, is but a local example of a global accident that we all now find ourselves living in the midst of, with seawaters already lapping at the parking lots of Miami and the subways of New York at high tide.[14] New Orleans, in this respect, won't be unique.

Just the first.

Twelve

Sichuan, 2008
The First Man-Made Earthquake

Seismic Event

Monday, May 12, 2008, Sichuan Province, China: at 2:28:01 P.M. local time, China was hit with its worst earthquake in thirty years, recalling the 1976 Tangshan quake which killed over 240,000 people. Measuring 7.9 on the Richter scale, and transpiring for just over two minutes, the seismic waves of the Sichuan quake tore the Longmenshan Fault in two sections, the first one ripping across seven yards of lithosphere, followed by a second one that cut along four more yards. The waves radiated out from an epicenter located 80 kilometers west-northwest of the city of Chengdu, the capital of Sichuan, killing over 90,000 people.

According to Japanese seismologists, the earthquake did so much damage because the seismic waves of the quake travelled a long distance without losing their power due to the firmness of the terrain in central China, and because of the density of the population in this particular region.[1]

Indeed, the media images of this event have become associated with one of its most unfortunate consequences, that, namely, of the massive destruction of thousands of primary schools that were then in session at the moment the quake hit. Many of these buildings were of shoddy construction and have been dubbed by the locals "tofu dregs schoolhouses," as though to imply that they had been merely stacks of bricks held together by tofu.[2] Strangely, most of the buildings surrounding these schoolhouses remained intact, as though the power of the quake had specifically — and rather bizarrely — sought out all the schoolhouses in this region. Of the approximately 90,000 people killed in the quake, 19,065 of these were school children crushed by the collapsing buildings, most of them from single parent families.

The Chinese government reported that over 7,000 poorly engineered schoolhouse buildings were destroyed in the quake. Instead of using steel rods for these buildings, they were built with thin iron wires for concrete reinforcement, inferior grade cement and fewer bricks were used than normal.

Attempts by Chinese reporters to document these inferior safety standards have led to a few imprisonments in China.

Geological Singularity

But the Sichuan quake was no normal earthquake. Far from it. Indeed, in the entire geological history of earthquakes, the Sichuan quake stands apart from this series like a bizarre geological mutation. It is, in fact, something of a singularity.

For the Sichuan quake was, many experts are now saying, the world's first man-made earthquake. According to the *New York Times*, a Columbia University scientist who studied the quake has said that it may have been triggered by the weight of 320 million tons of water in the Zipingpu Reservoir which is located only 3.4 miles from the quake's epicenter. Indeed, the Zipingpu Dam, which had its reservoir filled with water in 2004, sits right in between two fault lines, the Dujiangyan-Jiangyou Fault and the Yingxui-Beichan Fault. As U.S. engineer Dr. Philip Williams was quoted as saying: "I think there are substantial grounds for connecting the triggering of the earthquake to the filling of the reservoir as a Reservoir-Induced Seismicity event (RIS)."[3] The dam's reservoir is just 5 kilometers from the earthquake's epicenter and had only recently been filled. Both conditions are consistent with the phenomena of reservoir-induced seismicity in which increased pressure from water infiltrating into microcracks and fissures in the ground under and near a reservoir lubricates faults and induces slippage.

However, the *Times* is quick to point out that scientists generally agree that a reservoir by itself, no matter how large, cannot induce an earthquake. But they also point out that the impact of so much water *could* hasten an earthquake's occurrence if there was already a predisposition in the earth's crust for the eventual occurrence of a quake. One researcher, Dr. Leonardo Seeber, said that the weight of the water in the reservoir may have hastened the earthquake's occurrence by a few hundred years.[4]

The Chinese government, of course, denies all this as nonsense, but even some of their own engineers point out that this was, indeed, the likely cause of the quake. One Fan Xiao, the chief engineer of the Sichuan Geology and Mineral Bureau in Chengdu said he thought the connection was "very likely." He points out that though researchers haven't definitively proved a causative link between the filling of the dam's reservoir and the earthquake, he believes the evidence merits careful study before any more dams in the region are built.[5]

And indeed, the Zipingpu Dam, constructed between 2001 and 2006, is part of a larger dam building project that the Chinese have embarked upon in the past few decades. This particular dam was built on the Min River, a tributary of the Yangtze, but it is the Yangtze itself that has been the focus of China's efforts in recent years. Zipingpu is part of the so-called Three Gorges Dam project, an ambitious undertaking to harness and control the dangerously flood-prone waters of the Yangtze River.

Indeed, Three Gorges Dam, constructed between 1994 and 2008 on the Yangtze River in the town of Sandouping, is the world's largest hydroelectric dam. This project itself is a monstrous feat of human engineering: the dam's main wall is 610 feet high and spans 1.3 miles from bank to bank, which is five times longer than Hoover Dam. Its 26 turbines generate 18.2 million kilowatts of energy, the equivalent of 15 nuclear power plants. The water in its reservoir, moreover, rises to 574 feet and stretches back along the Yangtze for 360 miles at an average depth of 290 feet. The river's reservoir stretches back to the city of Chongqing, holding 11 trillion gallons of water. Some scientists — though they are in the minority — suspect that its reservoir may also have played a role in the Sichuan earthquake, since it is located about 326 kilometers from the city of Chengdu, not far from the quake's epicenter.

The project is something of a technological atavism left over from a previous age of global dam building that hit its peak in the 1950s and 60s and which originated in North America, with the construction in 1935 of Hoover Dam, the world's first dam behemoth and hidden (Platonic) Idea of which Three Gorges is but a local manifestation. Hoover Dam, at the time of its construction on the Colorado River, was recorded as having set off some minor seismic events of its own. Seismicity even fluctuates in accordance with water levels in the reservoir.

The 1930s was an age of technological gigantism, especially in America, during which time the Golden Gate Bridge, the Empire State Building,

Twelve. Sichuan, The First Man-Made Earthquake

dams along the Colorado and Columbia Rivers, and also in the Tennessee Valley were built. One of the engineers who worked on America's giant dams, John Savage, was sent to inspect an early version of the Three Gorges Dam when it was seriously being planned at the end of World War II under the Nationalist government of Chiang Kai-shek. The subsequent eruption of the Chinese civil war in the late 1940s, however, put an end to this Sino-American collaboration, and so Three Gorges Dam had to wait until the 1990s to begin construction under Li Peng.[6]

Three Gorges, and its associated dams on the Yangtze's tributaries, are thus delayed reactions from the era of what Zygmunt Bauman has termed "Heavy Modernity," which ended around the time of World War II, and which was characterized by colossal engineering projects and a gigantifying tendency in technology. "Light Modernity," by contrast, was an age of micro-technologies and electronics.[7]

But the construction of Three Gorges Dam was largely undertaken to control the flooding of the Yangtze River, which has a tendency toward catastrophic floods which occur many times during the course of a century, killing thousands of people. In 1954, a massive once-in-a-century flood killed some 33,000 people.[8] Another such flood occurred only half a century later in 1998, when the river flooded and killed 4,000 people and left 14 million homeless.[9]

The Yangtze's floods, throughout the twentieth century, have been coming with greater and greater frequency and devastation. Global warming is apparently accelerating snow melt on the Tibetan Plateau, where the Yangtze receives its water source, leading to ever more catastrophic and unpredictable floods as evaporated snow falls on the Yangtze basin in the form of ever more and more severe summer monsoons. Deforestation along the banks of the Yangtze have further contributed to flooding due to destabilized soils along the river, while deforestation near the source of the river has cut down trees that would have absorbed more of the falling snow and thus allowed more of it to enter the river, further contributing to flooding.

The floods, however, alternate with waves of drought. As of 2011, the Yangtze is suffering its worst drought and lowest water levels in half a century. The water level at Wuhan located in central China, east of the dam, has fallen to less than 14 meters for the first time since 1866. Of course, much of this water is locked up by the Three Gorges Dam, which is now having the effect of causing a global warming induced drought to be much worse than it would otherwise normally be. Currently, more than 4.23 million people are having difficulty finding adequate drinking water in the lower Yangtze basin and there is not enough water for farmers in the region to water their fields or their livestock.[10]

The dam has recently been ordered to release some of its water downstream, but there are currently fears that if the drought increases, there will not be enough water in the river for the dam to help alleviate the drought all that much.

In the previous summer, on the other hand, sustained rainfall during the monsoons caused widespread flooding and led to the deaths of more than 3,000 people.

Either way, then, the Yangtze River has been destabilized by human technological systems into a bipolar modality of swinging back and forth from the extremes of droughts and floods.

Nature Inside Civilization

The 2008 Sichuan earthquake, then, qualifies as a very special type of accident, one in which the human technosphere collides with the earth's lithosphere on a gigantic scale. The impact of the force of the water in the Zipingpu Dam's reservoir against the earth's crust has resulted in the world's first man-made earthquake, or at least, the first ever occurring on such a catastrophic scale. And now, with the recent revelation that the practice of fracking near Youngstown, Ohio — in which water and chemicals are sprayed down drilling holes deep into the earth in order to force out natural gas — has been linked with a series of earthquakes that have been occurring there since March of 2011 (the fracking began the year before), in a region, furthermore, that is not seismically active, it is beginning to look like manmade earthquakes may not be quite so rare after all. Eleven of them occurred in the region during 2011, and seismologists are saying that more will come as the water continues to destabilize the crustal plates. A magnitude 4.0 quake has already occurred, and if fracking continues, it could cause larger ones.[11]

There is now no such thing, then, as a natural disaster, for the occurrence of every such disaster — which, according to insurance companies, are indeed, on the rise — nowadays inevitably brings with it the suspicion lurking somewhere in the background of human technical interference with ecosystemic properties. The degree to which rising sea levels, for instance, contributed to the severity of the tsunamis in 2004 and 2011 is still being worked out by climatologists, but my guess is that such factors will, indeed, be entered into the equations.

In the world we are making nowadays — or perhaps, "unmaking" would be better — there is no longer any such thing as a natural disaster because nature now exists *inside* human civilization. All the ancient boundaries once erected by civilization against nature were based upon center-periphery models in which walls were erected to keep "Nature" out — barbarians, mudslides, floods, what have you — in order to preserve the city as a living miniature human terrarium against erosion by the forces of Chaos.

The preservation of this human terrarium was essential in order to set aside a space separate from Nature in which human beings could spend their waking hours creating culture, with the laws of natural chaos existing in a field of invisible suspension that hovered all about them. This was, in fact, the primary reason for the existence of state governments: it was their job, through the creation of things like militias or slave labor or corvee duty, to keep the laws of nature — i.e., chaos — in a state of perennial suspension so that a kind of tensor field called "society" could then be freed up to exist in a state in which people did not have to spend all their waking hours and energy fighting off natural predators and disasters. With the governments of the archaic city states doing that for them, the artists and poets, architects and prophets could set their minds to the task of bringing a mini-world, or cultural microcosm into being.

The culture creators did this by fashioning cosmospheres, spiritual-geographical itineraries, or maps of the cosmos, that created a maximum of cognitive resonance by situating the human inhabitant of these cities inside a sphere of world order and harmony in which spiritual energies organized a cosmic space that was largely free of technological encumbrances, for the technologies of the day — the ox and the plough, irrigation, mudbricks — were meanwhile devoted to building civilization's infrastructure, or its physical body. This was tantamount to the creation of a world space in which technology was mostly outer-directed at the elements and enemies of the civilizational project. For the most part, then, such technologies did not stray into the cosmospheric world pictures built by the prophets and poets.

In this world of the ancients, civilization was a closed container ini-

Part III: Planetary Scale Disasters

tiated by the building of the first walls during the Neolithic. In ancient China, walled towns first begin appearing around 3000 B.C. during the time of the so-called Lungshan cultures. By contrast with the earlier Yangshao farming cultures, whose villages did not, generally speaking, have walls, the towns and villages of the Lungshan — such as Cheng-tzu-yai or P'ing-liang-t'ai — come equipped with 3 meter high walls built out of sun dried clay bricks. The abrupt appearance of spear tips and arrowheads, the practice of scalping, and the presence of sacrificed human bodies suggest that, by contrast with the peaceful ways of the Yangshao village farmers of earlier days, the age of the proto-towns and palaces of the Lungshan was a very dangerous time indeed.[12]

By the time of the construction of China's first great empire under the emperor Shihuangdi, the Great Wall, in its earliest form, was built as an extension of this principle: the great city was now the World City of the Empire, and the Wall was constructed in China's north to keep the barbarian Xiongnu out.[13] The Age of the Qin Empire was a time of great technological acceleration in China: new roads were being built; a new currency and standardized form of writing was coming into being; new forms of architecture with higher buildings, etc., etc.[14] In such an age of technological and cultural acceleration, the principle of the erection of a membrane against *not*-civilization, i.e., Nature and the natural law of the struggle of the fittest to survive, was magnified to gigantic size. The barbarians must be kept *out* so that *we* civilized ones can bring a cosmos into being.

Of course, the attempt by the current Chinese government to build a wall across the Yangtze in the form of the world's biggest dam is but a modernized incarnation of this same way of thinking in terms of what is now outmoded center-periphery models in which Nature is over *there* on the other side of the wall, while civilization is over *here*, i.e., the lower Yangtze valley. But as we have seen, no sooner has the dam been built and the floodwaters taken care of, than a global warming induced drought proceeds to wreck the lives of the inhabitants of civilization in the lower Yangzte valley.

There is now no place where Nature is *not*, for in the present world, all the walls and boundaries demarcating Civilization from Nature have been effaced and erased by the degree to which our global engineering projects have taken on a planetary scale and size. They are, in other words, so inter-involved now with the planet's macroscale geological and bios-

Twelve. Sichuan, The First Man-Made Earthquake

pheric processes as to be inseparable from them. If something catastrophic happens in the technosphere, it sends ripples out into the planetary ecosphere that are impossible to avoid, and vice versa. The technosphere and the ecosphere have now become an impenetrable interinvolvement, or what the Chilean biologist Francisco Varela would have called "structural coupling."[15]

In other words, for the first time in human history we have created technologies that are so gigantic that they may as well be called "cosmospheric technologies," or "cosmo-technologies" for short. Our technologies are now actually invading the ancient cosmosphere, or the realm of cosmological maps and diagrams that used to be, for the most part, constructed out of spiritual and mythological components that were largely devoid of technological ones. Nowadays, however, our technologies are invading these ancient maps and reconstructing them in such a way that their mythological components are slowly being replaced, piece by piece, with technological components.

Consider the cosmosphere built by Dante: a vision in which Satan has crashed like a meteorite into the center of an earth that has been hollowed out by his impact to create Hell, while around this earth separate spheres of planetary angelic intelligences revolve to form a cosmic music that is audible only to the poets and, of course, the dead. These spheres whirl around the earth, composed of angels, saints and the souls of the blessed dead.

But now, as we have already discussed in the chapter on the *Hindenburg* disaster, we have rebuilt this cosmosphere from the ground up with technology: Dante's whirling spheres have been replaced by an upper sphere populated by satellites, space stations and bits of space junk, from which orbiting humans can look down at the earth just as Dante's angels once did from their own orbiting spheres. And immediately beneath this sphere of orbiting space junk is the ELF sphere of electromagnetic pulse signals beaming from these satellites to the various receiver towers spread over the surface of the earth to catch and capture these disembodied voices and images and decode them into luminous, though grainy and pixilated, avatars.

Down on the earth, meanwhile, Satan's lithosphere is being pumped, mined and invaded by drills and oil presses in search of hydrocarbons so that yet another new sphere can be constructed as an evolutionary atmospheric relic from the Carboniferous Age. We are extracting Satan's black blood from the earth and putting it back into the atmosphere in the form of CO2, from whence it was taken 300 million years ago by photosynthesizing plants and trees which pumped it down in order to use the carbon to construct the cellulose and lignin parts of their bodies, bodies which were then compressed into the earth and fossilized over jillions of years. We are currently in process of reconstructing this ancient Carboniferous greenhouse sphere by putting back all the carbon dioxide that these ancient plants once pulled out of a prehistoric sky. We are, in other words, using modern technologies to reconstruct Carboniferous Cosmology.

So, with technological projects on a scale and size that they have never been before in human history, there is now no longer any place that we can point to and say "that is nature" while over there, "that is civilization." Our civilization has become so bound up with natural processes that Nature must now be considered to exist *inside* civilization and consequently, any disaster that occurs on the surface of the earth, takes place *within* civilization itself.

The implications of this new cosmology, however, for the continuing creation of "culture" as a separate sphere carefully demarcated from Nature are, I'm afraid, rather dire, for with the integration of Nature into Culture, the realm of a free and secure cosmosphere within which our artists are enabled to go about the business of building civilization is beginning to vanish. As Nature invades civilization with increasing ferocity over the next century, there will be fewer and fewer places, and less and less free time, for these culture creators to create, and as a result, culture itself may become something of an endangered species along with all the planet's other species, which are, of course, disappearing at an alarming rate.

Thus, with the fusion of human civilization and the biosphere, we find ourselves in the midst of a planetary scale disaster that is unfolding in slow motion all around us and which we find ourselves looking at, now, from the *inside*. In the civilizations and societies of the past, on the other hand, the natural disasters could be looked at from behind the walls, as it were, of the society in question, while the besieged inhabitants of the cities watched the forces of destruction mounting all around them and eventually destroying their cities. The collapse of the Mayan cities around A.D. 900, or the American Indian civilization of the Southwest around A.D. 1300, or the destruction of Neolithic village sites like Ain Ghazal (due, in this case, to deforestation), were all episodes that could be watched from *inside* the permeable containers of the societies themselves. The difference today is

Twelve. Sichuan, The First Man-Made Earthquake

that the disaster is taking place inside the container of civilization itself and there is no longer any "safe" place from which it can be observed from an outside vantage point. The civilizational process can no longer be separated from the ecospheric one. The two are collapsing simultaneously.

Thus, the collision of the industrial technosphere with the earth's bio- and geospheres is resulting in a catastrophe that is now, for the very first time, of planetary magnitude. We are witnessing the disintegration of earth's present interglacial climate as global temperatures and sea levels rise all around us with the escalation of greenhouse gases. Today, we are indeed witnessing the first man-made planetary scale accident in human history.

Each day some new effect — record tornadoes, hurricanes, floods — results from the overall catastrophe of global warming, an accident that affects us all. There is now nowhere on the planet where we can go to find safety from natural chaos. In attempting to wall Nature out by erecting bridges and dams and skyscrapers to defend ourselves against it, we have actually ended up by building it right into the very substance of our civilizational containers. The Greeks would have loved the irony of our situation and would have written great tragedies depicting our hubris and folly.

Cities, in origin, draw circles around bits of geography in order to isolate them from nature. The earliest surviving clay map from ancient Babylon shows the city in the center of the map located between the Tigris and Euphrates rivers in the shape of a rectangle. Other cities are shown as tiny circles peripheral to it. The surrounding earth itself is a macro-circle, while another circle beyond it demarcates the Great Sea where huge mountainous islands float like fantasial images out of a Sinbad tale.[16]

The problem today, though, is that we are now drawing these same circles not around this or that piece of earth and calling it "civilization," but with the extension of our technologies into the Thermosphere around the earth, we have drawn the circle demarcating "civilization" around the entire planet. So the difference now is that there is no longer any piece of land on the surface of the earth to be set aside in order for this circle to demarcate itself from Nature, with the exception of outer space.

The old human historical dialogue of society vs. nature, then, is now one single macro system of society *plus* nature. And in between them, the old circle that once demarcated "culture" is being ground up into tiny pieces.

Part III: Planetary Scale Disasters

One day soon, it may cease to exist altogether as *all* of our energies are consumed in the struggle to adapt to the conditions of a warmer earth and a drastically altered climate.

Bailing out a sinking ship leaves one with little time for basking out on the deck, soaking up the sun's rays.

Thirteen

A Satellite Collision in the Exosphere
Some Ontological Consequences

Cosmic Crash

On February 10, 2009, at 16:56 Greenwich Mean Time, a pair of orbiting space satellites — for the first time ever — crashed into each other.

The event occurred approximately 789 kilometers above the Taymyr Peninsula in Siberia when a Russian satellite known as Kosmos-2251 collided with a U.S. satellite, Iridium 33, at speeds of over 26,000 miles per hour. The satellites were moving at right angles to one another, each orbiting the earth on a south to north trajectory which crossed the other's paths to form an "X," like the X which the ancients painted on their globospheric maps to indicate the crossing of the celestial equator with the ecliptic. A significant amount of debris was sent hurtling around the earth along these two vectors, some of it reportedly even falling to the ground in places like Texas and New Mexico.[1]

The Iridium 33 satellite was a telecommunications satellite owned by the U.S. company Iridium, and it had been launched in 1997 to join the company's fleet of approximately 66 such satellites. It was fully functional at the time, although the Russian satellite, launched in 1993 by Russian Space Forces, had gone out of service by 1995. The Kosmos satellite weighed 950 kilograms (2,094 lb); the Iridium satellite weighed 560 kilograms (1,235 lb). The Kosmos satellite, incidentally, was also a communications satellite.

Although there have been other collisions of space debris before, this was the first occasion on which two orbiting satellites crossed paths and slammed into each other. According to Nicholas L. Johnson, chief scientist of orbital debris at NASA: "Nothing to this extent has ever happened before.... We've had three other accidental collisions between what we call catalog objects, but they were all much smaller than this."[2]

Part III: Planetary Scale Disasters

Space Junk

The Thermosphere above the earth, together with the lower part of the Exosphere, as it turns out, is absolutely filled with space debris. Over 18,000 man-made objects currently circle the earth, and approximately 20,000 bits of debris large enough to be cataloged have been noted.[3] But there are most likely tens of thousands more such pieces of debris — discarded tools, screws, nuts, bolts, excreted waste from astronauts — hurtling around the earth. NASA reports, furthermore, have warned that the amount of space debris in orbit about the earth has reached a critical level, with enough currently in orbit to continually collide and create even more debris, raising the risk of spacecraft failures.[4]

There is a phenomenon that has been termed the "Kessler Syndrome" which says that, once space debris reaches a certain critical point, it will begin a process of cascading in which additional debris leads to more and more collisions, such that the rate of production of more debris becomes greater than the decay rate of existing debris.[5] This chain reaction of cascading collisions would then lead to the creation of smaller and smaller bits of junk, some of it only centimeters in size, but which would become so dense that it would render space travel too hazardous to undertake. In an earlier chapter, we have already seen how, in the case of the space shuttle *Columbia*— the wing of which was hit by a two and half pound piece of foam rubber insulation — it only takes One Small Thing to destroy an entire spacecraft. Or, as the National Academy of Sciences puts it: "A 1-kg object impacting at 10 km/s, for example, is probably capable of catastrophically breaking up a 1,000-kg spacecraft if it strikes a high-density element in the spacecraft."[6]

If we step far enough back from the earth, then, in order to view it from beyond its geosynchronous orbit with an attentive eye, we can picture it surrounded by a cloud of debris as dense as a swarm of gnats in a meadow at sunset in the failing orange light of evening.

The New Invisible Environment

Readers of Marshall McLuhan know that one of his favorite points to make was how, with the sending of Sputnik into orbit in 1957, the earth, for the first time in human history, was put *inside* of a mechanical environment.[7] This increased environmental awareness, furthermore, led within just a few years to the birth of the environmental movement with the publication of Rachel Carson's *Silent Spring* in 1962.

That was the event that inaugurated the Space Age, but now, just fifty years later, we are faced with the event that marks the beginning of its *end*. For what the first ever collision of a pair of telecommunications satellites in the Exosphere indicates is that the earth now finds itself, for the first time ever, *completely surrounded and encompassed by a man-made catastrophe*. Indeed, the planet now exists *inside* of a shell of pollution and debris that will soon be hatching accidents and disasters in the heavens all around it, while bits and pieces of this debris will tumble to the earth as burning micrometeorites of technological wreckage.

In other words, with the expansion and extension of the dromosphere of speeding objects into the Thermo- and Exospheres around the earth, collisions and accidents that are the daily fare on the streets of our cities below are now being extended into the realm of outer space. "*As above, so below*"; this phrase which once expressed the basic idea of ancient cosmology as an attempt to build cities on the earth patterned in imitation of transcendent, heavenly cosmic processes has now become a technological reality. Collisions between man-made objects in rapid motion will soon be as routine in the heavens as they now are upon the earth.

The fact that these were *telecommunications* satellites is not without its significance, either. Such satellites are tantamount to a cross-pollination of the dromosphere with the mediasphere, or a crossing of what Paul Virilio once termed the "transport revolution"—with its planes, trains and automobiles—with the "communications revolution" and its phantom realm of electric ghosts and avatars.[8] Indeed, the geosynchronous satellite is a means of making the entire sphere of communications nomadic, of placing it into the rapidly moving speeds of the dromosphere, where it is hurtled at tens of thousands of miles per hour in orbit about the earth. Whenever a call is made from a cell phone that utilizes this type of technology, it sends a pulse signal beaming at light speed to one of these satellites, which then relays the signal along a chain of such satellites which then bounce it back down to the earth. The communications grid thus created by these satellites, therefore, enwraps the earth with a kind of tensegrity of electromagnetic pulse signals, imprisoning it within an electrosphere of ELF radiation.

But with the inevitable proliferation of space debris as predicted by the Kessler Syndrome, these satellites will soon be knocking each other out, as the debris eats away at the pulsing grid of signals like some bizarre technological cancer.

Once again, it becomes clear that the world of marvels opened up by industrial civilization has its limits and will remain confined within a very narrow window of historical temporality, say, two or three centuries at most, before it disappears under the weight of its own technologically generated entropy.

Indeed, we have now surrounded ourselves with this Entropy, for every technological system that has ever been invented generates its own particular type of entropy, an entropy which eventually catches up with the system in question and paralyzes it to the point where it can no longer function. In ancient Mesopotamia, for instance, the salinization of the soils and the silting up of the canals led to a gradual shutting down and paralysis of its cities, which began in the far south with the cities of Eridu, Ur and Uruk and, as the pollution spread and the local soils became unusable, gradually migrated to the north with the Babylonians and then, as these soils, in turn, were polluted, further north to the period of the Assyrians.[9] Nor was this an anomaly, for the same thing happened to the Hohokam civilization in the Southwestern United States, a society which had also been situated in a harsh desert and was based on the clever manipulation of water through canals to grow crops. But when the canals silted up, they became gradually unusable.[10]

Our present global civilization, however, is a kind of *Gesamtkunstwerk* of civilization based upon the manipulation not of this or that particular resource, but rather *all* of the earth's resources. Consequently, due to its epic scale and size, it is using them all up and leaving behind huge scars of entropic waste from its industrial processing everywhere we look: to remind us, we have merely to look up at the brownish, poisoned atmosphere, filled with greenhouse gases; or else, look out at the great swaths of broken forests littered with the stumps of felled trees; or beyond them, to the undulating desertscapes of mile after mile of mountains, hillsides and open pits from which blue, green, red and gold minerals have been stripmined to exhaustion. All other civilizations have exerted one or another of these stresses upon its particular, local environment — just think of Gilgamesh laying waste to the Cedar Forest or the inhabitants of Easter Island running out of wood with which to transport and erect their statues — but since our civilization is unique for the scope of its planetary reach, the

Thirteen. Satellite Collision in the Exosphere

scale of the devastation is now world-wide, and there is no place on the earth, consequently, that remains unaffected by it. Now, for the first time in history, we are even polluting the orbital spaces around the earth with thousands of tiny microbits of techno-junk.

The collision of the two satellites in the lower part of the Exosphere must, therefore, be regarded as a planetary-scale accident. In this respect, it is an entirely *different* kind of accident from any that has ever occurred before. Accidents which take place on the ground — accidents, that is, of the dromospheric type which involve collisions between speeding objects — remain confined to very specific, localized coordinates. Their wreckage can be cleaned up and moved out of the way, so that civilization can resume its proper functioning once again on that particular spot.

However, with the collision of the satellites in orbit, the resulting wreckage, precisely because it is in orbit, does not remain confined to one place, but is immediately dispersed around the entire earth along the orbital tracks of two separate trajectories. It is like a mechanized version of the primordial planetary collisions — such as the collision of Thea with the earth approximately 5 billion years ago — that sent a ring of dust and debris in catastrophic orbit about the planet. The difference, of course, is that in the case of the planetary collisions, the debris was able to self-organize and clump together to form our earth / moon system. Its effect, therefore, was centripetal. The debris resulting from the collision of our satellites, on the other hand — and from the future thermospheric and exospheric collisions still to come — will not clump together into anything, but will actually continue, via the Kessler Syndrome, to crash and cascade into tinier and tinier bits of space debris that will eventually result in the formation of an effective *wall* around the earth, a Thermospheric wall barring all further attempts at space exploration. The inevitable creation of such a wall of space debris about the earth will effectively seal human beings off from outer space, ironically confining and condemning them to the earth as a prison in exactly the way that Dante once pictured it as the prison of Satan who crashed into it and was never allowed to escape from it back into the cosmos again.

Thus, the satellite collision marks the beginning of a singularity, a novelty — i.e., the extension of technological accidents from the earth to the Exosphere — which is the first step in a cascading series of collisions of space junk and satellites that will slowly, inevitably, close the human world-sphere back in on itself. The world-sphere, or rather zone of human habitation, will, at that point, contract backwards toward the earth until it is contiguous with the ground itself, as it once was in the days of the ancients. By that point, space travel — rendered too dangerous because of the ubiquity of the debris — will have disappeared back into myth and folklore as a legendary phase of human endeavor spoken of with the same kind of wonder which we reserve for imagining the construction of the pyramids or the temple of Angkor Wat in Cambodia.

The profusion of debris as the Kessler Syndrome sets in past its tipping point — and this is predicted by NASA researchers to begin within the next decade or so — will knock out one communications satellite after the next, until they all go dark. So not only will the thermosphere, with its swarm of tiny particles of space junk, be rendered too hazardous for the human being ever to leave the earth again — even to orbit it from space on a pleasure trip — but the knocking out of his satellites will slowly destructure and dismantle his global civilization — or at least, the outer shell that makes much of it possible — from space, while, with his own atmospheric pollutions, his earthly cities disappear beneath rising sea levels and increasingly ferocious hurricanes on the ground below.

With the creation of a thin metallic shell made out of a finely ground mixture of space debris surrounding his home planet, the human being will then be forced to turn back inward upon himself, his 1950s dreams of rocket-finned space travel having faded from his horizons like the dying ambitions of a man who has reached middle age and knows that most of his dreams are doomed to remain forever unrealized.

Thus, the first exospheric collision, precisely because it took place in orbit around the planet, has resulted in an asymmetric effect that is out of all proportion to the small size of the accident, namely, the surrounding and encompassing of the earth *inside* of a cosmic accident, the diffusion of whose consequences will become apparent only gradually over the following decades.

We now live *inside* the debris of the first man-made cosmic accident, and the ontological consequences of this should not be lost upon us, for it means that catastrophe has now *literally* become our new invisible environment. In other words, though it seems that we can isolate ourselves by mapping out particular accidents on the x and y axes of Cartesian grids, the reality is that we are surrounded by catastrophe as the new hidden ground of our Being. It is a total surround, comprising and encompassing humanity as the new hidden environment of the 21st century.

Thirteen. Satellite Collision in the Exosphere

Any efforts made in the process of bringing civilization into being must now take place with catastrophe as the hidden *ground* upon which civilization becomes the *figure*. In other words, catastrophe can no longer be filtered out, for we have literally walled ourselves *inside of it*, and now all attempts at the further articulation of civilization must take place by factoring catastrophe into all the equations. It can no longer be gotten rid of by building Great Walls and great dams to keep it out.

Catastrophe is *part* of civilization now, just the way a severe injury resulting from an accident must become a permanent part of a man's life from henceforth.

Life, then, *will* continue.

But it will never be the same again.

Fourteen

Tiny Blue Globe
Reflections on the BP Oil Spill

Planetary Stain

First, man-made earthquakes ... and now, man-made volcanoes...

The BP oil spill — the worst ever to occur — was the result of an accident that took place at approximately 9:45 on the evening of April 20, 2010. The accident occurred on a floating oil rig called the *Deepwater Horizon*, a rig that had been manufactured in South Korea and was being leased by BP, a major petroleum company and indeed, the fourth largest corporation in the world. The rig was built and manufactured by a company called Transocean, who hired Hyundai Heavy Industries in Ulsan, South Korea, to build it for them in 2001.

Even though *Deepwater Horizon* had already drilled the world's deepest oil well successfully in September of 2009 in the Gulf of Mexico's Tiber Field — where it drilled to the almost mythical depths of 35,000 feet — by the time of the accident in 2010, the rig was already nearly a decade old and was beginning to show its age. Over two dozen components and systems were in a state of disrepair, and computers on the rig crashed routinely, while many parts were in need of replacement.[1]

One of the units most in need of repair also happened to be one of the most important for guaranteeing the safety of drilling operations, the so-called blowout preventer, or BOP, for short. The blowout preventer is a rectangular-shaped box that sits atop the wellhead; its anatomy is composed of a number of pincher devices for clamping and sealing shut the central tube, called the drill pipe, which connects the well to the rig thousands of feet above. In the event of an emergency — and if, for some reason, the crew can't activate the BOP — it is supposed to go into action automatically, but in the case of *Deepwater Horizon*, the battery unit inside one of the control pods was running low, while the other control pod was mal-

Fourteen. The BP Oil Spill

functioning due to a faulty solenoid, so the BOP never activated. There was also another problem with the BOP: a rubber gasket called an annular, which was designed to close tightly around the drill pipe, was destroyed when a crewman accidentally bumped a joystick and exerted hundreds of thousands of pounds of additional pressure on it.[2] Thus, the very restrictor valve that was designed to seal the well shut in the event of a blowout simply wasn't up to its task.

The particular well which BP was drilling lay over 18,000 feet down — the sea floor was 5,000 or so feet below the rig, and this is where the wellhead with the BOP on top of it sat, while the well reservoir lay another 13,000 feet down below the seafloor — in an area of the Mississippi Canyon which BP had named the Macondo Prospect.[3] The oil and gas at this level lay under sandstone deposits formed 20 million years ago during the Miocene Epoch as the result of the sedimentation of dead bacteria layering the bottom of the seafloor. These hydrocarbons were in a highly compressed, pressurized state, a characteristic of the geology of the Mississippi Canyon as a whole.

A previous rig named the Marianas had been drilling this same well, with little success, since October of 2009. That rig had drilled down only about 4,000 feet when Hurricane Ida damaged the Marianas so severely that the rig had to be towed away and replaced by the *Deepwater Horizon* on February 6, 2010. By the middle of April, the project was already $58 million over budget.[4]

By April 19, the crew of the *Deepwater Horizon* had already finished drilling the well to a depth of 18,360 feet and lined it with a series of metal casings, one hanging on the rim of the other above it like a series of drinking straws within drinking straws.[5] At this point, they were ready to seal the well shut with a series of three different cement plugs, one at the bottom of the well, one in the middle and one at the top. (This was only an exploratory well, not a production well; *Deepwater Horizon*'s job was just to ascertain whether there was enough oil and gas in the "pay zone" for extraction to be profitable. Another rig, a production rig, was to come along later and actually harvest the hydrocarbons.) The inside of the well itself was pumped full of drilling fluid, a substance also known as "mud," which was meant to exert sufficient downward pressure to counteract the tendency of the highly pressurized oil and gas to shoot up the well.

BP had hired Halliburton to come in and create the three cement plugs needed to seal off the well. They did so, however, using a contro-

Part III: Planetary Scale Disasters

versial type of cement known as nitrified cement, a type of cement that is foamy in composition and therefore resists being absorbed into the cracks of the sandstone. However, nitrified cement is not normally used at these depths, and certain objections were made — mainly by the rig's OIM Jimmy Harrell — to the effect that the bubbles in the cement would be crushed out of it by the high pressures of so deep a well, thereby rendering it useless. Halliburton, however, having tested the cement to their satisfaction, chose to override these objections and went ahead and installed the three plugs using nitrified cement anyway.

After the cementing was completed, the crew ran a positive pressure test on April 20 at around noon to make sure that it worked. This test was designed to see if anything in the well was leaking *out*, which it wasn't. This was then followed by a negative pressure test designed to see if any of the hydrocarbons were leaking *in*, but this test was more ambiguous.

BP wanted to replace the heavy mud inside the well with much lighter seawater so that they could then reuse the expensive mud on other projects, and so they proceeded to siphon it out, while inserting a product called "spacer" which was a viscous chemical fluid designed to separate the mud from the seawater that they were pushing in to replace the mud. This particular spacer fluid, though, was unusual in that it was composed of a mix of two different kinds of fluid normally used as sealants, Form-a-Set and Form-a-Squeeze. The problem was that they had too much of this spacer fluid, 450 barrels of it, which they couldn't throw overboard because environmental laws stipulate that no watery fluids that have not first been sent down through the well bore can be tossed overboard, so they decided to use up all the sealant as spacer fluid. Normally, about 200 barrels of spacer are used, but the crew threw in all 450 barrels of the sealant in order to get rid of it. It is possible that the viscous nature of this unconventional spacer gummed up the works and caused certain ambiguities in the negative pressure test to result.[6]

Two important lines going through the blowout preventer are the kill line and the drill pipe, and both have some of these fluids pass through them. The crew was looking for pressure readings of zero on these two lines, which would tell them that the cement plugs had worked and that the hydrocarbons were not pushing their way into the well. The pressure in the kill line gradually reduced, finally going down to zero, but the pressure in the drill pipe, on the other hand, started to rise.

They scratched their heads, repeated the test several times, but because

Fourteen. The BP Oil Spill

the kill line read zero, they decided to ignore the reading of 1,400 psi (pounds per square inch) in the drill pipe as an anomaly. Everything else seemed fine.

BP had chosen not to conduct an expensive test known as a cement bond log test due to the good results of the positive pressure test. The cement bond log test, though, would have told them whether the cement had bonded properly or not, and in hindsight, it turned out to have been a major mistake to ignore this crucial test.

The workers, however, having falsely concluded that no hydrocarbons were entering the well, finished off their testing at 7:55 on the night of the 20th, and a few minutes later, began the process of siphoning out the mud and replacing it with the lighter seawater. Once they had finished with this task, they wandered off, dispersing throughout the rig to relax, eat, sleep, shower, etc.

A powerful jet of methane gas, meanwhile, had already entered the well and was making its way up the mile long riser toward the rig. At about 9:45, some of the crew noticed that it was raining black mud on the deck of the rig. Then, after this rain of mud mixed with cement, they heard a hissing sound as methane gas rushed up the riser through the derrick and began to soak the rig in a greenish fog. The gas made its way to engine room no. 3 and was sucked up by the engine, which began to over-rev and then shut down. The rig went dark. And five seconds later, the explosions began, everywhere, all over the rig.[7] A column of fire was soon blowing out of the derrick and towering into the night sky.

Eleven people were killed on the rig; the rest, a crew of 115, escaped via lifeboats, rafts, or else jumped from the rig's 75-foot drop to the oily, chemical-stained waters below.

The rig continued to burn through the night and on into the next day, spewing a column of heavy black smoke into the air as high as the stratosphere, where it then flattened out. At 10:22 A.M. on April 21, the rig tilted over in a mighty bloom of burning orange fire and sank beneath the waters of the Gulf. It remained attached to the riser, however, which the crew, after the rig's loss of power, had not been able to disconnect, and as it fell, it tore open a couple of holes in the riser.

On the bottom of the seafloor, huge inky plumes of black oil gushed from three different holes: two rips in the riser, and one directly from the top of the failed blowout preventer. The accident caused an estimated 53,000 barrels of oil per day to stain the waters of the Mississippi Gulf with an iridescent rainbow residue that was made famously visible by satellite photos which could clearly perceive the swirling, clockwise-turning stain from the vantage point of outer space. It looked like gasoline floating in a water puddle, blown up to cosmic proportions.

Needless to say, it took BP several months to contain the spill. After repeated attempts, they finally succeeded on July 15, 2010 (after 87 days) in capping the well and shutting off the flow. On August 4, they filled the well with a massive dose of cement, thus sealing it off forever. A total of 4.9 million barrels of oil had, by that point, spilled from the well, with 4.1 million barrels ending up in the Gulf and the rest siphoned off by BP's various ships and rigs. 25 percent of the oil dissolved, and another 16 percent was naturally dispersed. BP recovered 17 percent, chemically dispersed another 8 percent, while 5 percent of it was burned and only 3 percent skimmed. That left 26 percent of the oil unaccounted for.[8]

The environmental consequences of the disaster will undoubtedly continue to unfold for many years, as shoals of dead fish, whales, dolphins and birds wash ashore on the coasts of the Louisiana wetlands. The fishing industry in that region has been badly damaged and may never completely recover. Images of brown, oil-sodden pelicans have been circulated through the media so many times that they have, by now, become postcard images, banalizing the disaster.

Genesis Technologies

The first, and most obvious, point to notice about the accident is that it did not occur as the result of any one single cause. All commentators agree that it is difficult to pinpoint any one thing as the overriding factor contributing to the accident's occurrence: Halliburton's poor cement job is certainly crucial, but so also was the shoddy state of disrepair of the rig itself, including its malfunctioning blowout preventer. BP's failure to perform a cement bond log test was a main contributing factor, but so was the crewmembers' decision to use an unusually viscous type of spacer fluid in the well, and so on, etc., etc.

Multi-causal accidents are typical of those types of systems which theoretician Peter Sloterdijk has called "relative world islands," as opposed to "absolute world islands" like space stations or shuttles which, as we have seen, are much more fragile systems that can be brought down by a single

Fourteen. The BP Oil Spill

small error.[9] The *Deepwater Horizon* oil rig is an example of a relative world island, that is to say, a technological microcosm designed to support short-term human habitation by isolating it from a particular environment, such as in the case of Biosphere 2 (whereas an absolute world island is placed inside of a *completely* hostile environment). *Deepwater Horizon* was not embedded in a completely hostile environment, as is the case in outer space, but a merely difficult one since, after all, world-making parameters such as gravity, oxygen and protection from UV rays are, under such circumstances, provided for.

Oil rigs of this type — *Deepwater Horizon* floated on pontoons — are indeed mechanized islands which can go floating about through the world's deeps like one of those islands in Tolkien's *Silmarillion* that are towed about by sea gods. Mechanized islands of this type can remain habitable only so long as they do not suffer an *elemental disruption*, such as a flood, a fire, toxic gas, etc.

Islands, of course, though, are subject to geological catastrophes like earthquakes, volcanoes and tsunamis, so we should not be *too* surprised that the fate of this particular mechanized island ended by producing its own man-made volcano. Indeed, photo images of the burning oil rig on April 21 before it sank do resemble a sort of miniature volcanic eruption, complete with its own smokestack twirling up into the stratosphere just like a Plinian cloud.

Nowadays, our technologies are so gigantic that they have attained a cosmic scale unrivalled by any of those of the past. We are in the middle of an epoch that began back in the days of Heavy Modernity in the 1930s when the colossal scale of engineering monuments like the Golden Gate Bridge, Hoover Dam and the Empire State Building evoked a certain comparison to the engineering gigantism of the monuments from the time of Ramses II in Egypt (his tomb, for instance), or the gigantic ziggurats built by Ur-Nammu in ancient Sumer, or the Hellenistic period in which the Colossus of Rhodes was built. These were, indeed, gigantic monuments, but they differ from our own present colossalism in that they were not *planetary* in scale. That is, if something went wrong with them — if the Colossus, say, fell down during an earthquake — the consequences did not reverberate around the entire planet as they tend to do with today's technologies. A nuclear reactor accident that takes place in a small town in Russia is simultaneously an accident that affects the entire globe.

But today, we humans are becoming a geo-planetary force, with cosmotechnologies that are now capable of pushing the earth's crustal plates about or amplifying its hurricanes into asymmetric monsters or else producing man-made volcanoes. These kinds of technologies, in other words, are capable of mimicking the earth's Genesis forces, the very same Genesis forces which shaped the earth over the course of 5 billion years *without us*. (This time of the earth *without us* has been termed by the French philosopher Quentin Meillassoux, the "ancestral realm."[10]) But nowadays, of course, the epic scale and scope of our engineering projects are reconstructing an anthropic version of this geo-primitive epoch of earth's formative days. A technological equivalent of a volcanic eruption is, I think it is safe to say, something completely new in human — indeed, planetary — history.

This is a development which I think is cause for a certain alarm, though, because, as the reader of this book has figured out by now, the evolution of the catastrophes that it describes indicates that the events are becoming ever larger, more all-encompassing and impossible to predict, contain or control. They are, indeed, as Paul Virilio points out, becoming Biblical in scale: with 9/11 we saw a modern rehearsal of the Tower of Babel; with the 2004 tsunami, we witnessed a modern version of the Flood; and now with uprooted populations all over the globe shifting about, we are seeing a return of the Exodus.[11] And with the BP oil spill, I would add, we have a retrieval of that pillar of smoke by day and column of fire by night which, in the Book of Exodus, led the Hebrews, during the Mediterranean Dark Age of 1300 B.C., through the desert wildernesses of Sinai.

As Marshall McLuhan pointed out, furthermore, every new medium that comes along captures a previous medium as its content — the novel becomes the content, for example, of the film, just as the film becomes the content of television, while all previous electronic media whatsoever become the content of the Internet etc., etc. — and so, following the lines of McLuhan's logic, it becomes possible to see how the *content* of the BP oil spill is actually composed of previous disasters, specifically, the sinking of the *Titanic* and the explosion of the *Hindenburg*. Our disasters, as they grow ever larger and more spectacular in scope, do so precisely by encompassing, or *folding in* as Gilles Deleuze would put it, previous disasters. This is a process that structurally replicates how one organism in evolution swallows up another: the chloroplasts in plant cells, for instance, or the mitochondria in animal cells, were once free living bacteria that became endosymbiotically taken up into the larger architecture of the complex living cell, where they were relegated to the task of performing specialized functions.[12] It is, therefore, an alarming fact — to say the least — that disasters are now *evolving* into ever larger and more complex entities, just like biological forms.

The more complex our technologies become, paradoxically, the more primordial their characteristics.

But it is also the case that the BP oil spill is merely one example of a whole new species of accident — belonging in the same genus along with the 2008 Sichuan earthquake or Hurricane Katrina — in which the *planet itself* has become the content of the new cosmotechnologies which surround and encompass it. The earth, in other words, is borrowing evolutionary principles from the crustaceans and proceeding, through human beings, to cover itself with an exoskeleton. This technoskeletal outer shell, however, has imprisoned the earth as content of the new environment of technologically induced Biblical — or Genesis scale — disasters. The effect of this gigantism is to shrink the earth down to the point where all its distances have vanished and it has become correspondingly depotentiated of its powers. *The earth is no longer allowed to shape its own worlds anymore* because technology has, apparently, usurped that role from it. It is human technical systems now that have become the planetary geomorphic force.

Hence, the unintentional side effect of the famous satellite photo of the iridescent oil stain in the Gulf brings this hidden ground out of concealment and makes clear how the earth itself (with the satellite hovering *outside* and beyond it like a sentry guard holding watch over the inmates in the prison yard down below) has become a captive of human technologies. We are presently scaling the planet down to the size of that ball which the philosophers in the 1st century B.C. mosaic from the Villa Albani in Rome have gathered around to theorize about as a problem.[13] This mosaic thus becomes the surprising analogue to the satellite photo of the oil stain, because it too reveals that, by the 1st century B.C., the earth was no more mysterious to Greek philosophers by then than it is to us now. In both cases, it has become encompassed by the gigantism of human thought: modern industrial engineering projects in our case, and the vast and cumbersome ecumene of the Hellenistic cosmopolis in that of the ancients.

The problem is, then, that by the time civilization has reached this point of complexity in its development — a development in which it has come to encircle the entire globe with human thought forms — uncertainty begins to perfuse and destabilize its sense of direction. In the case of the

Part III: Planetary Scale Disasters

ancients in about the 1st century B.C., the only direction for civilization to go was to *contract*, and so the Punic Wars that made possible the geographical extensivity of the Roman Empire gave way to the intensivity of the civil wars that ruptured the social organization from within and dismantled the political machinery of the Republic in the process. In our present case, many of us believe that the direction to continue to expand is upward into outer space.

But either way, we now find ourselves gathered together in a convocation, just like that group of philosophers depicted in the Villa Albani mosaic, to theorize about the tiny blue globe that now sits upon a footstool in front of us, and has become a problem in and of itself.

A planet stripped of its mysteries.

What *now* should we do with it?

Fifteen

On the 2011 Tohoku Earthquake, Tsunami and Fukushima Meltdown

Planetary Event

The earthquake that hit Japan on March 11, 2011, was indeed a planetary scale disaster. The 9.0 magnitude quake — the largest ever recorded in Japan and the fourth largest earthquake ever recorded in history — actually altered the earth's axial tilt by about 25 centimeters and shortened the length of its day by 1.8 millionths of a second.[1] Japan itself is now wider than it was before: the quake stretched its eastern coastline another 13 feet out into the Pacific and dropped it by about 2 feet lower.

Other earthquakes, though, have exerted similar effects: the 8.8 magnitude quake that hit Chile in 2010 — and which also caused a tsunami — shortened the day by 1.26 millionths of a second and moved the earth's axis by about 3 inches; the 2004 earthquake — 9.1 on the Richter, and hence the third largest ever — that caused the famous Indian Ocean tsunami, likewise, shortened the day by 6.8 millionths of a second.[2]

It was Immanuel Velikovsky who, back in the 1950s, was scorned by the scientific community for daring to suggest that cosmic catastrophes in the earth's ancient past could have altered the length of its year and changed the degree of its axial tilt.[3] These days, it would appear, Velikovsky's ideas no longer seem quite so far-fetched.

We are all Velikovskians now.

Triple Disaster

The Tohoku earthquake, as it's called, struck Japan at 2:46 on a Friday afternoon, rumbling buildings and structures in various cities across the island for an inconceivable six minutes. The quake's epicenter lay 62 miles off the coast of Japan, to the east, and it sent powerful tsunami waves racing at 500 miles an hour across the ocean, which began slamming into its coasts about twenty minutes after the quake with, in some cases, waves that were over 40 meters high (133 feet). The powerful waves pushed inland for about 6 miles, destroying everything in their path and sweeping whole towns into a mass of wreckage — cars, buses, ships, houses, people — that crawled over the earth like a wall of black lava. Approximately 18,000 people were killed in the disaster, ground up into the waves like the people swept away by Apocalypse in the Last Judgment paintings of sixteenth-century Flemish artists like Hans Memling and Jan Van Eyck. Much of the coast was surrounded by 10-meter-high seawalls, but because the earthquake had lowered the coast by approximately one meter (or about 3 feet), the tsunami waves were much more damaging than they otherwise might have been.

At the Fukushima Daiichi Nuclear Power Station, located right on the coast, a six-meter-high seawall had been built, but this was not nearly enough to stop the waves which poured in over it, drowning out the backup diesel generators that were crucial for supplying energy to the plant after the earthquake had knocked out its electrical power. Seismic sensors had automatically triggered the shutdown of four nuclear power stations, including Fukushima no. 1, located 240 kilometers from Tokyo, but it was necessary to have power from the backup generators in order to insert the control rods into the reactor core to stop the nuclear chain reaction. However, with the backup generators drowned by the tsunami, this was no longer a possibility. The engineers at the plant were thus forced to rely on batteries, but the batteries only had 8 hours of life in them, and when they ran out, the cooling system died. Although the main nuclear reaction had been stopped by that point, radioactive atoms like Iodine 131 and Caesium 137 continued to decay, releasing heat as a by-product. Without a cooling system, there was nothing to stop the reactor from overheating and melting down.[4]

The day after the earthquake, an explosion blew away the walls and roof of reactor no. 1. As the fuel rods had heated up, the cloud gathering around them reacted with steam to produce hydrogen gas, which exploded and sent radioactive elements out into the atmosphere. Then, two more of the plant's six reactors exploded, and the levels of radioactivity surrounding the plant rose dramatically. Ultimately, the amount of radioactivity dispersed into the atmosphere was about 1/10th that of Chernobyl.

Fifteen. The 2011 Tohoku Earthquake

Approximately 200,000 people living within a thirty kilometer exclusion zone around the plant were evacuated, permanently losing their homes, which had to be left behind, too saturated with radiation ever again to serve as dwellings, just as the inhabitants of Pripyat during the Chernobyl meltdown had had to evacuate that city, leaving a ghostly shell of crumbling, radioactive buildings behind them. The landscape around Fukushima will remain for decades the site of empty buildings, shorn of all human habitation.

The radioactive plume was blown by the winds eastward across the Pacific and eventually over the United States, then across Europe and finally, full circle, back to Asia. It has, by now, covered the earth in a sheath of radioactive elements.[5]

To prevent further core damage, the workers at the plant began pouring seawater into the crippled reactors, but much of this water, now radioactive, began to leak through cracks at the plant, some of it making its way back into the ocean.

The workers were not able to achieve what is called "cold shutdown" at the plant until December of 2011. Cold shutdown is the level at which core temperatures fall below 100 degrees Celsius and are considered safe and stable.[6] However, in the case of Fukushima, the reactors are still leaking and require large amounts of water to be continually siphoned through them in order to keep them cool. During the next few decades, the workers at the plant will have to remove spent fuel rods and go back into the reactor cores to retrieve melted fuel which, together with the rods and other contaminated equipment, will have to be buried into the earth at some unspecified point.[7]

Fears still linger, however, about just how much control the Tokyo Electric Power Company really has over the plant. There have been reports that the temperatures in the reactors are actually much higher than Tepco is saying, and there have also been calls for the nationalization of the plant, in which case, clean up will have to be handled by the Japanese government.

Japan now has plans to phase out all of its nuclear reactors, and Germany, too, has pledged to decommission all their plants by 2022, proposing to make up for the energy shortage by stepping up funding for renewables. Italy, Israel and Indonesia, furthermore, are having second thoughts about their nuclear futures, while the debate in America goes on, both for and against. India and China, meanwhile, have apparently not the slightest reluctance to continue with their plans for building more reactors.

Part III: Planetary Scale Disasters

Integral Accidents

Paul Virilio once remarked that when we say that the average height of a man is 2 meters or so, then we are still speaking in the realm of men. But if we scale up a man to the height of, say, 20 meters, then we are no longer talking about a man, but something else entirely, a giant or a troll, perhaps, out of ancient mythology.[8] Likewise, when we scale up the size of a ship to the height of an eleven storey skyscraper—as in the case of the *Titanic*—then we no longer have a ship at all, but rather a floating city. The same principle, furthermore, applies to the matter of technology taken as a whole: when it is scaled up beyond humanly manageable proportions, then it can no longer be said to be the technology of humans, but rather a technology of giants who are capable of moving mountains, relocating rivers and shifting huge chunks of the earth's crust about like the characters out of a cosmogonic epic.

Gigantic technologies, furthermore, of planetary scale and scope attract gigantic disasters. It is as good as a mathematical axiom and may as well be written as such: the larger the technology, the bigger the resulting disaster will be when it strikes.

And disaster, as the reader of this book knows very well by now, *always* strikes, sooner or later.

Our present technological world system is the outgrowth of an industrial revolution largely crafted by the British who, with their bent toward geological Uniformitarianism, created a galaxy of slow-moving huffing and puffing steam engines that gradually eroded the earth's lithosphere and atmosphere in a manner not at all dissimilar from the way in which Lyell insisted in his *Principles of Geology* that the earth was laid out, over millions of years, without any appreciable catastrophic disruptions disturbing its gradual sedimentation, lithification and stratification of the creation of the earth's crusts and mountains. Darwin, who travelled on the *Beagle* with a copy of Lyell's text beside him, created a version of evolution by natural selection that was simply the translation into biology of the uniformitarian principles of slow, gradual evolution by natural selection. No sudden mutations or jumps in the evolutionary record for Darwin, despite the fact that this is exactly what the fossil record reflects. He was insistent that the gaps between the evolution of animal forms would eventually be filled in and that the fossil record would one day show the smooth gradation of one form evolving into the next over time.[9]

Fifteen. The 2011 Tohoku Earthquake

But that, of course, hasn't happened. Instead, we now live in an age governed by catastrophism in both the sciences and in our technological landscape. The British evolution of industrial forms has now given way to the more catastrophist vision of Cuvier, in which technological forms actually devolve through repeated catastrophes on an ever widening and gigantifying scale of planetary scope. Indeed, it is as though we were today constructing an Age of Catastrophes that serves as a technological equivalent of some dim and distant geological epoch of the past in which planetary scale catastrophes were of routine occurrence.

It is now known that the moon, for instance, in its present form is the result of two separate moons that once orbited the earth and eventually collided together.[10] The earth itself was formed in a planetary collision with another planet about the size of Mars called "Thea."[11] In the days of its Hadean epoch, furthermore, it was saturated with rains of meteorites that brought little crystals of water along with them from outer space, gradually forming the earth's oceans out of an immense catastrophe of falling bodies. Gigantic hurricanes of a kind now no longer possible on the planet whirled about through these oceans, churning them up into an elemental soup. Huge volcanoes pushed their way up through these oceans to create the world's first islands that would later join together into its first continent. As the gigantic moon, much closer to the earth in those days, slowly withdrew from the earth, the planet's rapid rotation on its axis — days then were only of six hours in duration — gradually slowed down and the days became longer and longer.

In other words, a primordial Age of Catastrophes shaped the earth into its present state, and it is a new Age of Catastrophes that our geo-technologies are now recreating right before our very eyes.

Everywhere we look nowadays, we are faced with extreme events: the biggest tornadoes ever, which swept through the American Midwest in 2011; two of the four biggest earthquakes ever to have occurred, both transpiring within a decade of each other (2004 and 2011); the biggest oil spill with the BP disaster of 2010; the fourth largest hurricane ever to make landfall in the U.S. in 2005; the record setting year of the worst "natural" catastrophes (2011); the two hottest years on record (2005 and 2010); and so forth and so on, an ever ascending spiral of record setting disasters such that one can no longer clearly discern how much of this is "natural" and how much man-made.

Indeed, the triple disaster of the Japan earthquake, tsunami and nuclear reactor accident is a seamless interpenetration of man-made disasters and apparently "natural" disasters, although the use of the word "natural" here still involves a certain amount of hesitation, for we must ask: to what degree might these tsunamis have been exacerbated by rising sea levels due to global warming? And what about the increasing frequency and severity of the earthquakes themselves? Is this a natural phenomenon, or one exacerbated by the weight of the earth's oceans from melting glaciers everywhere? How much of this present lithospheric activity is connected with human drilling, fracking, and mining of the earth's resources?

We don't know, and at present, it is impossible to tell. But all of these goings on have an apocalyptic feel about them, a feel that makes Biblical folk mutter about the arrival of the end times.

They are certainly right about one thing: the end of *something* seems to be portended by all of this, and that something is the life cycle of industrial civilization which is based upon an infinitely expanding economic model that is now coming up against the reality of a finite earth with finite resources and very definite limits to the endless extractions of those resources and the disturbances of the planet's atmospheric metabolism.

The Japan earthquake and tsunami, then, is best understood as a geo-technological event: one which is so large that, like the BP oil spill, it is composed out of earlier catastrophes which have been folded up into it. Chernobyl, the 2004 tsunami, the Sichuan earthquake: all are folded — like strands of DNA packed into a nucleus — up into it, and this leaves us with the dark suspicion that we are looking at the dawning of yet another new age of disasters, one in which multiple technological and geospheric systems will become increasingly more and more intertwined to form what Paul Virilio calls "integral accidents," that is to say, accidents that cause other accidents in an infinite chain of cascading causes.

Such are the consequences of a planetary scale technology in which multiple human systems are becoming entangled together with planetary weather and eco systems, so that now we can begin to say farewell to accidents of the single event type. The days of an industrially isolated event like the sinking of a *Titanic* or the explosion of a *Hindenburg* now seem like a lost Golden Age by comparison.

Disasters are beginning to connect with each other in an alarming way. Imagine a pattern, hitherto not yet visible, in which the fires in Texas and Australia, the hurricanes in the Pacific, the tornadoes in the Midwest, and earthquakes in the Pacific basin are all interconnected together, one accident slowly linking up with another to form a densely interwoven patchwork of catastrophes, each one mutually implying and causing another, to such an extent that the human ability to manage them is eventually overwhelmed. This frightening possibility may be the "pattern that connects" the coming disasters together into ever larger and larger chains, gradually rendering human life, in its present mode, an impossibility.

To put it starkly: the biggest technological civilization that the earth has ever seen may also have unwittingly brought into being along with it the biggest stage of human-caused disasters that history has ever seen.

No Biblical Book of Revelation is necessary to make sense out of these phenomena. They are simply the end result of an industrial civilization that has slowly integrated itself into the planetary bio-metabolism to such a degree that it is becoming impossible to tell where human systems end and the natural order begins. It is precisely planetary industrial civilization itself that forms the pattern that is connecting all of these disasters together into one gigantic Global Accident that is slowly beginning to surface into view before us in the form of these record setting phenomena.

We are, then, moving into a frightening new age in which the planet is gradually becoming more and more hostile to human technological civilization.

One by one, the safety zones of the earth — those quiet little suburban towns and communities where, as the cliché goes, "nothing ever happens"— will slowly disappear as planetary catastrophes surround them on all sides.

The privileged rich who can afford beach front properties the world over will slowly become the misfortunates who are hit first, as hurricanes, tsunamis and rising sea levels gradually inundate all the world's coastal zones. These will be followed by the disappearing river systems of the planet's interiors — dissolved by rising global temperatures — which will gradually empty out towns, suburbs and cities everywhere, leaving behind huge landscapes full of empty houses, weed-blown neighborhoods and the silent, rotting skeletons of buildings and rusting automobiles.

And, as nuclear reactors melt down one by one — America's 104 reactors were mostly built in the 1970s and 80s, and so are now reaching the age when they will begin to malfunction routinely (witness the recent reactor shutdown in January 2012 at the Byron Nuclear plant in Springfield, Illinois[12])— those areas of the landscape that will be free of radioactive contamination will be fewer and fewer. Areas like Pripyat and the towns in

Part III: Planetary Scale Disasters

the exclusion zone around Fukushima will begin to spread across the planet like a cancer eating away at the landscape, leaving less and less space for arable soils to grow anything of any kind upon which to live.

As a result of the inevitable population displacements, furthermore, refugee camps like those at Darfur will begin to become common, spreading across entire continents. One by one, whole cities — like Detroit, Michigan or East Saint Louis — will begin to empty out as populations look for better lives elsewhere and begin to take to the road.

If all of this frightens you, it should. It is not an exciting prospect, and it is not the kind of world that I look forward to living in.

But then maybe these are just the visions of an anxiety-prone hysteric, and we will turn out, after all, to find some way to save civilization and to manage these catastrophes as they pop up one by one.

The problem is, though, that the more of them there are — and, as the existence of this book testifies, they do seem to be on the rise — the more such disasters will tax entire economies and exhaust the resources of the various cities and nations who will have to provide the disaster relief to combat them. With 2011 now the most expensive year on record for disasters — establishing a new precedent for their severity and ubiquity — how many more such years can we afford before whole economies start to go under in an effort to manage it all?

Life always finds a way, as the saying goes, and I'm sure that the human race will manage, one way or another, to survive all this.

But in what form, and under what reduced conditions of "civilization," will remain to be seen.

Postscript: Global Accident

So what, then, today, can we *do* about all this?

Absolutely nothing, in my opinion.

For what we need to understand is that what is unfolding all around us today is happening with the rigorous necessity of the final steps of a geometrical proof whose axioms make the conclusions inevitable. In geometry, if you want to change the outcome — find a case, say, where all three angles of a triangle *do not* add up to 180 degrees — then you have to change the initial axioms (in this case you have to shift the entire foundation of the geometry from planar to curved space). Changing the ontological foundations of the game, in other words, will shift things onto a different track with a different outcome.

But Western civilization was a World — in Heidegger's sense of the term — created by Gothic monks in the twelfth century who were fascinated with machines. Roger Bacon, Petrus Peregrinus, Robert Grosseteste, Witelo: these men preoccupied themselves with the properties of optics, magnetism, time and space. They made the first mechanical clocks, the first eyeglasses, the first magnetic compasses and the first mirrors.[1] And they did so as a kind of sacramental imitation of a cosmology in which they imagined God as a master craftsman, a maker of the cosmos-as-machine, whose cosmic task they were simply performing in miniature. These men set down the ontological foundations of Western European (Atlantic) civilization and we are *still* living inside the world they created. What is happening on the planet all around us right now is the direct outcome of their vision of the earth as invaded by a swarm of machines manifesting the Godly Light of supernal Reason. The huge mechanical armies that we have sent out across the earth to build giant bridges and dams, monstrous skyscrapers and tunnels; to strip minerals from the ground and cut away whole forests; to redirect the course of entire rivers and actually shift the tectonic plates; these armies of machines were sent out into the world by the monks of the 12th and 13th centuries. These machines were born — like the gods materializing out of subtle matter in the mind of the Hindu creator god Brahma —*inside* their skulls and they have sprung forth, like Athena cracking open the head of Zeus, into our world today, where they are playing out the final chapters of the novel that was composed by these monks.

Nothing can stop them.

For they are manifestations of an entire World Picture — which is still, to this day, in process of realizing its virtualized tendencies (in the sense in which Deleuze sees all matter as incarnating Ideas which are then realized through morphogenetic processes)[2] — and as we have seen, accidents and catastrophes haunt them because such catastrophes realize in three dimensional physical space the turbulence that is already contained, built *a priori, into* this very World Picture. A flaw in the World Picture will translate into physical reality as a flawed machine. The *a priori* assumption, for example, that human beings, those tiny ants with God-like intelligence, are capable, with all their flaws, of creating a *perfect machine*—an unsinkable ship, say, or a skyscraper that cannot be knocked down — led to the disasters of the sinking of the *Titanic*— a disaster so overloaded with hubris and arrogance that it has become proverbial — and the 9/11 terrorist attacks in which the failure to provide sufficient routes of escape to a population doomed in a burning tower was part of the initial arrogance in the design and building of that tower. The elimination of Death and the Underworld, likewise, from the cosmology of the suburbs, as we have seen, led to the attempt to *work death into* the suburbs in the form of the bloody myth of the primordial sacrifice by a couple of disaffected teenagers who were tired of living in the semiotic vacancy of the nihilism which had brought them into being. The cold impersonality of airports, as we have also seen, constrained to operate along inflexible lines that do not take human processes of decision making into account, bound Captain van Zanten's decision to take off from the airport in defiance of good common sense, and the result was an enormous tragedy. A World Picture, finally, in which human lifeworlds matter *less* than the creation of artificial chemical spheres led to the disaster of Bhopal. And so on.

So accidents, in a certain sense, are not accidental at all, but realizations of imprecisions or mistaken assumptions made in the designs of the world maps drawn up by the men who created Western civilization in its primordial Gothic days when its mind was first beginning to awaken. The present conquest of the earth by these cosmotechnologies facilitated and realized by governments and multinational corporations is the inevitable outcome of those first principles that were constitutive parts of a World Picture in which the earth becomes the plaything of human beings using the spark of God to help them conquer it.

The course of this megamachine can, I believe, neither be stopped, nor slowed, nor even altered. We have geared it up and set it rolling, and it *will* continue its course no matter what we do at this point. There is simply too much inertia behind it to slow it down or derail it. It is in process, right this very moment, of slowly colliding with the biosphere, the lithosphere and the cosmosphere; it is, indeed, a single gigantic accident that is taking place now in slow motion and *inside which* we find ourselves contained, moving at a slower temporal biometabolism that gives us the illusion that we *might* be able to stop it.

But Paul Virilio's Integral Accident that he has prophesied for years is, in fact, *already* happening all around us, and to try and stop it would be like attempting to stop a bullet that is already mid-way through its course.[3] We are presently in the middle of a Cambrian explosion of machines whose fragments are in mid-flight across the earth, and they are impacting the biosphere in ways that are profoundly reshaping it.

The standard cliché is, of course, that it is not too late for us to change things if we only conserve more energy, recycle, go green, use power more efficiently, etc. But these activities will ultimately have little effect on this global accident that is already in full swing because its enormous momentum will average them out due to the truly *massive* scale of the cosmotechnological explosion that is in force all around us. Such strategies do not attack the roots of the problem, which are the *fundamental assumptions* made cosmologically and ontologically by Western — now Planetary — civilization. It is those very assumptions that would have to be changed in order to alter the course that we are now locked onto, but of course, it is now far too late in the game to change *any* of those assumptions. Going green will only prolong the life cycle of a civilization and a way of life that *is itself* the problem.

In order to halt this cosmotechnological explosion or slow it down, we would have to shut off all the machines right this very minute: simply unplug them, tell the multinationals to forget about their profits and let it all go to ruin before our very eyes. But as we know very well, this is an impossibility: billions of people, out of work, displaced, rendered homeless, exurban and nomadic, would starve to death, and in addition, riots and civil wars the likes of which the planet has never seen would then descend upon us.

The machines, at this point, are keeping all seven billion of us alive. But as Thom Hartmann puts it: "There's obviously a collision coming between our growing population, with its increasing consumption of dwindling supplies of ancient sunlight, and our ability to sustain that population."[4]

Moreover, there is a clear conflict of interest between implementing regulations against these corporations and doing further damage to an already debilitated world economy. The more they are regulated and told to conserve, the more money they lose and the more people find themselves out of work, and so, the worse the economy gets. The political right doesn't want to conserve energy because of the profits they know that doing so will cost them. The left, on the other hand, seems prepared to accept the massive unemployment and impoverishment that will result from implementing such measures. Both sides are caught in a deadlock in which neither can win.

So the machines aren't going to go away any time soon. They *will* continue spewing CO_2 and other greenhouse gases into the atmosphere no matter how many Kyoto Protocols are signed, and that means that the global temperature *will* continue to rise, along with sea levels, bringing more and more ferocious storms, hurricanes and earthquakes along with them. Indeed, most climate scientists are already saying that it is too late to halt global climate change, for even if all emissions ceased tomorrow, the amount of CO_2 presently in the atmosphere would require *centuries* to cycle back down. We have the words of climatologist Mark Lynas to this effect, as he writes in *Six Degrees*:

> Even if we stopped increasing atmospheric CO_2 tomorrow, it would take many centuries for the Earth to once again reach thermal equilibrium in a new, hotter state. Expecting today's Pliocene CO_2 levels [i.e., 400 ppms] to equate to Pliocene temperatures [i.e., 3 degrees hotter than now] straight away would be like expecting a kettle to boil instantly.[5]

Or, as the atmospheric chemist James Lovelock puts it: "Even if we stopped immediately all further seizing of Gaia's land and water for food and fuel production and stopped poisoning the air, it would take the Earth more than a thousand years to recover from the damage we have already done, and it may be too late even for this drastic step to save us."[6]

Postscript

So, as a result of this thermal inertia, we are locked in for another degree, or possibly even two, of global mean temperature rise, no matter *what* scenario transpires. And that means diminishing food, drought, famine, drying rivers, and resource scarcity that will begin to fuel ever more and more tribal conflicts which will result in larger and larger groups of displaced peoples and refugees. Shanty towns and refugee camps like the one in Dadaab in Kenya — the world's largest — will soon be proliferating everywhere. As Paul Virilio has written:

> The twenty-first century will be the century of mass migrations. A billion people will move. The whole world situation will be disrupted. Disrupted by the crisis in localization. The old societies were connected to a territory, a native land. Today they're adrift due to the delocalization of jobs and never-ending conflicts. There is also, clearly, the major issue of climate: the disappearance of archipelagoes, submersion of coastlines. This means all of history is on the move again. All of history is taking to the road. A billion people moving over half a century — that's never been seen before... It's almost as though the sky, and the clouds in it, and the pollution of it, were making their entry into history.[7]

In other words, we are looking at the coming Africanization of the entire globe.

So, find yourself a good seat in the stadium and make yourself comfortable, if you can. Because the drama of the machines *will* continue to unfold as they go crashing into each other and into the planetary biospheric systems until they, and our civilization, are ground to pieces. Count on it.

The exurbanization of the planet, meanwhile, will soon begin. Our coastal cities, not too far from now, will be finding themselves caught in an ever spiraling economic battle of building dykes, dams and seawalls with which to defend themselves against an ocean that *will not stop rising* no more than the sun will stop rising. The dilemma of counting the costs involved in building up these walls vs. simply abandoning the cities — which Katrina has already given us a glimpse of — will soon be preoccupying the minds of most of our city politicians. Eventually, though, they will lose the battle and the ocean will win, for even the most conservative models are predicting the submerging, *first*, of their airports and subways, *then* their downtown city streets and *finally* their suburbs within the next 50 or so years. Bit by bit, they will have to be abandoned and their populations will drift away to the north to cooler, drier latitudes.

But the good that will come out of this devastation is that the present civilization, with its terrific and terrifying depredations, its basic hostility to a properly human way of life, will finally be put to rest and will become a gigantic junkyard, the largest the world has ever seen. Indeed, the countryside all around us will be filled with ancient rusting hulks of rotting, broken down machines and corroding heaps of steel and iron. Piles of charred, burnt metal and blown out machines; the cracked and crumbling walls of former skyscrapers, their girders exposed to the air like broken ribs; and the silence, all around us, of an aviation-free sky. When that happens, new plans for a new civilization may then be drawn up, with new premises and new axioms that will result in a completely different outcome.

Hopefully, the next one will be more sane.

Appendix: A Disaster Timeline

A complete timeline of all the disasters that have taken place since the year 1900 would demand a book unto itself. Suffice it to say, then, that I have listed only the most prominent disasters, of both the technological and the "natural" kind, since it is becoming increasingly more and more difficult to tell the difference between them. I have, however, not listed any "natural" disasters that occurred prior to the last decade of the twentieth century, since this corresponds in time to the period of the first noticeable effects of global warming.

June 15, 1904: The passenger steamboat *General Slocum* catches fire in New York's East River; more than 1,000 people are killed.

February 23, 1910: Great Northern Railway Disaster, in which an avalanche tumbles down over a train in the Cascade Mountains, leaving 96 people dead.

March 25, 1911: Triangle Shirtwaist fire; 146 people, most of them young girls, are killed due to lack of safety exits in the ten storey building they were working in.

April 14, 1912: Sinking of the *Titanic;* 1,504 dead.

May 7, 1915: *Lusitania* is torpedoed and sinks; 1,198 killed (first attempt to deliberately mimic a technologically induced disaster, for the event is a simulacrum of the sinking of the *Titanic*).

December 6, 1917: Halifax explosion, in which a French cargo ship, carrying war munitions, accidentally collides with a Norwegian ship, causing the largest man-made explosion in history prior to Hiroshima, and killing over 2,000 people.

August 23, 1921: Crash of the British airship R38, which kills 44 people onboard.

December 18, 1923: Crash of the French airship the *Dixmude* while on a flight around the Mediterranean.

September 2, 1925: Crash of the American airship the *Shenandoah* in a violent storm above Ohio. Fourteen of the 43 people onboard are killed.

Appendix

March 12, 1928: collapse of William Mulholland's Saint Francis Dam in Santa Clarita, California; 600 people killed.

May 25, 1928: Crash of the airship *Italia* into Arctic ice; 8 or so killed; survivors stranded on the ice for almost two months before being rescued.

October 5, 1930: Crash of the British airship R101, on a voyage to India from Britain. Forty-eight people of the 54 onboard are killed. This ends the airship service for the British.

April 3, 1933: Crash of the U.S. Navy airship the *Akron* into the ocean off the shore of New Jersey. Seventy-two of the 76 men onboard are killed.

February 12, 1935: Crash of the airship the *Macon* off the coast of Point Sur, California. Nobody is killed, but the crashes of the *Macon* and the *Akron* end the airship business for the Americans.

May 6, 1937: *Hindenburg* explodes in a 34 second fire; 33 people killed; this ends the rigid airship permanently as a mode of passenger transport.

November 7, 1940: Tacoma narrows bridge collapses due to wind perturbations.

August 6, 1945: Hiroshima as the first disaster of Neomodernity, in which long term consequences from radiation poisoning extend across generations. Approximately 100,000 people killed in the blast.

January 10, 1954: British Overseas Airways Corporation Flight 781 suffers an explosive decompression at high altitude and crashes into the Mediterranean, killing all 35 people onboard.

October 10, 1957: Windscale Fire nuclear facility accident near Cumberland in Britain; reactor core caught fire.

1959: Simi Valley nuclear facility accident.

December 8, 1963: Pan Am Flight 214, a flight from Baltimore to Philadelphia, crashed after being struck by lightning, killing all 81 people onboard.

January 17, 1966: Palomares Incident: A U.S. B-52 bomber collided with a KC-135 tanker during mid-air flight refueling over the coast of Spain. The tanker was completely destroyed in the incident, while the B52 broke apart, spilling four hydrogen bombs from its broken fuselage. The non-nuclear weapons in two of the bombs detonated on impact, contaminating a 490 acre area with radioactive plutonium.

June 5, 1966: Feyzin, Rhone, France: explosion at the Feyzin refinery.

March, 1967: the first major oil spill occurs when the supertanker the Torrey Canyon spills 35 million gallons of Kuwaiti oil off the shores of Cornwall and Brittany.

January 21, 1968: Thule accident: cabin fire aboard a B-52 forced the crew to abandon their craft; bomber then crashed onto sea ice near Thule Air Base in Greenland, causing the nuclear payload to rupture, which resulted in widespread radioactive contamination.

A Disaster Timeline

June 22, 1969: the Cuyahoga River in Ohio catches fire as the result of an oil slick in the river that is possibly ignited by a spark from a passing train. The fire burns for only thirty minutes, but it does $50,000 worth of damage, primarily to railroad tracks. This helps to spur the Cleanwater Act of 1972.

July 28, 1976: Seveso, Italy; dioxin gas leak from Icmesa factory.

March 27, 1977: Tenerife, Canary Islands: two 747 jumbo jets collide on runway killing 583 people in the deadliest aviation accident in history.

March 17, 1978: Portsall, Finistere, France: wreck of the tanker *Amoco Cadiz*, which spills 69 million gallons of Iranian crude oil into the ocean around Brittany.

May 25, 1979: American Airlines Flight 191 out of O'Hare International Airport in Chicago crashes moments after takeoff, killing all 271 people onboard.

March 28, 1979: Three Mile Island.

April 2, 1979: Sverdlovsk Incident in which at a Soviet biological facility a cloud of anthrax was released, spreading the disease to 96 people. Approximately 100 people died.

June 3, 1979: the Ixtoc I, a Mexican drilling rig, blows out and explodes, leaking 140 million gallons of crude oil in the Gulf of Mexico.

July 17, 1981: Hyatt Regency hotel balcony collapse in Kansas City, Missouri, kills 114 people and injures 216 others.

January 13, 1982: Air Florida Flight 90 crashes into the Potomac, killing 78 people.

December 4, 1984: Bhopal, India; poison gas leak from the Union Carbide Factory.

May 29, 1985: Heysel stadium disaster in which 39 people were killed and over 600 injured in a brawl between English and Italian soccer fans; the people died when a wall collapsed.

July 19, 1985: The Val di Stava dam collapses near Tessero in northern Italy, killing 268 people.

August 10, 1985: Russian nuclear submarine K-439 Chazhma Bay accident: 10 sailors killed, 49 injured with radiation.

January 28, 1986: explosion of the space shuttle *Challenger*.

April 26, 1986: Chernobyl disaster.

December 22, 1988: Lockerbie, Scotland; crash of Pan Am Boeing 747; 247 killed as the result of a terrorist bomb exploding onboard.

March 6, 1987: Zeebrugge Ferry disaster results in the deaths of 193 people.

September 13, 1987: Goiana, Brazil, radiation accident from opening of an abandoned radiation therapy machine at a junkyard; several city blocks had to be demolished.

Appendix

July 6, 1988: Piper Alpha oil drilling platform explodes in the North Sea, killing 167 men.

April 1, 1989: *Exxon Valdez* oil spill: after altering its course to avoid ice, the crew is unable to steer the ship and Bligh Reef slices it open, spilling 11 million gallons of Alaskan crude oil.

April 22, 1992: Guadalajara gas explosions in the sewer system kill 252 people.

October 4/5, 1992: Amsterdam, Netherlands: crash of a cargo plane into two high rise apartment buildings; 43 people killed.

September 22, 1993: the Amtrak train Sunset Limited derails and some of the cars crash into the water off a bridge near Mobile, Alabama.

January 17, 1995: A 6.9 earthquake hits Kobe, Japan, and kills 5,500 people, injuring 26,000.

March 20, 1995: Aum Shinrikyu nerve gas attack in Tokyo subway (deliberate attempt to mimic a poison gas leak, such as at Bhopal).

June 29, 1995: Sampoong Department Store in Seoul, South Korea, collapses, killing 501 people.

May 11, 1996: ValuJet Flight 592 crashes into Florida Everglades, killing all 110 people onboard.

July 17, 1996: TWA Flight 800 crashes 12 minutes after takeoff from JFK on its way to Rome, just off the coast of East Morches, New York, killing all 230 people onboard.

November 21, 1996: Humberto Vidal gas explosion in a building in Puerto Rico kills 33 and wounds more than 80.

August 9, 1997, Kingman, Arizona: derailment of a passenger train after passing over a bridge that was damaged by a storm.

February 3, 1998: Cable car accident in the Italian town of Cavalese occurs when a low-flying Grumman EA-6B Prowler of the United States Marine Corps severs a cable and causes the cable car to crash to the ground below, killing all occupants.

June 3, 1998: Eschede, Germany: ICE train derailment; 70 killed.

March 24, 1999: Nairobi, Kenya: derailment of train; 32 killed.

April 20, 1999: Columbine High School near Littleton, Colorado; 12 killed.

May 3–6, 1999: 66 tornadoes break out in Oklahoma and Kansas, killing 50 people.

September 30, 1999: Tokaimura nuclear facility accident, northeast of Tokyo.

October 5, 1999: Paddington Rail Disaster: a London-bound express train collides with a commuter train, killing 32 people.

December 13, 1999: Brest, France: sinking of the oil tanker *Erica*.

July 25, 2000: Air France Flight 4590, a Concorde, crashes just after takeoff in Gonesse, France, on its way to New York; all one hundred passengers

A Disaster Timeline

and nine crewmembers killed; the Concorde as a type of craft was retired after this crash; 113 people killed, four of them on the ground in a hotel where it crashed.

August 12, 2000: Russian nuclear submarine Kursk sinks in the Barents Sea after an onboard explosion, killing all 118 crewmembers.

November 11, 2000: Kaprun railway car fire in Austria results in the deaths of 155 skiers, who were trapped in the train car in an ascending tunnel.

September 11, 2001: World Trade Center attack.

November 12, 2001: crash of Flight 587 in Queens, New York (terrorism or accident? Fatal confusion).

November 21, 2001: Krefeld, Germany; fire on a cargo vessel at Bayer chemical company wharf; toxic fumes and nitric acid leak into the Rhine.

February 1, 2003: space shuttle *Columbia* explodes.

December 26, 2004: Indian Ocean tsunami killed approximately 300,000 people.

March 23, 2005: BP oil refinery in Texas City, Texas, explodes, killing 15.

August 29, 2005: Hurricane Katrina kills nearly 2,000 people.

March 2, 2006: BP spills 200,000 gallons of oil in Prudhoe Bay, due to corrosion in oil pipes, and failure to properly clean or "pig" them.

April 16, 2007: Virginia Tech massacre; 33 people killed.

August 1, 2007: I-35W Mississippi River Bridge collapses in Minnesota, killing 13 people and injuring 145.

May 12, 2008: 8.0 earthquake in Sichuan, China, set off by Zipingu Dam, kills 90,000.

September 13, 2008: Los Angeles commuter train crash; 25 killed.

June 1, 2009: Air France flight 447 crashes into the Atlantic on its way from Rio de Janeiro to Paris as a result of automated systems failure and kills all 200 plus people onboard.

January 12, 2010: 7.0 magnitude earthquake in Haiti; death toll somewhere between 100,000—300,000.

February 22, 2011: 6.3 earthquake in Christchurch, New Zealand, the second deadliest ever recorded there, kills 181 people.

April 5, 2010: Upper Big Branch coal mine disaster, in which an explosion killed 29 miners.

April 20—July 15, 2010: BP oil spill in which offshore drilling rig Deepwater Horizon caught fire, killing 11 people and spilling up to 4.9 million barrels worth of oil into the Mississippi Gulf.

March 11, 2011: 9.0 earthquake, tsunami and Fukushima reactor accident in Japan kills 18,000 people.

April, 2011: worst tornado outbreak in U.S. history occurs in Midwest, killing 43 people with 179 tornadoes across 16 states. A second, much worse, wave later in the month of 336 tornadoes kills 346 people throughout the Midwest in the worst tornado outbreak ever recorded.

July 22, 2011: Anders Breivik shootings at a summer camp in Norway result in 77 deaths and 151 injuries.

August 20–29, 2011: Hurricane Irene travels up the eastern coast of the United States as a tropical storm that kills 56 people and inflicts massive flooding in Vermont and New Jersey, causing a total of 10 billion dollars worth of property damage. For the first time in a century, New York is targeted by the bull's eye of the hurricane, but it downgrades to tropical storm at the last moment.

September, 2011: the most catastrophic wildfires in Texas history rage through the state, burning over 34,000 acres and destroying 1,554 homes. The fires are exacerbated by an ongoing Southern U.S. drought and desertification, possibly due to global warming.

September 16, 2011: airplane crash at an airshow in Reno, Nevada; 11 people killed.

October 23, 2011: Earthquake in Van, Turkey, measuring 7.2, kills over 600 people.

January 13, 2012: the cruise ship *Costa Concordia* partially sinks and runs aground at Isola del Giglio, Tuscany. Fifteen people are killed, including 14 passengers and one crewman. Sixty-four others are injured and 23 are missing.

January 22–23, 2012: Outbreak of 28 tornadoes in Mississippi, Alabama, Tennessee, Illinois, Kentucky, Indiana and Missouri; 3 fatalities.

Summer, 2012: Worst drought in the United States in half a century erupts across Midwest, inviting comparison with the Great Dust Bowl of the 1930s.

June, 2012: Wildfires erupt across Colorado, causing nearly half a billion dollars in damage and forcing the evacuations of over 34,000 people. Five people are killed and over 600 homes are destroyed.

July 20, 2012: largest shooting spree in American history occurs when one James Eagan Holmes kills 12 and injures 58 more at a movie theater in Aurora, Colorado.

August 6, 2012: a large fire erupts at a Chevron Refinery in Richmond, California.

Chapter Notes

Introduction

1. See "NOAA: 2010 Tied for Warmest Year on Record" on the National Oceanic and Atmospheric Administration website: http://www.noaanews.noaa.gov/stories/2011/20110112_globalstats.html.

2. See "Chinese Earthquake May Have Been Man-Made, Say the Scientists" on the *Telegraph* website: http://www.telegraph.co.uk/news/worldnews/asia/china/4434400/Chinese-earthquake-may-have-been-man-made-say-scientists.html.

3. See Mark Lynas, *Six Degrees: Our Future on a Hotter Planet* (Washington, D.C.: National Geographic, 2008), 68.

4. Paul Virilio, *Unknown Quantity* (London: Thames & Hudson, 2003), 59.

5. See "2009: Second Warmest Year on Record; End of Warmest Decade" on the NASA website: http://www.nasa.gov/topics/earth/features/temp-analysis-2009.html.

6. See "Big Quake Question: Are They Getting Worse?" online at www.msnbc.msn.com/id/35618526/ns/world_news-chile_earthquake/t/big-quake-question-are-they-getting-worse/

7. See Eric Niiler, "Geologists Say Ohio Quakes Directly Tied to Fracking," MSNBC, January 6, 2012, http://www.msnbc.msn.com/id/45903873/ns/technology_and_science-science/t/geologists-say-ohio-quakes-directly-tied-fracking/—.TycN08VYutY.

8. See "Earthquake Predictions: Alarming Facts About Earthquake Trends," www.small-farm-permaculture-and-sustainable-living.com/earthquake_predictions.html.

9. See, for example, Kiefer's "Monumenta 2007" art exhibition in Paris at the Grand Palais. A video version of the exhibit can be viewed on YouTube at http://www.youtube.com/watch?v=zV-QXn6C_T0.

A Brief Note

1. Martin Heidegger, *History of the Concept of Time: Prolegomena* (Bloomington: Indiana University Press, 1992), 187–88.

2. Oswald Spengler, *Man and Technics: A Contribution to a Philosophy of Life* (New York: Alfred A. Knopf, 1932).

3. Lewis Mumford, *Technics and Civilization* (New York: Harcourt Brace, 1934).

4. Marshall McLuhan, *The Mechanical Bride: Folklore of Industrial Man* (Corte Madera, CA: Gingko Press, 2002).

5. Jacques Ellul, *The Technological Society* (New York: Vintage Books, 1967).

6. Marshall McLuhan, *Understanding Media: The Extensions of Man* (Cambridge: MIT Press, 1994).

7. Arnold Toynbee, *A Study of History: Abridgement of Volumes I-VI* (New York: Oxford University Press, 1987), 255.

8. For the decline in funerary standards after the 21st century, see John H. Taylor, *Death and the Afterlife in Ancient Egypt* (Chicago: University of Chicago Press, 2001), 87.

9. See Thorkild Jacobsen, *Salinity and Irrigation Agriculture in Antiquity: Diyala*

Chapter Notes

Basin Agricultural Report on Essential Results, 1957–58 (Malibu: Undena Publications, 1982), 63.
10. See Barbara Stoler Miller, ed., *Love Song of the Dark Lord: Jayadeva's Gita Govinda* (New York: Columbia University Press, 1977).

Part I

1. See especially Zygmunt Bauman, *Liquid Modernity* (Cambridge, UK: Polity Press, 2000), 54.
2. Ulrich Beck and Johannes Williams, *Conversations with Ulrich Beck* (Cambridge, UK: Polity Press, 2004), 115.
3. Ulrich Beck, *World at Risk* (Cambridge, UK: Polity Press, 2009), 68.

Chapter One

1. See the National Geographic documentary *Seconds from Disaster: Sinking of the Titanic*, which can be found online at http://www.youtube.com/watch?v=0_cDl XEwaDU.
2. Peter Sloterdijk, *Spheres I: Bubbles* (Los Angeles: Semiotexte, 2011), 24–25.
3. Benedict Anderson, *Imagined Communities* (London: Verso, 1991).
4. Siegfried Giedion, *Space, Time and Architecture* (Cambridge: Harvard University Press, 1982), 179.
5. Paul Virilio, *Negative Horizon* (New York: Continuum, 2006), 154–55.
6. J.P. Mallory, *In Search of the Indo-Europeans* (London: Thames & Hudson, 1991), 198.
7. See the website CO2 Now at http://co2now.org/.
8. Mark Lynas, *Six Degrees* (Washington, D.C.: National Geographic Society, 2008), 86–87.
9. Ibid., 216–17.
10. James Lovelock, *The Revenge of Gaia: Earth's Climate Crisis and the Fate of Humanity* (New York: Basic Books, 2007), 55.

Chapter Two

1. See the National Geographic documentary *Seconds from Disaster: The Hindenburg*, which can be found online at www.youtube.com/watch?v=ShFLID PoSoA.
2. Douglas Botting, *Dr. Eckener's Dream Machine: The Great Zeppelin and the Dawn of Air Travel* (New York: Henry Holt, 2001), 28.
3. Rick Archbold and Ken Marschall, *Hindenburg: An Illustrated History* (New York: Warner Books, 1994), 48.
4. Gilles Deleuze and Félix Guattari, *A Thousand Plateaus* (Minneapolis: University of Minnesota Press, 1987), 351.

Part II

1. Ulrich Beck and Johannes Williams, *Conversations with Ulrich Beck* (Cambridge, UK: Polity, 2004), 4–5.
2. See the interview with Peter Sloterdijk entitled "Spheres Theory: Talking to Myself About the Poetics of Space," which can be found online at eyondentropy.aa school.ac.uk/?p=689.

Chapter Three

1. See the PBS documentary made by Nova, *The Deadliest Plane Crash* (2007).
2. Martin Heidegger, *A History of the Concept of Time* (Bloomington: Indiana University Press, 1992), 34.
3. Marc Auge, *Non-Places: Introduction to an Anthropology of Supermodernity* (New York: Verso, 1995).
4. Michel Foucault, *Discipline and Punish* (New York: Vintage Books, 1979), 193.
5. See especially Alain Badiou, *Ethics: An Essay on the Understanding of Evil* (New York: Verso, 2002).
6. On the annihilation of the culturally authentic "thing" by scientific values, see Martin Heidegger, *Poetry, Language, Thought* (New York: Harper Perennial, 2001), 168.

7. My conception of "world" vs. "antiworld" runs parallel with, but does not borrow from, Jean-Luc Nancy's opposition of "globalization" vs. "unworld" or *globalisation* vs. *immonde*. See Jean-Luc Nancy, *The Creation of the World or Globalization* (Albany: SUNY Press, 2007), 34.

8. Ibid., pp. 111–12.

Chapter Four

1. See the National Geographic documentary *Seconds from Disaster: Bhopal Nightmare*, which can be found online at http://www.youtube.com/watch?v=iOgfzUh02lA.

2. See the BBC documentary *One Night in Bhopal*, which can be found online at http://www.youtube.com/watch?v=uz73rcdSG80&feature=related.

3. See the article "Methyl isocyanate" on Wikipedia, http://en.wikipedia.org/wiki/Methyl_isocyanate.

4. See the article "Bhopal disaster" on Wikipedia, http://en.wikipedia.org/wiki/Bhopal_disaster.

5. Ibid.

6. Tim Edwards, "How Many Died in Bhopal?" online at http://www.bhopal.net/oldsite/death-toll.html.

7. Peter Sloterdijk, *Terror from the Air* (Los Angeles: Semiotexte, 2009), 10.

8. Paul Hawken, *The Ecology of Commerce* (New York: Harper Business, 1994), 31.

9. Gilles Deleuze, *The Fold: Leibniz and the Baroque* (Minneapolis: University of Minnesota Press, 1992).

10. See Titus Burckhardt, *Alchemy: Science of the Cosmos, Science of the Soul* (Louisville: Fons Vitae, 1997).

11. See Lucretius, *The Nature of Things* (New York: Penguin Classics, 2007), "Book I: Matter and Void."

12. Zygmunt Bauman, *Liquid Modernity* (London: Polity Press, 2000), 54–59.

13. Fernand Braudel, *Civilization and Capitalism, Volume I: The Structures of Everyday Life* (New York: Harper & Row, 1985), 23–24.

Chapter Five

1. See the documentary *The Last Flight of the Space Shuttle Challenger* which can be found online at http://www.youtube.com/watch?v=gOpq_IYjZ_g&feature=related.

2. Roger Boisjoly, "A Management Decision Overrides a Recommendation Not to Launch," Online Ethics Center, http://www.onlineethics.org/Topics/ProfPractice/Exemplars/BehavingWell/RB-intro/Override.aspx.

3. See the NASA documentary *Challenger Accident Investigation* (1986), which can be found online at http://www.youtube.com/watch?v=MKG4bvZGWag.

4. This quote has been taken from the following video: *Seconds from Disaster: Columbia's Last Flight* which can be found on YouTube, http://www.youtube.com/watch?v=RUHcJeEyZvw&feature=fvwrel.

5. And this "small thing," it should be noted, is not the same thing as the famous Butterfly Effect of Chaos Theory, in which a sensitivity to the initial conditions of a system explodes in a nonlinear manner which can cause catastrophic failure in the later evolution of that system. In accidentology, the One Small Thing, rather, is an effect of the random, the uncertain, the aleatory: the wheel of the Concorde which (on July 25, 2000) at takeoff, just happens to run over a piece of metal that causes a blowout which eventually causes the crash of the plane; the piece of foam rubber that just happens to crash into the space shuttle's wing, etc. The Butterfly Effect, by contrast, is a type of nonlinear effect that results from a structural flaw that is intrinsic to the system.

6. See Peter Sloterdijk, *Neither Sun Nor Death* (Los Angeles: Semiotexte, 2011), 220–21.

7. Martin Heidegger, *Basic Writings* (New York: Harper Perennial, 2008), 317.

Chapter Six

1. Indeed, Svetlana Alexeivitch has called it "the largest technological disaster of the twentieth century." See Svetlana Alexeivitch, *Voices from Chernobyl: The Oral History of a Nuclear Disaster* (New York: Picador, 2006), 1.
2. Piers Paul Read, *Ablaze: The Story of Chernobyl* (London: Mandarin Paperbacks, 1994), 56.
3. "Chernobyl disaster," Wikipedia, http://en.wikipedia.org/wiki/Chernobyl_disaster.
4. *Disaster at Chernobyl*, Discovery Channel documentary which can be found on YouTube, http://www.youtube.com/watch?v=Qe_sD7bPSvg&NR=1.
5. Pierpaolo Mittica, *Chernobyl: The Hidden Legacy* (London: Trolley Books, 2007), 42–43.
6. Read, 321.
7. *The Battle of Chernobyl*, documentary which can be found on YouTube at http://www.youtube.com/watch?v=yiCXb1Nhdlo.
8. Mittica, 23.
9. Ibid., 17.
10. Robert Polidori, *Zones of Exclusion: Pripyat and Chernobyl* (Göttingen: Steidl, 2003), 9, 11.
11. John David Ebert, *The New Media Invasion: Digital Technologies and the World They Unmake* (Jefferson, NC: McFarland, 2011), 19–21.
12. See Alain Badiou, *Being and Event* (London: Continuum, 2007), 173.
13. See Ibn Khaldun, *The Muqqadimah: An Introduction to History* (Princeton: Princeton University Press, 1967), 43.

8. See the essay "Strong Observation for a Space Station Philosophy" by Peter Sloterdijk in *Native Land: Stop Eject*, edited by Paul Virilio and Raymond Depardon (Paris: Actes Sud, 2009), 29–36.

Chapter Seven

1. The foregoing is based largely on the scenario described in the National Geographic documentary *Seconds from Disaster: Amsterdam Air Crash* which can be found online at http://www.youtube.com/watch?v=Lganu0iYxu0.
2. See the National Geographic documentary entitled *Seconds from Disaster: High Speed Train Wreck*, which is available online at http://www.youtube.com/watch?v=O-UNxGSZUJc.
3. See "Eschede train disaster," http://en.wikipedia.org/wiki/Eschede_train_disaster.
4. For the "dromosphere," see the concluding chapter of Paul Virilio, *The University of Disaster* (London: Polity Press, 2010).
5. Gilles Deleuze and Félix Guattari, *A Thousand Plateaus* (Minneapolis: University of Minnesota Press, 1987). See the chapter "1227: Treatise on Nomadology — the War Machine."
6. Alain Badiou, *Being and Event* (New York: Continuum, 2007).
7. See Paul Virilio, *Desert Screen: War at the Speed of Light* (London: Continuum, 2005), 7.
8. Again, see Paul Virilio, in this case, *Speed and Politics* (Los Angeles: Semiotexte, 2006), 35–36.
9. See, of course, the works of Marija Gimbutas, especially *The Civilization of the Goddess* (New York: HarperCollins, 1994).
10. See Mircea Eliade, *A History of Religious Ideas*, Volume 1 (Chicago: University of Chicago Press, 1982): for the Asvins, see page 193; for Indra, see pages 205–08; for Thor, see Volume 2, pages 163–66; for Gaia and the Titans, see pages 247–48.
11. For the story of Lugalbanda, see Jeremy Black, Graham Cunningham, Eleanor Robson, Gábor Zólyomi, *The Literature of Ancient Sumer* (Oxford: Oxford University Press, 2006), 22.

Chapter Notes

12. James Hillman, *Re-Visioning Psychology* (New York: Harper & Row, 1976), 128.
13. Michel Foucault, *Security, Territory, Population: Lectures at the College de France 1977-1978* (New York: Picador, 2007), 325.
14. Gilles Deleuze, *The Fold: Leibniz and the Baroque* (Minneapolis University of Minnesota Press, 1992).

Chapter Eight

1. Haruki Murakami, *Underground: The Tokyo Gas Attack and the Japanese Psyche* (New York: Vintage, 2000), 10.
2. David E. Kaplan and Andrew Marshall, *The Cult at the End of the World: The Terrifying Story of the Aum Doomsday Cult, from the Subways of Tokyo to the Nuclear Arsenals of Russia* (New York: Crown, 1996), 124.
3. Ibid., 25.
4. Ibid., 35.
5. Akira Sadakata, *Buddhist Cosmology: Philosophy and Origins* (Tokyo: Kosei, 1998), 27-33.
6. For an image of this map, see the photo on http://www.henry-davis.com/MAPS/AncientWebPages/103.html.
7. For an image of a Medieval T-O map, see the photo on http://www.mapsanddirections.us/cartography.htm.
8. See Marshall McLuhan, *Understanding Me: Lectures and Interviews* (Cambridge: MIT Press, 2005), 264.
9. The term "socius" comes from Gilles Deleuze and Félix Guattari, *Anti-Oedipus: Capitalism and Schizophrenia* (New York: Penguin, 2009), 139.
10. See Arnold Toynbee, *A Study of History: An Abridgment of Volumes I—VI by D.C. Somervell* (New York: Oxford University Press, 1974), 375.
11. Gilles Deleuze and Félix Guattari, *A Thousand Plateaus* (Minneapolis: University of Minnesota Press, 2005), 111.
12. See *The Mahabharata, Volume I: The Book of the Beginning*, trans. J.A.B. Van Buitenen (Chicago: University of Chicago Press, 1980).
13. For a diagram of a Japanese tombstone see Sadakata, 24.
14. See the Patrick Olivelle translation of *The Upanishads* (New York: Oxford University Press, 1996), 289-90.
15. Louis G. Perez, *The History of Japan* (Westport, CT: Greenwood, 2009), 84.

Chapter Nine

1. See the documentary *The Columbine Killers*, which can be found online at http://www.youtube.com/watch?v=l853KaRheqw&feature=results_video&playnext=1&list=PL1DB9BB59A1DCF6DC.
2. See the documentary *Zero Hour: Massacre at Columbine High*, which can be found online at http://www.youtube.com/watch?v=FZZCwLeaAJQ&feature=related.
3. The image of the cops hiding behind the fire truck is clearly visible at 2:39 in the documentary *Columbine Shooting: The Final Report 2/5*, which can be found here: http://www.youtube.com/watch?v=5R80uTxQg6c&feature=related.
4. Jürgen Habermas, *The Structural Transformation of the Public Sphere* (Cambridge: MIT Press, 1991), 159-75.
5. See, for example, Thompson's discussion of how the ancient Paleolithic goddess figurines illustrate this primordial iteration of how the One becomes Two in William Irwin Thompson, *Coming Into Being: Artifacts and Texts in the Evolution of Consciousness* (New York: St. Martin's Press, 1996), 108.
6. The opening montage of the Showtime television show *Weeds* captures this principle of suburban seriality and repetition perfectly.
7. Unfortunately, it is precisely this process of the interjection of singularity as difference into a series of *spatial* universals which Deleuze does *not* discuss in his famous book, which deals with Repetition

Chapter Notes

only as a temporal phenomenon. See Gilles Deleuze, *Difference and Repetition* (New York: Columbia University Press, 1994).

8. See Heiner Mühlmann, *MSC Maximal Stress Cooperation: The Driving Force of Cultures* (Wien: Springer, 2005).

9. René Girard, *Violence and the Sacred* (Baltimore: Johns Hopkins University Press, 1977), 49.

10. See Emmanuel Levinas, *Basic Philosophical Writings* (Bloomington: Indiana University Press, 2008), 54.

11. See, for example, Christopher Hitchens, *God Is Not Great: How Religion Poisons Everything* (New York: Twelve, 2009) or Sam Harris, *The End of Faith: Religion, Terror and the Future of Reason* (New York: W.W. Norton, 2005).

12. Zygmunt Bauman, *Community: Seeking Safety in an Insecure World* (Cambridge, UK: Polity Press, 2001), 54.

13. Dave Cullen, *Columbine* (New York: Twelve, 2009), 239.

Part III

1. See Arjun Appadurai, *Modernity at Large* (Minneapolis: University of Minnesota Press, 1996), 22.

2. Appadurai has elsewhere termed this an opposition of cellular vs. vertebrate structures. International terrorist groups, such as Al Qaeda or the Tamil Tigers, etc., are cellular in opposition to vertebral nation state formations. See Arjun Appadurai, *Fear of Small Numbers: An Essay on the Geography of Anger* (Durham: Duke University Press, 2006), 21–31.

3. Ulrich Beck, *World At Risk* (Cambridge, UK: Polity Press, 2009), 68.

4. Paul Virilio, *Negative Horizon: An Essay in Dromoscopy* (London: Continuum, 2007), 59.

5. See Manav Taneeru, "It's Official: 2005 Hurricanes Blew Records Away," http://articles.cnn.com/2005-12-19/weather/hurricane.season.ender_1_intense-storms-national-hurricane-center-hurricane-season?_s=PM:WEATHER.

6. See Mark Hertsgaard, *Hot: Living Through the Next 50 Years on Earth* (New York: Houghton Mifflin, 2009), 9.

7. Elaine Chow, "Was the Sichuan Earthquake Man-Made?" http://shanghaiist.com/2009/02/03/was_the_sichuan_earthquake_manmade.php.

Chapter Ten

1. Anthony Summers and Robbyn Swan, *The Eleventh Day: The Full Story of 9/11 and Osama bin Laden* (New York: Ballantine, 2011), 74.

2. See "Spheres Theory: Talking to Myself about the Poetics of Space by Peter Sloterdijk," which can be found online at beyondentropy.aaschool.ac.uk/?p=689.

3. Rick Archbold and Ken Marschall, *Hindenburg: An Illustrated History* (New York: Warner Books, 1994), 38.

4. W.G. Sebald, *On the Natural History of Destruction* (New York: Random House, 2003), 26–28.

5. The consequences of this are first evident in the Dutch art of the 17th century, for with the world ceiling now out of the way, the heavens become visible for the first time in the vast, spatially expansive canvases of Jan van Goyen or Jacob Ruisdael.

6. See Gilles Deleuze and Félix Guattari, *A Thousand Plateaus* (Minneapolis: University of Minnesota Press, 1987), especially the "Treatise on Nomadology," 351–423.

7. See also Paul Virilio, *Speed and Politics* (Los Angeles: Semiotexte, 2006), especially the opening chapter on "The Dromocratic Revolution," for a discussion on how cities step down the power of the dromosphere with obstructions.

8. Ibn Khaldun, *The Muqqadimah: An Introduction to History* (Princeton: Princeton University Press, 1967), 43.

9. Albert Hourani, *A History of the Arab Peoples* (Cambridge, MA: Belknap Press, 1991), 334.

Chapter Notes

10. Lawrence Wright, *The Looming Tower: Al-Qaeda and the Road to 9/11* (New York: Alfred A. Knopf, 2006), 25.
11. For a discussion of the symbolism of this cosmic sky pillar, the classic work to consult is, of course, Hertha von Dechend, *Hamlet's Mill: An Essay Investigating the Origins of Human Knowledge and its Transmission Through Myth* (Boston: David R. Godine, 1977).
12. See Andrew George, *The Epic of Gilgamesh: A New Translation* (New York: Barnes and Noble Books, 1999), 46.
13. See the article "Nuwa" on Wikipedia at http://en.wikipedia.org/wiki/N%C3%BCwa.
14. See the opening discussion of weapons of destruction vs. weapons of obstruction in Paul Virilio, *Desert Screen: War at the Speed of Light* (New York: Continuum, 2005).
15. Heiner Mühlmann, *MSC Maximal Stress Cooperation: The Driving Force of Cultures* (Wien: Springer, 2005), 60.
16. See the article "B-25 Empire State Building crash" on Wikipedia at http://en.wikipedia.org/wiki/B-25_Empire_State_Building_crash.
17. See the article "Siege of Ta'if" on Wikipedia at http://en.wikipedia.org/wiki/Siege_of_Ta%27if.

Chapter Eleven

1. See the article "Danziger Bridge shootings" on Wikipedia at http://en.wikipedia.org/wiki/Danziger_Bridge_shootings.
2. The clip from *60 Minutes* can be found online at www.youtube.com/watch?v=FYhkjvJ-XG8.
3. Douglas Brinkley, *The Great Deluge: Hurricane Katrina, New Orleans, and the Mississippi Gulf Coast* (New York: William Morrow, 2006), 27–29.
4. See the article "2005 Atlantic hurricane season" on Wikipedia at http://en.wikipedia.org/wiki/2005_Atlantic_hurricane_season.
5. Brinkley, 76.
6. Jed Horne, *Breach of Faith: Hurricane Katrina and the Near Death of a Great American City* (New York: Random House, 2008), 18.
7. Mark Lynas, *Six Degrees: Our Future on a Hotter Planet* (Washington, D.C.: National Geographic Society, 2008), 65–66.
8. Ibid., 68.
9. See the interview with Sloterdijk, "Beyond Entropy: When Energy Becomes Form" online at beyondentropy.aaschool.ac.uk/?p=689.
10. See Giorgio Agamben, *Homer Sacer: Sovereign Power and Bare Life* (Stanford: Stanford University Press, 1998).
11. Michel Foucault, *Security, Territory, Population: Lectures at the College de France, 1977–1978* (New York: Picador, 2007), 325.
12. See Mary Settegast, *Plato Prehistorian: 10,000– 5,000 BC Myth, Religion, Archaeology* (Hudson, NY: Lindisfarne Books, 1990), 196.
13. See, for example, William Irwin Thompson, "This Time, Let's Build a New Venice and Not Another New Orleans," which can be found online at http://www.williamirwinthompson.org/essays.html.
14. For those in need of ocular proof, they can consult the video "Sea Level Rise Impacts on Florida and Miami," a video which can be found here: http://www.youtube.com/watch?v=O0KB19eOP8Q.

Chapter Twelve

1. See "2008 Sichuan Earthquake," en.wikipedia.org/wiki/2008_Chinese_earthquake.
2. See "Sichuan schools corruption scandal" on Wikipedia at http://en.wikipedia.org/wiki/Sichuan_schools_corruption_scandal.
3. From the following online article: http://www.probeinternational.org/catalog/contentfullstory.php?contentId=6840&catid=7.

Chapter Notes

4. Sharon LaFraniere, "Possible Link Between Dam and China Quake," *The New York Times*, Feb. 5, 2009, which can be found online here: http://www.nytimes.com/2009/02/06/world/asia/06quake.html?pagewanted=all.
5. See the following online article: http://blogs.discovermagazine.com/80beats/2009/02/02/did-a-new-hydropower-dam-trigger-chinas-deadly-2008-earthquake/.
6. Deirdre Chetham, *Before the Deluge: The Vanishing World of the Yangtze's Three Gorges* (New York: Palgrave-Macmillan, 2002), 145.
7. See Zygmunt Bauman, *Liquid Modernity* (Cambridge, UK: Polity Press, 2000), 54.
8. See "1954 Yangtze River Floods," http://en.wikipedia.org/wiki/1954_Yangtze_River_Floods.
9. See "Flooding in China Summer 1998," wf.ncdc.noaa.gov/oa/reports/chinaflooding/chinaflooding.html.
10. See "Worst Drought in 50 Years Along the Yangtze," usa.chinadaily.com.cn/epaper/2011-05/25/content_12576632.htm.
11. See Eric Niiler, "Geologists Say Ohio Quakes Directly Tied to Fracking," MSNBC website, January 6, 2012, found at http://www.msnbc.msn.com/id/45903873/ns/technology_and_science-science/t/geologists-say-ohio-quakes-directly-tied-fracking/—.TycN08VYutY.
12. K.C. Chang, *The Archaeology of Ancient China* (New Haven: Yale University Press, 1987), 255.
13. Mark Edward Lewis, *The Early Chinese Empires: Qin and Han* (Cambridge: Belknap Press of Harvard University Press, 2007), 55.
14. Ibid., 54–55.
15. Humberto R. Maturana and Francisco Varela, *The Tree of Knowledge: The Biological Roots of Human Understanding* (Boston: Shambhala Books, 1992), 75.
16. For an image of this clay map, see the picture on the website http://www.henry-davis.com/MAPS/AncientWebPages/103.html.

Chapter Thirteen

1. Bill Harwood, "U.S. and Russian Satellites Collide," http://www.cbsnews.com/stories/2009/02/11/tech/main4792976.shtml.
2. William J. Broad, "Debris Spews Into Space After Satellites Collide," *New York Times*, http://www.nytimes.com/2009/02/12/science/space/12satellite.html.
3. See "The Objects Orbiting the Earth: What Is Space Junk and Where Does it Come From?" http://www.guardian.co.uk/technology/2009/feb/13/space-junk-orbits-earth.
4. See Christian Torres, "Report says space debris past 'tipping point,' NASA needs to step up action," http://www.washingtonpost.com/national/health-science/reports-says-space-debris-past-tipping-point-nasa-needs-to-step-up-action/2011/08/31/gIQAo6WTuJ_story.html.
5. See the article "Kessler syndrome" on Wikipedia at http://en.wikipedia.org/wiki/Kessler_syndrome.
6. National Research Council, *Orbital Debris: A Technical Assessment* (Washington, D.C.: National Academies Press, 1995), 4.
7. Marshall McLuhan, *McLuhan Unbound* (Corte Madera, CA: Gingko Press, 2005), "At the Moment of Sputnik the Planet Became a Global Theater in Which There Are No Spectators but Only Actors."
8. See Paul Virilio, *Negative Horizon: An Essay on Dromoscopy* (New York: Continuum, 2006), 154–55.
9. See Thorkild Jacobsen, *Salinity and Irrigation Agriculture in Antiquity: Diyala Basin Agricultural Report on Essential Results, 1957–58* (Malibu: Undena Publications, 1982), 63.
10. See Robert H. Lister and Florence C. Lister, *Those Who Came Before: South-*

Chapter Notes

western Archaeology in the National Park System (Tucson: Southwest Parks & Monuments Association, 1993), 28.

Chapter Fourteen

1. Carl Safina, *A Sea in Flames: The Deepwater Horizon Oil Blowout* (New York: Crown, 2011), 9.
2. See the "The Blowout," *60 Minutes* http://www.youtube.com/watch?v=db 9T0XYKhrA&feature=related.
3. John Konrad and Tom Shroder, *Fire on the Horizon: The Untold Story of the Gulf Oil Disaster* (New York: Harper, 2011), 56.
4. Safina, 5.
5. Ibid., 6–7.
6. Joel Achenbach, *A Hole at the Bottom of the Sea: The Race to Kill the BP Oil Gusher* (New York: Simon & Schuster, 2011), 221.
7. Ibid., 26–27.
8. Ibid., 233.
9. See Peter Sloterdijk, "Spheres Theory: Talking to Myself About the Poetics of Space," http://beyondentropy.aaschool.ac.uk/?p=689.
10. See Quentin Meillassoux, *After Finitude: An Essay on the Necessity of Contingency* (New York: Continuum, 2008), esp. "Chapter 1: Ancestrality."
11. See Paul Virilio, *The Administration of Fear* (Los Angeles: Semiotexte, 2012), 29–30.
12. This was the endosymbiosis theory of microbiologist Lynn Margulis. See my interview with her in John David Ebert, *Twilight of the Clockwork God: Conversations on Science & Spirituality at the End of an Age* (San Francisco: Council Oak Books, 1999), 68–87.
13. See Peter Sloterdijk, *Spheres I: Bubbles* (Los Angeles: Semiotexte, 2011), illustration on page 65.

Chapter Fifteen

1. See the BBC documentary "Japan Earthquake: A Horizon Special" which can be found online at http://www.youtube.com/watch?v=klUcDJKfsfE&feature=relatedd.
2. Kenneth Chang, "Quake Moves Japan Closer to U.S. and Alters Earth's Spin," *The New York Times*, March 13, 2011, http://www.nytimes.com/2011/03/14/world/asia/14seismic.html?scp=4&sq=japan%20earthquake%20march%202011&st=csee.
3. See Immanuel Velikovsky, *Worlds in Collision* (New York: Doubleday, 1950).
4. See the Frontline documentary "Nuclear Aftershocks," which can be found online at http://www.pbs.org/wgbh/pages/frontline/nuclear-aftershocks/.
5. According to physicist Michio Kaku, interviewed on *60 Minutes*, found at http://www.youtube.com/watch?v=DcOol3KJscc&feature=related.
6. Geoff Brumfiel, "Fukushima Reaches Cold Shutdown," Nature.com, December 16, 2011, http://www.nature.com/news/fukushima-reaches-cold-shutdown-1.9674.
7. "Japan PM Says Fukushima Site Finally Stabilised," www.bbc.co.uk/news/world=asia=16212057.
8. Paul Virilio, *Grey Ecology* (New York: Atropos Press, 2009), 33.
9. Immanuel Velikovksy, *Earth in Upheaval* (New York: Doubleday, 1955), 21–30.
10. Richard Lovett, "Early Earth May Have Had Two Moons," Nature.com, August 3, 2011, http://www.nature.com/news/2011/110803/full/news.2011.456.html.
11. See the National Geographic documentary "Earth: the Making of a Planet," found online at http://www.youtube.com/watch?v=e1-F4lxJPo0.
12. See "Byron Generating Station, Illinois Nuclear Plant, Shutdown Investigated by Officials," AP, January 31, 2012, http://www.huffingtonpost.com/2012/01/31/byron-generating-station-illinois-nuclear_n_1243335.html.

Postscript

1. See the chapter "The Monastery and the Clock" in Lewis Mumford, *Technics and Civilization* (New York: Harcourt, Brace, 1963), 12.

2. See Gilles Deleuze, *Difference and Repetition* (New York: Columbia University Press, 1994), 244–54.

3. See Paul Virilio, *The Original Accident* (Cambridge, UK: Polity Press, 2007), 70.

4. Thom Hartmann, *The Last Hours of Ancient Sunlight: The Fate of the World and What We Can Do Before It's Too Late* (New York: Broadway, 2004), 19.

5. Mark Lynas, *Six Degrees: Our Future on a Hotter Planet* (Washington, D.C.: National Geographic, 2008), 134.

6. James Lovelock, *The Revenge of Gaia: Earth's Climate Crisis & The Fate of Humanity* (New York: Basic Books, 2007), 6.

7. Paul Virilio, Raymond Depardon, et. al., *Native Land: Stop Eject* (Paris: Fondation Cartier, 2009), 7–8.

Bibliography

Achenbach, Joel. *A Hole at the Bottom of the Sea: The Race to Kill the BP Oil Gusher.* New York: Simon & Schuster, 2011.

Agamben, Giorgio. *Homo Sacer: Sovereign Power and Bare Life.* Stanford: Stanford University Press, 1998.

Alexeivitch, Svetlana. *Voices from Chernobyl: The Oral History of a Nuclear Disaster.* New York: Picador, 2006.

Anderson, Benedict. *Imagined Communites.* London: Verso Books, 1991.

Appadurai, Arjun. *Fear of Small Numbers: An Essay on the Geography of Anger.* Durham: Duke University Press, 2006.

____. *Modernity At Large.* Minneapolis: University of Minnesota Press, 1996.

Archbold, Rick, and Ken Marschall. *Hindenburg: An Illustrated History.* New York: Warner Books, 1994.

Auge, Marc. *Non-Places: Introduction to an Anthropology of Supermodernity.* London: Verso Books, 1995.

"B-25 Empire State Building crash." Wikipedia, the Free Encyclopedia. 16 January 2012. http://en.wikipedia.org/wiki/B-25_Empire_State_Building_crash

Badiou, Alain. *Being and Event.* New York: Continuum, 2007.

____. *Ethics: An Essay on the Understanding of Evil.* London: Verso Books, 2002.

Battle of Chernobyl, The. Online documentary. http://www.youtube.com/watch?v=yiCXb1Nhdlo.

Bauman, Zygmunt. *Community: Seeking Safety in an Insecure World.* Cambridge, UK: Polity Books, 2001.

____. *Liquid Modernity.* Cambridge, UK: Polity Press, 2000.

Beck, Ulrich. *World at Risk.* Cambridge, UK: Polity Press, 2009.

____, and Johannes Williams. *Conversations With Ulrich Beck.* Cambridge, UK: Polity Press, 2004.

"Bhopal disaster." Wikipedia, the Free Encyclopedia. 23 January 2012. http://en.wikipedia.org/wiki/Bhopal_disaster.

"Big Quake Question: Are They Getting Worse?" MSNBC. February 27, 2010. www.msnbc.msn.com/id/35618526/ns/world_news-chile_earthquake/t/big-quake-question-are-they-getting-worse/.

Black, Jeremy, Graham Cunningham, Eleanor Robson and Gábor Zólyomi, eds. *The Literature of Ancient Sumer.* Oxford: Oxford University Press, 2006.

Boisjoly, Roger. "A Management Decision Overrides a Recommendation Not to Launch." Online Ethics Center. http://www.onlineethics.org/Topics/ProfPractice/Exemplars/BehavingWell/RB-intro/Override.aspx.

Botting, Douglas. *Dr. Eckener's Dream Machine: The Great Zeppelin and the Dawn of Air Travel.* New York: Henry Holt, 2001.

Braudel, Fernand. *Civilization and Capitalism, Volume I: The Structures of Everyday Life.* New York: Harper & Row, 1985.

Brinkley, Douglas. *The Great Deluge: Hurricane Katrina, New Orleans, and the Mississippi Gulf Coast.* New York: William Morrow, 2006.

Broad, William J. "Debris Spews Into

Bibliography

Space After Satellites Collide." *The New York Times*, February 11, 2009. http://www.nytimes.com/2009/02/12/science/space/12satellite.html.

Brumfiel, Geoff. "Fukushima Reaches Cold Shutdown." Nature.com, December 16, 2011. http://www.nature.com/news/fukushima-reaches-cold-shutdown-1.9674.

Burckhardt, Titus. *Alchemy: Science of the Cosmos, Science of the Soul.* Louisville: Fons Vitae, 1997.

"Byron Generating Station, Illinois Nuclear Plant, Shutdown Investigated by Officials." Associated Press, January 31, 2011. http://www.huffingtonpost.com/2012/01/31/byron-generating-station-illinois-nuclear_n_1243335.html.

Challenger Accident Investigation. NASA documentary. http://www.youtube.com/watch?v=MKG4bvZGWag.

Chang, K.C. *The Archaeology of Ancient China*. New Haven: Yale University Press, 1987.

Chang, Kenneth. "Quake Moves Japan Closer to U.S. and Alters Earth's Spin." *The* New York Times, March 13, 2011. http://www.nytimes.com/2011/03/14/world/asia/14seismic.html?scp=4&sq=japan%20ear thquake%20march%202011&st=csee.

"Chernobyl Disaster." Wikipedia, the Free Encyclopedia. 16 January 2012. http://en.wikipedia.org/wiki/Chernobyl_disaster.

Chetham, Deirdre. *Before the Deluge: The Vanishing World of the Yangtze's Three Gorges*. New York: Palgrave-Macmillan, 2002.

Chow, Elaine. "Was the Sichuan Earthquake Man-Made?" Shanghaiist.com. 3 February 2009. http://shanghaiist.com/2009/02/03/was_the_sichuan_ear thquake_manmade.php

The Columbine Killers. Online documentary. http://www.youtube.com/watch?v=l853KaRheqw&feature=results_video&playnext=1&list=PL1DB9BB59 A1DCF6DC.

Columbine Shooting: The Final Report. Online documentary. http://www.youtube.com/watch?v=5R80uTxQg6c&feature=related.

"Court Issues Arrest Warrant for Former CEO of Union Carbide in Gas Leak Case." Associated Press. *The Guardian UK*. http://www.guardian.co.uk/world/2009/jul/31/warren-anderson-arrest-warrant.

Cullen, David. *Columbine*. New York: Twelve, 2009.

"Danziger Bridge Shootings." Wikipedia, the Free Encyclopedia. 24 January 2012. http://en.wikipedia.org/wiki/Danziger_Bridge_shootings.

The Deadliest Plane Crash. Dir. Chantal Hebert. Nova Documentary, 2006.

Deleuze, Gilles. *Difference and Repetition.* New York: Columbia University Press, 1994.

———. *The Fold: Leibniz and the Baroque.* Minneapolis: University of Minnesota Press, 1992.

———, and Félix Guattari. *Anti-Oedipus: Capitalism and Schizophrenia*. New York: Penguin Books, 2009.

———, and ———. *A Thousand Plateaus*. Minneapolis: University of Minnesota Press, 1987.

Disaster at Chernobyl. Discovery Channel documentary. http://www.youtube.com/watch?v=Qe_sD7bPSvg&NR=1.

Earth: The Making of a Planet. National Geographic documentary. http://www.youtube.com/watch?v=e1-F4lxJPo0.

"Earthquake Predictions: Alarming Facts About Earthquake Trends." Fantastic Farms.com.au. www.small-farm-permaculture-and-sustainable-living.com/earthquake_predictions.html.

Ebert, John David. *The New Media Invasion: Digital Technologies and the World They Unmake*. Jefferson, NC: McFarland, 2011.

———. *Twilight of the Clockwork God: Conversations on Science & Spirituality at the End of an Age*. San Francisco: Council Oak Books, 1999.

208

Bibliography

Edwards, Tim. "How Many Died in Bhopal?" http://www.bhopal.net/oldsite/death-toll.html.

Eliade, Mircea. *A History of Religious Ideas, Volume 1*. Chicago: University of Chicago Press, 1981.

———. *A History of Religious Ideas, Volume 2*. Chicago: University of Chicago Press, 1982.

Ellul, Jacques. *The Technological Society*. New York: Vintage Books, 1967.

"Eschede Train Disaster." Wikipedia, the Free Encyclopedia. 23 January 2012. http://en.wikipedia.org/wiki/Eschede_train_disaster.

"Flooding in China Summer 1998." NCDC website. 20 August 2008. http://lwf.ncdc.noaa.gov/oa/reports/chinaflooding/chinaflooding.html.

Foucault, Michel. *Discipline and Punish*. New York: Vintage Books, 1979.

———. *Security, Territory, Population: Lectures at the College de France, 1977–1978*. New York: Picador, 2007.

George, Andrew. *The Epic of Gilgamesh: A New Translation*. New York: Barnes and Noble Books, 1999.

Giedion, Siegfried. *Space, Time and Architecture*. Cambridge: Harvard University Press, 1982.

Gimbutas, Marija. *The Civilization of the Goddess*. New York: Harper Collins, 1994.

Girard, René. *Violence and the Sacred*. Baltimore: Johns Hopkins University Press, 1977.

Habermas, Jürgen. *The Structural Transformation of the Public Sphere*. Cambridge: MIT Press, 1991.

Harris, Sam. *The End of Faith: Religion, Terror and the Future of Reason*. New York: W.W. Norton, 2005.

Hartmann, Thom. *The Last Hours of Ancient Sunlight: The Fate of the World and What We Can Do Before It's Too Late*. New York: Broadway, 2004.

Harwood, Bill. "U.S. and Russian Satellites Collide." CBS News online. http://www.cbsnews.com/stories/2009/02/11/tech/main4792976.shtml.

Hawken, Paul. *The Ecology of Commerce*. New York: Harper Business, 1994.

Heidegger, Martin. *Basic Writings*. New York: Harper Perennial, 2008.

———. *History of the Concept of Time: Prolegomena*. Bloomington: Indiana University Press, 1992.

———. *Poetry, Language, Thought*. New York: Harper Perennial, 2001.

Hertsgaard, Mark. *Hot: Living Through the Next 50 Years on Earth*. New York: Houghton Mifflin, 2009.

Hillman, James. *Re-Visioning Psychology*. New York: Harper and Row, 1976.

Hitchens, Christopher. *God Is Not Great: How Religion Poisons Everything*. New York: Twelve, 2009.

Horne, Jed. *Breach of Faith: Hurricane Katrina and the Near Death of a Great American City*. New York: Random House, 2008.

Hourani, Albert. *A History of the Arab Peoples*. Cambridge, MA: Belknap Press, 1991.

Jacobsen, Thorkild. *Salinity and Irrigation Agriculture in Antiquity: Diyala Basin Agricultural Report on Essential Results, 1957–58*. Malibu: Undena Publications.

Japan Earthquake: a Horizon Special. BBC documentary. http://www.youtube.com/watch?v=klUcDJKfsfE&feature=relatedd.

"Japan PM Says Fukushima Site Finally Stabilised." http://www.bbc.co.uk/news/world-asia-16212057.

Kaplan, David E., and Andrew Marshall. *The Cult at the End of the World: The Terrifying Story of the Aum Doomsday Cult, from the Subways of Tokyo to the Nuclear Arsenals of Russia*. New York: Crown Books, 1996.

"Kessler Syndrome." Wikipedia, the Free Encyclopedia. 20 January 2012. http://en.wikipedia.org/wiki/Kessler_syndrome.

Khaldun, Ibn. *The Muqqadimah: An In-*

Bibliography

troduction to History. Princeton, NJ: Princeton University Press, 1967.

Konrad, John, and Tom Shroder. *Fire on the Horizon: The Untold Story of the Gulf Oil Disaster.* New York: Harper, 2011.

LaFraniere, Sharon. "Possible Link Between Dam and China Quake." *The New York Times*, Feb. 5, 2009. http://www.nytimes.com/2009/02/06/world/asia/06quake.html?pagewanted=all.

The Last Flight of the Space Shuttle Challenger. Online documentary. http://www.youtube.com/watch?v=gOpq_IYjZ_g&feature=related.

Levinas, Emmanuel. *Basic Philosophical Writings.* Bloomington: Indiana University Press, 2008.

Lewis, Mark Edward. *The Early Chinese Empires: Qin and Han.* Cambridge: Belknap Press of Harvard University Press, 2007.

Lister, Robert H., and Florence C. Lister. *Those Who Came Before: Southwestern Archaeology in the National Park System.* Tucson: Southwest Parks & Monuments Association, 1993.

Lovelock, James. *The Revenge of Gaia: Earth's Climate Crisis & The Fate of Humanity.* New York: Basic Books, 2007.

Lovett, Richard. "Early Earth May Have Had Two Moons." Nature.com, August 3, 2011. http://www.nature.com/news/2011/110803/full/news.2011.456.html.

Lucretius. *The Nature of Things.* New York: Penguin Classics, 2007.

Lynas, Mark. *Six Degrees: Our Future on a Hotter Planet.* Washington, D.C.: National Geographic, 2008.

Mallory, J.P. *In Search of the Indo-Europeans.* London: Thames & Hudson, 1991.

Maturana, Humberto, and Francisco Varela. *The Tree of Knowledge: The Biological Roots of Human Understanding.* Boston: Shambhala Books, 1992.

McLuhan, Marshall. *McLuhan Unbound.* Corte Madera, CA: Gingko Press, 2005.

———. *The Mechanical Bride: Folklore of Industrial Man.* Corte Madera, CA: Gingko Press, 2002.

———. *Understanding Me: Lectures and Interviews.* Cambridge: MIT Press, 2005.

———. *Understanding Media: The Extensions of Man.* Cambridge: MIT Press, 1994.

Meillassoux, Quentin. *After Finitude: An Essay on the Necessity of Contingency.* New York: Continuum, 2008.

"Methyl Isocyanate." Wikipedia, the Free Encyclopedia. 23 December 2011. http://en.wikipedia.org/wiki/Methyl_isocyanate.

Miller, Barbara Stoler. *Love Song of the Dark Lord: Jayadeva's Gita Govinda.* New York: Columbia University Press, 1977.

Mittica, Pierpaolo. *Chernobyl: The Hidden Legacy.* London: Trolley Books, 2007.

Moore, Malcolm. "Chinese Earthquake May Have Been Man-Made, Say Scientists." *The Telegraph*, February 2, 2009. http://www.telegraph.co.uk/news/worldnews/asia/china/4434400/Chinese-earthquake-may-have-been-man-made-say-scientists.html.

Mühlmann, Heiner. *MSC Maximal Stress Cooperation: The Driving Force of Cultures.* Wien: Springer, 2005.

Mumford, Lewis. *Technics and Civilization.* New York: Harcourt Brace, 1934.

Murakami, Haruki. *Underground: The Tokyo Gas Attack and the Japanese Psyche.* New York: Vintage, 2000.

Nancy, Jean-Luc. *The Creation of the World or Globalization.* Albany: SUNY Press, 2007.

National Research Council. *Orbital Debris: A Technical Assessment.* Washington, D.C.: National Academies Press, 1995.

Niiler, Eric. "Geologists Say Ohio Quakes Directly Tied to Fracking." MSNBC. January 6, 2012. Found at http://www.msnbc.msn.com/id/45903873/ns/technology_and_science-science/t/geologists-say-ohio-quakes-directly-tied-fracking/—.TycSGsVYutZ.

Bibliography

"1954 Yangtze River Floods." Wikipedia, the Free Encyclopedia. 3 September 2011. http://en.wikipedia.org/wiki/1954_Yangtze_River_Floods.

"NOAA: 2010 Tied For Warmest Year on Record." National Oceanic and Atmospheric Administration website. http://www.noaanews.noaa.gov/stories2011/20110112_globalstats.html.

Nuclear Aftershocks. Frontline documentary. http://www.pbs.org/wgbh/pages/frontline/nuclear- aftershocks/.

"Nuwa." Wikipedia, the Free Encyclopedia. 13 December 2011. en.wikipedia.org/wiki/Nüwa.

Olivelle, Patrick, trans. *The Upanishads*. London: Oxford University Press, 1996.

One Night in Bhopal. BBC documentary. http://www.youtube.com/watch?v=uz73rcdSG80&feature=related.

Perez, Louis G. *The History of Japan*. Westport, CT: Greenwood, 2009.

Polidori, Robert. *Zones of Exclusion: Pripyat and Chernobyl*. Göttingen: Steidl, 2003.

Read, Piers Paul. *Ablaze: The Story of Chernobyl*. London: Mandarin Paperbacks, 1994.

Sadakata, Akira. *Buddhist Cosmology: Philosophy and Origins*. Tokyo: Kosei, 1998.

Safina, Carl. *A Sea in Flames: The Deepwater Horizon Oil Blowout*. New York: Crown, 2011.

Sea Level Rise Impacts on Florida and Miami. Online video. http://www.youtube.com/watch?v=O0KB19eOP8Q.

Sebald, W.G. *On the Natural History of Destruction*. New York: Random House, 2003.

Seconds from Disaster: Amsterdam Air Crash. National Geographic film. http://www.youtube.com/watch?v=Lganu0iYxu0.

Seconds from Disaster: Bhopal Nightmare. National Geographic film. http://www.youtube.com/watch?v=iOgfzUh02lA.

Seconds from Disaster: Columbia's Last Flight. National Geographic film. http://www.youtube.com/watch?v=RUHcJeEyZvw&feature=fvwrel.

Seconds from Disaster: High Speed Train Wreck. National Geographic film. http://www.youtube.com/watch?v=O-UNxGSZUJc.

Seconds from Disaster: The Hindenburg. National Geographic film. www.youtube.com/watch?v=ShFLIDPoSoA.

Seconds from Disaster: Sinking of the Titanic. National Geographic film. http://www.youtube.com/watch?v=0_cDlXEwaDU.

Settegast, Mary. *Plato Prehistorian: 10,000—5,000 BC Myth, Religion, Archaeology*. Hudson, NY: Lindisfarne Books, 1990.

"Sichuan Schools Corruption Scandal." Wikipedia, the Free Encyclopedia. 26 October 2011. http://en.wikipedia.org/wiki/Sichuan_schools_corruption_scandal.

"Siege of Ta'if." Wikipedia, the Free Encyclopedia. 18 October 2011. http://en.wikipedia.org/wiki/Siege_of_Ta%27if.

Sloterdijk, Peter. *Spheres I: Bubbles*. Los Angeles: Semiotexte, 2011.

_____. "Spheres Theory: Talking to Myself About the Poetics of Space." eyondentropy.aaschool.ac.uk/?p=689.

_____. "Strong Observation for a Space Station Philosophy." In Paul Virilio, Raymond Depardon, Diller Scofidio, Renfro, Mark Hansen, Laura Kurgan, Ben Rubin. *Native Land: Stop Eject!* Paris: Fondation Cartier, 2009.

_____. *Terror from the Air*. Los Angeles: Semiotexte, 2009.

_____, and Hans-Jürgen Heinrichs. *Neither Sun Nor Death*. Los Angeles: Semiotexte, 2011.

Spengler, Oswald. *Man and Technics: A Contribution to a Philosophy of Life*. Alfred A. Knopf. 1932.

Summers, Anthony, and Robbyn Swan. *The Eleventh Day: The Full Story of 9/11 and Osama bin Laden*. New York: Ballantine, 2011.

Bibliography

Taneeru, Manav. "It's Official: 2005 Hurricanes Blew Records Away." CNN. com. http://articles.cnn.com/2005-12-19/weather/hurricane.season.ender_1_intense-storms-national-hurricane-center-hurricane-season?_s=PM:WEATHER.

Taylor, John H. *Death and the Afterlife in Ancient Egypt*. Chicago: University of Chicago Press, 2001.

Thompson, William Irwin. *Coming Into Being: Text and Artifacts in the Evolution of Consciousness*. New York: St. Martin's Press, 1996.

———. "This Time, Let's Build a New Venice and Not Another New Orleans." William Irwin Thompson Worldwide Web Site. http://www.williamirwinthompson.org/essays.html.

Torres, Christian. "Report Says Space Debris Past 'Tipping Point,' NASA Needs to Step Up Action." *The Washington Post*, August 8, 2011. http://www.washingtonpost.com/national/health-science/reports-says-space-debris-past-tipping-point-nasa-needs-to-step-up-action/2011/08/31/gIQAo6WTuJ_story.html.

Toynbee, Arnold. *A Study of History: Abridgement of Volumes I-VI*. New York: Oxford University Press, 1987.

"2005 Atlantic Hurricane Season." Wikipeida, the Free Encyclopedia. 7 January 2012. http://en.wikipedia.org/wiki/2005_Atlantic_hurricane_season.

"2008 Sichuan Earthquake." Wikipedia, the Free Encyclopedia. 9 January 2012. http://en.wikipedia.org/wiki/2008_Sichuan_earthquake.

"2009: Second Warmest Year on Record; End of Warmest Decade." NASA website. http://www.nasa.gov/topics/earth/features/temp-analysis-2009.html.

Van Buitenen, J.A.B., trans. *The Mahabharata, Volume I: The Book of the Beginning*. Chicago: University of Chicago Press, 1980.

Velikovsky, Immanuel. *Earth in Upheaval*. New York: Doubleday, 1955.

———. *Worlds in Collision*. New York: Doubleday, 1950.

Virilio, Paul. *The Administration of Fear*. Los Angeles: Semiotexte, 2012.

———. *Desert Screen: War at the Speed of Light*. New York: Continuum, 2005.

———. *Grey Ecology*. New York: Atropos Press, 2009.

———. *Negative Horizon*. New York: Continuum, 2006.

———. *The Original Accident*. Cambridge, UK: Polity Press, 1994.

———. *Speed and Politics*. Los Angeles: Semiotexte, 2006.

———. *University of Disaster*. Cambridge, UK: Polity Press, 2010.

———. *Unknown Quantity*. London: Thames & Hudson, 2003.

Von Dechend, Hertha. *Hamlet's Mill: An Essay Investigating the Origins of Human Knowledge and Its Transmission Through Myth*. Boston: David R. Godine, 1977.

"Worst Drought in 20 Years Along the Yangtze." USA *China Daily*. usa.chinadaily.com.cn/epaper/2011-05/25/content_12576632.htm.

Wright, Lawrence. *The Looming Tower: Al-Qaeda and the Road to 9/11*. New York: Alfred A. Knopf, 2006.

Zero Hour: Massacre at Columbine High. Online documentary. http://www.youtube.com/watch?v=FZZCwLeaAJQ&feature=related.

Index

Ablaze: The Story of Chernobyl 200
Abraham (Biblical figure) 115
Achaemenid Empire 104
Achenbach, Joel 205
The Administration of Fear (Virilio) 205
advertising 113
Aeschylus 93
Afghanistan 135
Africa 136
After Finitude (Meillasoux) 205
Agamben, Giorgio 8, 71, 145, 203
Age of Catastrophes 19, 181
Ain Ghazal 67, 158
Akihabara Station 98
Akimov, Alexander 73
Alaska 6
Al-Banna, Hasan 135
alchemy 56–57, 58
Alchemy: Science of the Cosmos, Science of the Soul 199
Aleppo 129
Aleutian Islands (2011 earthquake) 6
Alexandria (ancient) 56
Alexeivitch, Svetlana 200
Al Ghafiqi, Abdul Rahman 104
al–Jihad (Islamic group) 125
Almoravids 56
al–Qaeda 125, 126, 129, 130, 136, 137, 138
al–Zawahiri, Ayman 135
America 135, 146–47, 152, 153, 179;
 American Midwest 26, 143, 181, 182; American Southwest 144, 158, 164; Americans 131

American Airlines Flight 11 129
American Airlines Flight 77 129
American Indians 67, 158, 164
Amsterdam 40, 46, 85, 93, 126, 144
Amsterdam Schiphol Airport 85, 86, 89
Anderson, Benedict 21, 198
Angkor Wat 166
Angst 126
Anima mundi 55
Antarctica 6
Anthropogenic World Islands 37, 69, 71
Anthropos 47
Anti-Oedipus 201
anti-world 43–44, 47–48
Antwerp 31, 132
Apocalypse 178, 182
Apollo (Greek god) 93
Appadurai, Arjun 125, 202
aquifers 6
Arabs 56, 134, 135
Aral Sea (drying up of) 26
arcades (Paris) 22
Archaeology of Ancient China 204
Archbold, Rick 198, 202
Archons 128
Arctic ice 27
Aristotle 56, 57
Around the World in 80 Days (novel) 24
asabiyyah 134
Asahara, Shoko 97, 99, 105
Asia 179
Assyrians 13, 164
astral body 33
Astral Teleporters 100
astronauts 32, 61–62

Asvins 94
Athena (Greek goddess) 4, 186
Athenians 104
Atlantic Ocean 61
Atlantis 4
atomic bomb 74
atoms 57, 58, 83
Atta, Mohammad 129
Attica 104
Auge, Marc 10, 44, 48, 198
AUM Shinrikyo cult (attacks) 38, 53, 97–108, 123
Austin, Texas 148
Australia 1, 101
Australian wildfires 1, 182
Axial Age 83
axial tilt of earth 177
axis mundi 136

B-25 bomber crash into Empire State Building 137–38
Baal 94
Babylon (ancient city) 102, 159; Babylonian myth 104; Babylonians 13, 164
Bacon, Roger 185
Badiou, Alain 10, 45, 80, 90, 198, 200
Barmbek 132
Basic Philosophical Writings (Levinas) 202
Basic Writings (Heidegger) 199
Battle of Marathon 104
Battle of Tours 104
Bauman, Zygmunt 10, 17, 57, 117, 153, 198, 199, 202, 204
Bayer (corporation) 57
BBC (British Broadcasting Corporation) 39

213

Index

Beagle 180
Bechtel 54
Beck, Ulrich 17–18, 37, 126, 198, 202
Bedouins 80, 90, 134
Before the Deluge 204
Being and Event 200
Belarus 78
Belfast 20
Belorussia 77
Benjamin, Walter 44
benzene ring 57
Beqaa Valley 136
Berbers 134
Berlin 57
Bernini 32
bhakti cults 13
Bhopal 18, 37, 50–60, 186
Bijlmer suburb 85, 86
Billwerder Ausschlag 132
Bingham Valley, Utah 6
bin-Laden, Osama 135
Bioscope 24
Biosphere 2 173
Black, Jeremy 200
Blix, Hans 77
blowout preventer 168, 170
blues (music) 142, 148
Boisjoly, Roger 61, 199
Bosch, Hieronymus 14
Boston Logan International Airport 129
Botting, Douglas 198
Boundary Act 103–104
Bourbon Street 148
bourgeois family 113–114
Boyle, Robert 57
BP oil spill (2010) 125, 168–176
Brahma (Hindu deity) 79, 186
Braudel, Fernand 59, 199
Brazil 143
Breach of Faith 203
Brinkley, Douglas 142, 203
Britain 28, 126; British 180–81
Broad, William J. 204
Bronze Age 106
Brown, Brooks 110
Brueghel, Pieter 14
Brumfiel, Geoff 205
Buddha 99
Buddhism 13, 24, 83, 105; Buddhist cosmology 102, 106, 107

Buddhist Cosmology (book) 201
Buras, Louisiana 139
Burckhardt, Titus 199
Byron Nuclear Plant 183

Caesium 137 75
Cain and Abel (myth of) 115
Cairo 129, 135
California 1
Cambodia 166
Canada 27
Canary Islands 40, 45
canopic jars 13
Cantor Fitzgerald 129
capitalism 59, 60, 103, 107, 108, 114, 135
car crashes 4, 14, 25
carbon 57
carbon dioxide 21, 25, 52, 127, 158, 188
Carboniferous Age 21, 157–58
Carcassone 22
Carpathia (ship) 20
Carson, Rachel 163
Cartesian phase space 166
Caspian Sea 23
Castaldo, Richard 110
Çatalhöyük 71, 148
Catastrophism (geological) 181
cement bond log test 171, 172
Ceylon 13
Challenger (space shuttle) 61–62, 65, 68
Chang, K.C. 204
Chang, Kenneth 205
Chaos theory 14
Charles, Jacques 30
Chauvet (cave) 82
Chengdu 150, 152
Cheng-tzu-yai (archaeological site) 156
Chernobyl 18, 37, 72–84, 178, 179, 182
Chernobyl (book) 77, 200
Chetham, Deidre 204
Chevron 119
Chile (2010 earthquake) 5, 177
China 2, 6, 25, 125, 150, 151, 153, 156, 179; civil war 153; civilization 3;

cosmology 64; government 152; mythology 136
Chinese Neolithic 80, 156
chlorine gas 53, 57
Chongqing 152
Chou Dynasty 3
Christ, Jesus 115, 116
cities (coastal drowning of) 26
Civilization (television series) 39
Civilization and Capitalism (book) 59, 199
The Civilization of the Goddess 200
Clark, Kenneth 39
climate: hottest years on record 5, 126, 142–43, 181
climate inertia 188–89
climate scientists 6
clocks (mechanical) 14, 185
closed-circuit machinic symbiosis 46
CNN 1, 137
coal mines 6
Coast Guard 145
codex (parchment) 147
coffee houses 113
cold shutdown 179
Colorado River 152, 153
Colossus of Rhodes 173
Columbia (space shuttle) 33, 34, 62–64, 65, 68, 162
Columbia River 153
Columbia University 151
Columbine (book) 202
Columbine (shootings) 8, 37, 38, 96, 109–123
Columbine High School 109, 121
Coming Into Being (Thompson) 201
communications revolution 163
Community (Bauman) 202
Conservatory of the Jardin des Plantes 22
Conversations with Ulrich Beck 198
Cook, Captain 13
Copernican cosmology 21, 32, 33, 131
Copernicus, Nicolaus 65

214

Index

copper mines 6
Corsica 75
cosmospheric technologies 157, 175, 187
cosmotopia 102, 103
The Creation of the World or Globalization 199
Crystal Palace 22, 108
Cullen, Dave 122, 202
Cult at the End of the World 201
culture industry 113
Cunard 20
Cunnigham, Graham 200
Cuvier, Georges 181

Dadaab, Kenya 189
Daedalus (Greek myth) 30
daimon 47
dams 6, 22, 25
Dante 32, 157, 165
Danziger Bridge Incident 140
Darfur refugee camp 184
Darius 104
Dark Age (Mediterranean) 174
Darwin, Charles 180
Day of the Dead 121
DeAngelis, Frank 111
Death and the Afterlife (book) 197
Deepwater Horizon 168, 169, 173
Deir el-Medina 72
DELAG (*Deutsche Luftshiffahrts-Aktiengesellschaft*) 28, 31
Deleuze, Gilles 31, 55, 90, 91, 96, 105, 134, 174, 186, 198, 199, 200, 201, 202, 206
democracy 107
Depardon, Raymond 200, 206
Dereivka 23
Derrida, Jacques 2, 4, 5, 82
Descartes, René 44, 57
Desert Screen 200, 203
desertification 26
Detroit 184
Deutsche Bahn AG 87, 88, 89
Difference and Repetition 202, 206

Dirgha-tamas 94
dirigibles 30
Discipline and Punish 198
Dittmann, Jörg 87–88
Dr. Eckener's Dream Machine 198
Dolní Věstonice 144
Dow Chemical 52, 58
dromosphere 23, 24, 25, 26, 29, 31, 32, 33, 50, 55, 59, 89–91, 92, 127, 133, 134, 137, 144, 146, 148, 163, 165, 200
DSM Manual 123
Duamutef (Egyptian god) 13
Dujiangyan-Jiangyou Fault 151
Duralumin 28
Dyatlov, Anatoli 73, 74

Early Chinese Empires 204
Earth in Upheaval (Velikovsky) 205
earthquakes 1, 2, 3, 5, 6, 14, 127, 150–60, 173, 177–84, 188
East St. Louis 184
Easter Island 13, 164
Eastern Europe 75
Ebert, John David 200, 205
The Ecology of Commerce 54, 199
Edwards, Tim 199
Egypt: ancient Egyptians 12, 13, 136, 173; modern regime 135
Eiffel Tower 22
Eilbek 132
El Al Flight 1862 85–86, 89, 91, 92, 95, 96, 126
Elbe 132
electronics 17, 39, 58, 79
elemental disruption 173
The Eleventh Day 202
Eliade, Mircea 200
Ellul, Jacques 12, 197
Emperor (Japanese) 107
Empire State Building 138, 152, 173
End of Faith 202
England 21
Enkidu 80, 136
entropy 14, 22, 117, 120, 144, 146, 164

environmental movement 163
The Epic of Gilgamesh 136, 203; *see also* Gilgamesh (character)
Eridu 164
Eschede 87, 88
Ethics (Badiou) 198
Euphrates River 13, 159
Europe 22, 76, 77, 131, 143, 179, 185
Existenz 38
Exodus (Biblical) 174
Exodus, Book of 174
Exosphere 125, 127, 128, 136, 161, 162, 163, 165, 166
Ezekiel 30

FDA (Food & Drug Administration) 59
Fear of Small Numbers (Appadurai) 202
Feith, Greg 28
fifth century 12
fifth millennium BC 23
film 174
Fire on the Horizon 205
firebombing of European cities 132
First Gulf War 135
Five Weeks in a Balloon (novel) 24
Flood (Biblical) 174
Florence, Italy 149
Florida 1
The Fold 199, 201
Fontaine, Pierre 22
Form-a-Set 170
Form-a-Squeeze 170
Fortune 500 141
Foucault, Michel 45, 92, 95–96, 145, 198, 201, 203
four elements 33, 56, 57, 105
fracking 6, 154
France 28, 30, 75
Frankfurt, Germany 28
Franks 104
French 131; culture 22
French Quarter (New Orleans) 148
Fuchs, Yitzhak 85, 86
Fuerzas Armadas Guanches 40

215

Index

Fukushima Daiichi Nuclear Power Station 178; meltdown 83, 125, 177–84
Fuller, Buckminster 144

Gaia (climate theory) 188
Gaia (Greek myth) 94
Galen 9
Galerías Preciados 40
Galerie d'Orléans 22
Galileo 65
Ganesha 94
Ganymede (Greek myth) 30
Gardner, Neil 110–111
Garuda (Hindu myth) 30
Garuda Airlines 30
Gatlin gun 24
GATT (Global Agreement on Trade and Tariffs) 37
Geb (Egyptian god) 3
Genesis, Book of 33
Genesis Technologies 174, 175
genetic engineering 17, 79; genetically modified organisms 59
geologists 6
geo-planetary force (humans as) 173–74
George, Andrew 203
geosynchronous satellites 133
Germanic barbarians 128
Germans 31, 53, 131, 179; culture 22
Gesamtkunstwerk 164
Giedion, Siegfried 198
Gigantic (ship) 20, 24
gigantic technologies 180
Gilgamesh (character) 94, 136, 164; see also *The Epic of Gilgamesh*
Gimbutas, Marija 200
Girard, René 115–116, 202
Gita Govinda 13
glaciers (melting) 6, 182
global accident 149, 183, 185–90
Global Free Trade Agreements 37
global mean temperature 25, 26
global warming 4, 6, 26, 63, 126, 142, 143, 153,

159, 160, 182, 183, 188, 189
globalization 19, 37, 107, 126, 135
Gnosticism 47, 128
God Is Not Great 202
Golden Gate Bridge 152, 173
golf courses 119
Gong Gong (Chinese deity) 136
gospel (music) 142, 148
Gospels 115, 147
Gran Canaria airport 40, 48
Graves, Sean 110
The Great Deluge 203
Great Dust Bowl 26
Great Wall of China 156
Greek fire 34
Greeks 12, 13, 93, 131, 159; philosophy 56, 175
greenhouse gases 2, 21, 159, 164, 188
Greenhouses of the Botanical Gardens, Paris 22
Greenland 27; ice sheet (melting) 6, 20, 25, 127
Greenpeace 77
Greenwich Mean Time (GMT) 161
Grey Ecology (Virilio) 205
Groeneveen apartment building 86, 91
Grosseteste, Robert 185
growth hormones 59
Grubbs, Captain Victor 41, 42
Guatemala 6
Guattari, Félix 90, 91, 105, 134, 198, 200, 202
Gulf of Mexico 141, 143, 148, 168, 171
Gulf Stream 20, 143
Gulf War see First Gulf War
gunpowder 96, 131

Haber, Fritz 57
Habermas, Jürgen 113, 201
Hadean epoch 181
Haiti (2010 earthquake) 5
Halafian 94; pottery 56
Halliburton 169–70, 172
Halloween 120–21
Hamburg 87, 132

Hamlet's Mill 203
Hammerbrook 132
Hamm-Nord 132
Hamm-Süd 132
Hanover 87
Harland and Wolff 20
Harrell, Jimmy 170
Harris, Eric 109, 111, 112, 114, 115, 116, 121, 122–23
Harris, Sam 117, 202
Hartmann, Thom 188, 206
Harwood, Bill 204
Hawken, Paul 54, 199
Hayashi, Ikuo 97
Hayashi, Yasuo 98
Hebrews 174
Heidegger, Martin 3, 11, 12, 43, 46, 48, 65, 66–67, 71, 126, 185, 197, 198, 199
Hell 157
Hellenistic Age 13, 173, 175
Hertsgaard, Mark 202
Hesiod 94
Hillman, James 94, 201
Hinayana Buddhists 13
Hindenburg 18, 19, 28–35, 33, 34, 65, 157, 174, 182
Hindenburg: An Illustrated History 198, 202
Hinduism 105, 107; Hindus 12; mythology 30, 79, 99, 110; Trimurti 79
Hirose, Kenichi 97–98
Hiroshima 74
A History of Japan 201
A History of Religious Ideas 200
A History of the Arab Peoples 202
History of the Concept of Time (Heidegger) 197, 198
Hitchens, Christopher 117, 202
Höchst (corporation) 57
Hohokam 67, 164
A Hole at the Bottom of the Sea 205
Holy Land 136
Holy Spirit 15, 29, 33, 56, 58
Homer 65, 94
Homo Sacer (book) 8, 145, 203

216

Index

Hoover Dam 152, 173
Horne, Jed 203
Horus 3, 136
Hot (Hertsgaard) 202
hot air balloons 30, 31, 32
hottest years on record *see* climate
Hourani, Albert 135, 202
Houston, Texas 148
Huelva, Spain 143
Huracán (Mayan god) 3
hurricanes 7, 141–43, 159, 174, 181, 182, 183, 188; Ida 169; Irene 1, 2; Katrina 4, 8, 37, 71, 125, 126, 127, 139–49, 175, 189; Vince 143
Husserl, Edmund 44
hydrocarbons 157, 169, 171
hydroelectric dam 152
hydrogen 57
hydrogen chloride 52
hydrogen cyanide 52
Hyundai Heavy Industries 168

Ibaraki 97
ibn Khaldun 80, 134, 200, 202
Imagined Communities 198
IMF (International Monetary Fund) 37
In Search of the Indo-Europeans 198
India 13, 50–51, 179
Indian Ocean 5, 177; tsunami 177
Indo-Europeans 23, 94
Indonesia 179
Indra (Hindu god) 94
Indus River 148
industrial accidents 19
Industrial Revolution 17, 180
industrial society 35, 105, 143, 164, 182
integral accidents 180–84, 187
InterCityExpress train 87, 95
internal combustion engine 30, 31, 54
internal proletariat 105
International Atomic Energy Agency 77
Internet 37, 125, 174

Iodine 131 75
iPad 148
iPhones 148
iPod 149
Iran 56
Iraq 56, 72, 80
Iridium-33 (U.S. satellite) 161
irrigation systems 13, 67, 155
Islam 135; Islamists 135, 136
Islamic fundamentalists 49, 121, 134
Islamic Group 125
Ismay, J. Bruce 18
Israel 147, 179; Israeli air force 72
Italy 131, 179

Jacobsen, Thorkild 13, 197, 204
Japan 1, 2, 97–108, 177–84
Japanese tombstones 105
Jayadeva 13
jazz 142, 148
Jericho (Neolithic town) 80
Jerusalem 147
Jewish Christians 147
Jewish Wars 147
Jews 53, 56, 104
JFK International Airport 40
Joachim of Flora 14
John (Evangelist) 115
Johnson, Nicholas L. 161
Journey to the Center of the Earth (novel) 24
Joyce, James 39
Judaea 104
Jupiter 65

Kaiser Wilhelm Institute 57
Kai-shek, Chiang 153
Kaku, Michio 205
Kapilavastu 83
Kaplan, David E. 201
Kasumigaseki Station 97, 101
Keio Hospital 97
Kekule, Friedrich 57
Kenya 189
Kepler, Johannes 65
Kermadec Islands (2011 earthquake) 6

Kessler Syndrome 127, 162, 164, 165, 166
Kiefer, Anselm 7, 197
Kiev 72
Kindle 148
Kinetoscope 24
Kirkland, Lance 110
Klebold, Dylan 109, 111, 112, 114, 115, 116, 121, 122–23
Klee, Paul 91
Klein-Kruitberg apartment building 86
KLM Flight 4805 40–43
Kogakuin University 98
Konrad, John 205
Korea 107
Kosmos-2251 (Russian satellite) 161
Krishna 13
Kung Bushman 47
Kusky, Tim 141
Kyoto Protocol 188

Labrador 20
Lafayette, Louisiana 148
LaFraniere, Sharon 204
Lake Constance 30
Lake Gooimer 86
Lake Pontchartrain 139–40, 141
Lakehurst, New Jersey 19, 28
Lakehurst Naval Air Station 28
Lao-tzu 83
Lapis exilis 56
The Last Hours of Ancient Sunlight 206
Last Judgment 178
Levinas, Emmanuel 3, 116, 202
Lewis, Mark Edward 204
Liege 31
limes 128
Liquid Modernity 198, 199, 204
Lister, Florence C. 204
Lister, Robert H. 204
The Literature of Ancient Sumer 200
lithosphere 6
Littleton, Colorado 109
logosphere 80, 82, 83
London 22, 31, 132
Longmenshan Fault 150

217

Index

The Looming Tower 203
Los Angeles 40, 129
Los Rodeos Airport 40, 41
Louisiana 139, 140; wetlands 172
Love Song of the Dark Lord 198
Lovelock, James 27, 188, 198, 206
Lovett, Richard 205
Lower Dnieper basin 23
Lower Ninth Ward 139–40, 146
LSD 100
Lucretius 199
Lugalbanda 94
Lungshan 80, 156
Lyell, Charles 180
Lynas, Mark 27, 143, 188, 197, 198, 203, 206

Maccabean Revolt 104
Maccabeus, Judas 104
Macondo Prospect 169
Madrid 126
The Mahabharata 105, 201
Mallory, J.P. 198
Malta 94
Man and Technics (Spengler) 12, 197
Manchuria 107
Mardi gras 148
Margulis, Lynn 205
Marianas (oil rig) 169
Mars 55, 181
Marschall, Ken 198, 202
Marshall, Andrew 201
Martel, Charles 104
Martu 80
Mary (Virgin) 115
Mathy, Heinrich 132
Matsomoto, Chizuo 99
Matsumoto 101
Mattathias the Hasmonean 104
Maturana, Humberto 204
Maximal Stress Cooperation 115
Mayans 3, 81, 158
McAuliffe, Christa 61
McLuhan, Marshall 12, 104, 162, 174, 197, 201, 204
McLuhan Unbound 204
The Mechanical Bride (McLuhan) 12, 197
Medicaid 144

Mediterranean 143
Meiji Restoration 106, 107
Meillassoux, Quentin 174, 205
Memling, Hans 178
Memphis Tennessee 148
mercury 56
Mesopotamia 12, 13, 102, 131, 144, 164
methane 21, 171
methyl isocyanate 50–52, 54, 59
Meurs, Klaas 41
Miami, Florida 149
Michelangelo 68
Michigan 184
Middle Ages 9, 22, 96, 117, 119
Middle East 135
Midgard Serpent 94
Midwest (American) 26, 143, 181, 182
Miller, Barbara Stoler 198
Min River 152
Miocene Epoch 169
Mississippi Canyon 169
Mississippi delta 141
Mississippi Gulf 171–72, 175
Mississippi River 3, 141, 143
Mittica, Pierpaolo 77, 200
Miyazaki, Hayao 25
Modernity 33
Modernity at Large 202
Mohammad 83
Mohenjo-daro 71, 148
monomethyl amine 52
Monsanto 54, 59
Moon 65, 181
Morocco 40
Morton Thiokol 61, 62
Mount Buzhou 136
Mount Fuji 97, 99, 106
Movement for Self-Determination and Independence of the Canary Archipelago 40
MSC Maximal Stress Cooperation (Muhlmann) 202, 203
Mühlmann, Heiner 115, 137, 202, 203
mujahideen 135
multinational corporations 53, 54, 59, 187

Mumford, Lewis 12, 90, 197, 206
Munich 87
The Muqqadimah 200, 202
Murakami, Haruki 101, 106, 201
Muse 47
Muslim Brotherhood 135
mustard gas 53, 57
Muybridge, Eadweard 24

NAFTA (North American Free Trade Agreement) 37
Nagin, Ray 139
Nancy, Jean-Luc 199
nanotechnology 58
Naraka (Buddhist underworld) 102
NASA 61–62, 63, 161, 162, 166
National Academy of Sciences 162
National Transportation Safety Board 28
Native Land: Stop Eject 200, 206
natural gas 6, 154
The Nature of Things 199
Nazis 122
Near East 80
Negative Horizon (Virilio) 198, 202, 204
Neither Sun Nor Death (Sloterdijk) 199
Neolithic 23, 67, 80, 94, 148, 156, 158
Neomodernity 17–18, 19, 21, 26, 37–39, 125
Nerdrum, Odd 38
Nestorian Christians 56
Netherlands 85
neutrons 73
New Jersey 1, 19, 129, 130
The New Media Invasion (book) 79, 200
New Mexico 161
New Orleans 71, 125, 139, 141, 142, 144, 147, 148–49; police department 140
New York 20, 40, 85, 125, 130, 149
New York Times 1–2, 151
New Zealand 1, 5

218

Index

Newark International Airport 130
Newfoundland 19, 20
newspapers 113
Newton, Isaac 44, 57, 65, 66, 90
Nielson, Patti 111
Nietzsche, Friedrich 9
nihilism 48, 122
Niiler, Eric 197, 204
9/11 7, 8, 125, 126, 129–138, 174, 186; conspiracy theories 130–131
nineteenth century 11, 22, 23, 24, 30, 131
nitrogen 52, 57
nomads 26–27, 31, 39, 80, 90, 91, 94, 134, 135, 137, 188
non-places 44, 48
Non-Places (book) 198
North America 6, 75, 119, 141, 146, 152
North Atlantic Civilization 27, 185
North Atlantic Ocean 19, 20, 24
North Korea 107
North Sea 27
Northern Arctic Civilization 27
Nova Scotia 20
nuclear technology 78, 80, 81; power plants 79, 178; reactors 72–77, 178, 182, 183
Nuremberg 87

Ochanomizu Station 98
Ohad, Arnon 85, 86
oil drilling 6
oil reserves (vanishing) 26
Okamura Ironworks 100
Oklahoma City bombing 109
Old Silk Road 56
Olivelle, Patrick 201
Olympic (ship) 20, 24
OM (Sanskrit syllable) 105
On the Natural History of Destruction 202
One Small Thing (as cause of accident) 64, 67–68, 69, 70, 162, 199
Operation Gomorrah 132
Oresme, Nicholas 66

The Oresteia 93
Orestes 93
The Original Accident (Virilio) 206
O-rings 61, 62, 68
Osiris 63, 94
oxygen 57

Pacific Ocean 2, 177, 179, 182
Palais Royal 22
Paleomodernity 17–19, 20
Palestine 104, 136
Palmyra 13
Pan Am Flight 1736 40–43
Pandava brothers 105
Paris 22
PCBs 130
Peng, Li 153
Pentagon 129
Pentecost 29
Peregrinus, Petrus 185
Perez, Louis G. 201
Perfect Salvation Initiation 100
Pergamene 13
Persian Gulf 13
Persians 104
Petra 13
Phaeton (Greek myth) 30
Pharisees 147
Philippines 2
Philistines 137
phosgene gas 51, 53, 57
physis 66–67, 70
Picasso, Pablo 49
Pilâtre de Rozier, Jean-François 30
P'ing-liang-t'ai (archaeological site) 156
plane crashes 4, 40–49, 85–86, 126
plate tectonics 6, 7
Plato 65, 83, 152
Plato Prehistorian (Settegast) 203
Plenum 128
Plinian cloud 173
Pliocene CO_2 levels 188
Plotinus 83
plough 155
Plutonium 239 75
Poetry, Language, Thought 198
poiesis 66–67
police (origins of) 95–96

Polidori, Robert 77, 200
polisphere 23, 24, 31, 37, 55, 59, 78, 80, 81, 82, 83, 91–93, 134, 144, 145, 147
Polynesians 13
pop culture 39
population explosion 188
Poseidon (Greek god) 3, 4
pottery, Neolithic 56
Principles of Geology 180
Pripyat 72, 76, 77, 81, 179, 183
Pruss, Max 29
Ptolemy 9
Punic Wars 176

Qebehsenuef (Egyptian god) 13
Qin Empire 156
quantum mechanics 17
"The Question Concerning Technology" (Heidegger) 12, 66
Qutb, Sayyid 135

radionuclides 75
Rahman, Sheikh Abdul 135
Rameses II 173
Rameses III 72
Read, Piers Paul 200
Reservoir-Induced Seismicity Event 151
Revelation, Book of 183
Revenge of Gaia 198, 206
Revisioning Psychology 94, 201
Rift Valley (Africa) 136
rivers (drying up) 26
Robert, Marie Noel 30
Robson, Eleanor 200
rock and roll 142, 148
Rodin, Auguste 49
Rohrbough, Danny 110
Rolls Royce 31
Roman Empire 176; Romans 13, 128, 147
Roman Republic 176
Rome 175
Rouhault, Charles 22
Ruisdael, Jacob 202
Russia 77, 161, 173
Russian Space Forces 161
Ryuku Islands (2010 earthquake) 5

219

Index

Sadakata, Akira 201
Safeway 119
Safina, Carl 205
Sahara 26
St. Georg (German city) 132
Saint Louis University 141
Saint Matthew Island 54
Saint Theresa 32
Sakamoto, Tsutsumi 100
salinization (of riverine soil) 13, 67
Samarran pottery 56
Samson (myth of) 137
samurai 106
San Francisco 130
Sanders, Dave 111
Sandouping 152
Sanskrit 105
Sapta Sindu 94
sarin gas 53, 97, 98, 99, 101
Satan 157, 165
satellite collision (2009) 125, 127, 161–67
Saudi Arabia 135
Savage, John (engineer) 153
Scandinavian mythology 136
Schreuder, Willem 42
Scott, Rachel 110
A Sea in Flames 205
sea-level rise 26, 127, 142, 149, 155, 159, 183, 189
Sebald, W.G. 132, 202
Security, Territory, Population (Foucault) 201, 203
Seeber, Dr. Leonardo 151
Seleucids 104
semiotic vacancy 120–22
September 11 terrorist attacks *see* 9/11
Seriality and Repetition 114, 115, 119
Set (Egyptian god) 94
Settegast, Mary 203
7 Eleven 119
seventeenth century 57, 95
Sevin 50–51
shamanism 29
Shang Dynasty 3
Shanghai, China 49
Shanksville, Pennsylvania 130

Shihuangdi (Chinese Emperor) 156
Shinjuku 98
Shiva 79, 80, 94, 99
Shroder, Tom 205
Shyamalan, M. Night 117, 120
Siberia 27, 161
Sichuan earthquake (2008) 2, 5, 25, 125, 127, 150–60, 175, 182
Sichuan Geology and Mineral Bureau 152
Silent Spring 163
The Silmarillion 173
Sinai 174
Sinbad (character) 159
Six Degrees (book) 188, 197, 198, 203, 206
sixteenth century 95, 145, 178
60 Minutes (television show) 141
Sloterdijk, Peter 21, 37, 53, 64, 69, 144, 172, 198, 199, 200, 202, 203, 205
Smith, Captain Edward J. 20
Social security 144
sociosphere 78, 121, 122
Sofer, Gedalya 85
Solomon, Anat 85
South Atlantic 143
South Korea 168
Southampton 20
Soviet Union 72, 76, 135
Space Age 163
space junk 157, 162, 163–64, 165, 166
Space, Time and Architecture 198
Spain 40, 48, 143
Sparwood, British Columbia 6
Speed and Politics (Virilio) 200, 202
Spengler, Oswald 12, 197
Spheres I: Bubbles 198, 205
Spielberg, Steven 7
spiritual cartographies 106
Springfield, Illinois 183
Sputnik 133, 162
Starčevo 94
Star-shaped city 131
steam engine 30
Steiner, Rudolf 82

stirrups 12
Stockhausen, Karlheinz 8
Stratosphere 32
Strontium 90 75
Structural Transformation of the Public Sphere 113, 201
A Study of History (Toynbee) 12, 197, 201
subtle body 105
suburbs 114, 115, 117, 118, 119, 120, 123, 186
Sudbury, Ontario 6
Sufi mystic 47
sukshma technologies 79
Sulphur 56
Sumerians 3, 13, 94
Sumeru (Mount) 102, 106
Summers, Anthony 202
Superdome (New Orleans) 139–40, 146
Suriname 85
Swan, Robyn 202
SWAT team 111–112
Sweden 75
Syria 56

Taiwan 107
Taneeru, Manav 202
Tangshan earthquake (1976) 150
Taoism 83
Taylor, John H. 197
Taymyr Peninsula 161
Technics and Civilization (Mumford) 12, 197, 206
The Technological Society (Ellul) 12, 197
technologies of ballistics 25, 137
technologies of obstruction 25, 137
technology (theories about) 11, 12, 15, 43–44
technopolis 48
Tel Aviv 85, 86
telegraph 6, 107
Tell es Sawwan 80
Tenerife (plane crash) 40–49, 50
Tennessee Valley 153
tensegrities 144, 163
The Terminator (film) 15
Terror from the Air 53, 199
Teshub 94
Texas 1, 161; wildfires 1, 182

220

Index

Thea (primordial planet) 165, 181
Thermosphere 3, 32, 106, 128, 133, 136, 159, 162, 163, 165, 166
Third Age (of the Holy Spirit) 14
thirteenth century 14
Thompson, William Irwin 201, 203
Thor (Norse god) 94
Those Who Came Before 204
A Thousand Plateaus 198, 200, 201, 202
Three Gorges Dam 6, 25, 152, 153
Tiamat (Babylonian deity) 104
Tiber Field 168
Tibetan Plateau 153
Tigris River 13, 80, 159
Titanic (ship) 8, 18, 19, 20–27, 29, 127, 143–44, 174, 180, 182, 186
Titans (Greek myth) 30, 94
tofu dregs schoolhouse scandal 150
Tohoku earthquake (2011) 125, 177–84
Tokai 97
Tokai University 98
Tokugawa Shogunate 102, 106, 107
Tokyo 53, 97, 101, 102, 105, 107, 108, 123, 178
Tokyo Electric Power Co. 179
Tokyo Metro 97
Tokyo University 98
Tolkien, J.R.R. 173
Toptunov, Leonid 73, 74
Torah 147
Tornado outbreak (2011) 1, 181
Torres 143
Torres, Christian 204
Tower of Babel 174
Toynbee, Arnold 12, 105, 197, 201
Toyoda, Toru 98
train derailments 4, 87–89, 95
Transocean 168

transport revolution 23, 91, 163
The Tree of Knowledge (Maturana) 204
A Trip to the Moon (novel) 24
Trisiras 94
Troposphere 30, 31, 32, 33
tsunamis 3, 7, 14, 173, 182, 183; 2004 tsunami (Indian Ocean) 5, 155, 174; 2010 tsunami (Chile) 177; 2011 tsunami (Japan) 155, 177–84
Tuileries 30
Turkey 1, 6
Turner, J.M.W. 24
Twain, Mark 46
twelfth century 14
twentieth century 37, 53
twenty-first century 166, 189
20,000 Leagues Under the Sea (novel) 24
Twilight of the Clockwork God 205
Typhon (Greek myth) 94

Ukraine 72, 76, 77
Ulsan, South Korea 168
Umayyad Caliphate 104
Underground (Murakami) 201
Understanding Me (McLuhan) 201
Understanding Media (McLuhan) 12
Uniformitarianism 180
Union Carbide India, Ltd. 50–52, 53, 54, 55, 57, 58
United Airlines Flight 93 130
United Airlines Flight 175 129
United Nations 37
United Nations Scientific Committee on the Effects of Atomic Radiation 77
United States 28, 140, 179; government 140
United States Capitol Building 130
United States Congress 141

The University of Disaster 200
Unknown Quantity (Virilio) 197
The Upanishads 105, 201
Ur 164
Uranium 235 58, 75
Ur-Nammu 173
Uruk 94, 164
U.S. Army Corps of Engineers 3, 141

Vaishnava technologies 79
Van Buitenen, J.A.B. 201
Van Eyck, Jan 178
Van Goyen, Jan 202
Van Zanten, Captain Jacob 41, 42, 46, 47, 186
Varela, Francisco 157, 204
Velikovsky, Immanuel 177, 205
Venice 144, 148, 149
Vent Gas Scrubber 51
Venus 65
Vermont 1, 2
Verne, Jules 24
Versailles 30
Vikings 39
Villa Albani mosaic 175–76
The Village (film) 117–18, 120
Violence and the Sacred 115–116, 202
Virilio, Paul 5, 23, 31, 89, 91, 92, 163, 174, 180, 182, 187, 189, 197, 198, 200, 202, 203, 204, 205, 206
Vishnu 79
Voices from Chernobyl 200
volcanic eruptions 7, 173, 174, 181
von Dechend, Hertha 203
Vorhandenheit 44, 45, 46, 65, 71

Waggoner, Colonel 141
Walgreens 119
Wandsbek 132
War of the Worlds (novel) 7
War of the Worlds (Byron Haskin film) 7
War of the Worlds (Steven Spielberg film) 7
Warhol, Andy 7
Waseda University 98

221

Index

Washington, D.C. 125
Washington Monument 2
waterwheels 14
Wegener, Alfred 7
Welles, Orson 7
Wells, H.G. 7
West Antarctic ice sheet (melting of) 127
Western civilization 14, 185, 187
White Star Line 18, 20
Wilber, Ken 55
Williams, Dr. Philip 151
windmills 14
Witelo 185
World at Risk 198, 202
World Bank 37
World Health Organization 77
world islands (Sloterdijk) 172
World Trade Center 136; North Tower 129, 130, 137; South Tower 129, 130, 153
World Trade Organization 37
World War I 21, 30, 51, 57, 131
World War II 10, 17, 20, 26, 37, 53, 107, 132, 153
Worlds in Collision 205
Wright, Lawrence 203
Wuhan, China 153

Xenon-135 73
Xiao, Fan 152
Xiongnu barbarians 156

Yajnavalkya 83
Yam (Canaanite deity) 94
Yangshao culture 156
Yangtze River 152, 153, 154, 156
Yellow River 80
Yingxui-Beichan Fault 151

yoga 13, 83
Yokoyama, Masato 98
Yotsuya Station 98
Youngstown, Ohio (2011 earthquake) 6, 154
Ypres (battle of) 53
Yucatan peninsula 81

Zeppelin, Count Ferdinand von 30, 31
Zeus (Greek myth) 30, 94, 104, 186
Zhu Rong (Chinese deity) 136
ziggurats 173
Zipingpu Dam 127, 151, 152, 153
Zoescope 24
Zólyomi, Gábor 200
Zones of Exclusion (book) 77, 200
Zuhandenheit 44, 65
Zyklon B 53

www.ingramcontent.com/pod-product-compliance
Ingram Content Group UK Ltd.
Pitfield, Milton Keynes, MK11 3LW, UK
UKHW041918140426
5217IPUK00013B/211